BODYGUARD

BODYGUARD
MY LIFE ON THE FRONT LINE

CRAIG SUMMERS WITH TONY HORNE

Biteback Publishing

First published in Great Britain in 2012 by
Biteback Publishing Ltd
Westminster Tower
3 Albert Embankment
London
SE1 7SP

ISBN 978-1-84954-223-4

10 9 8 7 6 5 4 3 2 1

A CIP catalogue record for this book is available from the
British Library.

Set in Caslon Pro and Franchise by Selina Swayne
Cover design by Namkwan Cho

Printed and bound in Great Britain by
CPI Group (UK) Ltd, Croydon CR0 4YY

CONTENTS

ACKNOWLEDGEMENTS

It goes without saying that there are so many people to thank that I could never do it justice. In my book alone, there are hundreds of characters who passed through my life, without whom there would be no story.

From inside the BBC, huge gratitude goes to Jon Williams, Paul Greeves, Stuart Hughes, John Glendinning, Colin Pereira, Fred Scott, Richard Stacey, Nick Woolley, Tony Fallshaw, Sam Bagnall, Tom Giles, Paul Simpson and John Simpson.

I have to mention the High Risk Team, too. You know who you are – it's been brilliant. Chris Cobb-Smith, Ian White and Dylan in the Baghdad Bureau – you are masters in your field.

At Sky, a special mention for Sarah Whitehead – it's great to be back working with you again, and to my old buddy Chas Staines – you made it into the book! And John Iley – brilliant website!

To Iain Dale, and James, Sam, Katy and Ella – only you believed in this adventure so thank you, and to Tony Horne, my brilliant ghost writer – what skill, speed and sense you made of my ramblings. An incredible job, and friends for life.

Finally, to Mum, Kate, Charlotte, Nicole, Sam and Ella. Of course, this book would not have been possible without the love and support from my darling wife Sue; you can finally read what I was up to on all those trips. Lots of love always.

And, to you, for buying my book. Let the rollercoaster begin...

FOREWORD

There was a time when journalists, like businessmen, diplomats, contract workers and the other strange characters who work in dangerous places for a living, had to look after their own safety. No bodyguards, no body armour, no nothing. But those were the days before we became natural targets for the world's terrorists – and before the habit caught on of suing one's employers if something went wrong. The journalists who covered the first Gulf War in 1991 had no security advisors and scarcely any body armour. My team in Baghdad had two flak jackets between six of us; dishing them out wasn't an easy task.

Twelve years later, in the second Gulf War, even the journalists who covered the situation in Doha, far away from any possible threat, were given full nuclear, biological and chemical warfare suits, and had excellent ex-special forces characters working with them. Some elderly hacks did a lot of harrumphing about all these changes; it was better in the old days, they said. Not me – but then I had the enormous benefit of working with Craig Summers.

Craig was, it's fair to say, a mildly rough diamond in those early stages. A veteran of the Falklands War, he was tough and imposing; when he and I walked down the street in Northern Iraq in the run-up to the American-led invasion of Iraq in 2003, I never had the slightest fear of being attacked. When the critical moment of danger came, and an American navy plane managed to drop a 1,000 lb bomb on the wrong people (as American planes have traditionally done in war after war), Craig's training kicked in superbly. He did what he could for our dying translator, and he salvaged all our television gear and even our personal bags from our burning car, with explosives and live ammunition going off all round him. If ever there was a moment when close protection showed its value, it was then.

In the years that followed, Craig and I worked together in various parts of the globe, as he describes in this excellent and very accurate account. I always knew I'd be fine as long as Craig was there. And although he became smoother, and learned to adopt the ways of the BBC executive, people still didn't mess with us when we wandered round the streets of Baghdad or Kabul together.

Now Craig has gone on to grander things, and I don't have the advantage of working with him any more. I miss his company, and I miss the sense of security he exuded. No one was better at finding good places to sleep, good vehicles to drive, decent food, a cup of tea when there was nothing else. I used to try to give the impression he was my personal bodyguard, though he was always a great deal more than that. But he was not simply superb to work with, he was great company; even if I sometimes had to ask him not to tell any more of his ripest stories.

This book is a great account of his career so far, and an accurate if generous one, too. I count myself extremely lucky to have worked alongside him so often over the years.

John Simpson

END OF THE ROAD

Cheeky bastard.

> Not really an office-based person, strong aversion to paperwork ... rarely seen at a desk – unless it's doing his expenses. If not, he was at other people's desks doing what Craig really does in the office, which is generating his next trip out of the office. Often on the most tenuous of security or safety reasons, Craig was always ready to leap on a plane – somehow always at least Upper Class if not Business Class. It's been a colourful and action-packed ten years.

That's how Paul Greeves, Head of BBC Safety, summed me up at my leaving do on 19 August 2011. It's also why I was leaving. After a decade travelling the world, filming undercover at football tournaments and all but snorting coke with gangsters in the name of News, I had taken redundancy. With cuts being made to our High Risk Team of six, the Beeb wanted me more desk-bound and less on the road. The man had said it himself: Craig Summers didn't work like that.

At first I thought I had been forced out by Paul Easter. He had arrived as my boss in February and we had a blazing row straightaway. With me in Iraq for the elections, he had taken one look at the calendar and rung me in Baghdad. 'I've cancelled your trip to America,' he'd said. 'You can do it on videophone or over the phone.'

I was livid. 'That's a £250,000 project agreed by Newsgathering. You can't just do that. You don't just buy armoured cars over the phone.'

I knew what people at the BBC wanted. None of my journalists wanted to read a 25-page-long Health and Safety form – and you couldn't run an op from thousands of miles away in London. When it came to security, those reporters cared about three things: can we get new kit, have we got the right vehicles and will we do it better next time? That was the kind of work I was into but this was the new politics.

Over the past decade, like everyone else, the BBC had gone Health and Safety mad.

But I left with mixed emotions. I'd had some great times and worked with some brilliant people. Many of those whom I had come to know over the years weren't there to hear Paul speak because of the Libyan coverage – my last job had been organising the crews for the London riots that summer, ironically where my work had begun all those years ago.

Paul Easter had asked me what would stop me leaving. '£5,000 and let me do my job,' I'd replied, but I only felt it was a token question. It had never been about the money – I could have earned more cash as a freelance. I loved the BBC. I had only had two proper jobs in my life and gradually over the years the two jobs had intertwined. First I was military, and then I was risk assessment-cum-journo. On both jobs, I was often undercover.

As a soldier in Bosnia I had watched the way Colonel Bob Stewart operated with Kate Adie in tow. That excited me. It was the first inkling I had about making the transition from army to media, and from that moment all I did was watch the BBC. A decade on, that great generation of classic reporters was beginning to fade and the Corporation was swamped with middle managers pulling purse strings. Everything from 9/11 to the Freedom of Information Act had changed the landscape. I didn't know where the next golden era of journos would be coming from, nor that once common determination to get the story that I had so admired. In Alex Crawford and Stuart Ramsay at Sky, I could see that the dream was still alive.

I still adored the BBC and would always watch the Ten but I was done, and there would never now be another Craig Summers in the Beeb. Over a period of six months, Sky had been courting me to become their Broadcast Security Operations Manager; an unpublicised incident in Afghanistan had set their alarm bells ringing, and they were looking to recruit somebody with my skill set. They were working in really tough terrain out there.

Head of News Fran Unsworth took me out to lunch to Jamie Oliver's restaurant to tell me she couldn't believe I was going. One of the assignment editors, Jonathan Paterson, told me it was crazy that they wanted me desk-bound, and my former producer Peter Leng told me he was devastated not to be going on the road again with John Simpson and me. As the alcohol flowed that night, I reminded myself not to put my foot in it as I so often had in the past. Don't be bitter, I told myself. Be polite, and walk out of there with your head held high.

It took me back to Gibraltar in 1984 when I had been on a mini exercise in the army stripping down vehicles. 'That fucking wanker put the radio in the back of the vehicle when we need it in the front,' I shouted entering the training room.

'So I am the wanker, am I?' said the officer from behind the desk.

'Yes, you are Sir,' I continued.

I got bollocked and was reminded of protocol!

I didn't want to leave with a ruined reputation. Anything could happen and I might be back here in the future but the truth remained that since Easter had arrived, I was no longer the first of the High Risk Team out of the door, preparing the ground for a global network of reporters in wildly varying scenarios. Four had left since he had arrived. Forty years of experience in this field down the drain.

It was a far cry from where it had all begun.

HUMBLE ORIGINS, FALSE DAWNS

I was born in Woolwich Military Hospital in 1960. My dad was in the army and my childhood took me to Malaya, Germany and back home to the UK. Predictably, I hated school and was out by sixteen. I became an apprentice sprayer at the local garage on my way to becoming the real deal Phil Mitchell – their speciality was cuts 'n' shuts, which wasn't illegal at the time. I had no qualifications: basketball at county standard was as good as it got. Of course, I had also been in trouble with the law.

Bored, like so many teenagers, and apathetic to education, my mates and I used to pass a café with Whitbread lorries outside of it – your classic truck stop fry-up gaff. We were thrill-seekers. Well, the uncovered cases in the back of the vehicles were too much to resist – and we didn't try to, until the day we got caught. My dad had me straight home from school that night and the police let us off with a warning.

Stupid arrogant me learned nothing. A week later, it was more of the same. At the age of fifteen, I was pinching cars with my mates in Bow, East London.

This time, when the police rang home, Dad said: 'I'm not coming to collect him, leave him in jail overnight.'

The next morning he came to court with me and bullshitted the judge. 'I'll make it sure it doesn't happen again,' he said. 'I've got him something lined up in the army.'

I was fined thirty quid – a lot of money back then – and from court I went straight to the Careers Office. My father had already been on the phone to some old contacts. But I was a Jack the Lad from East London. I didn't want the discipline.

My first port of call was Nuneaton in 1977. I hated it instantly. I had joined the Boys Service Junior Leaders Royal Artillery. Like the dickhead that I was, I turned up on the train with four cans of lager to use as bargaining tools! It was only an ex-Hells Angel, Lieutenant Dickey, who brought me to my senses, telling me I could make a good soldier and I should stick with it. He would put me down for Commando training, and that would enable me to fly around the world. I owe my twenty-three years in the army to my dad and Dickey.

From there, I joined 29 Commando in Plymouth, deployed to the Falklands during the war, before going to Belize, and next spent five years alongside the Special Boat Forces in Poole, Dorset. I went undercover for two years in Northern Ireland, toured Bosnia and did a UN tour of Cyprus. I had been there, done that and bought the t-shirt. When I was twenty-one, in 1982, the Falklands War was unbelievable; in 1991 I was itching to get to the Gulf. It was in my blood. I had to get to the heart of the action.

In Bosnia, the worst moment was witnessing the ethnic cleansing of Kiseljak, about thirty miles west of Sarajevo. The Mujahideen were rampant and told us to fuck off. Villagers were screaming, buildings were burning, and we just had to drive past. Afterwards, nobody believed that our soft-skinned vehicles had been down that road, where only armoured cars were supposed to go. It was horrific, not so much for the blood and guts and appalling racial slaughter, but for our helplessness at being unable to intervene.

For my last eighteen months, I returned to London to train the Territorial Army. I had also had a brief dalliance with the Foreign Legion but was turned away for being too pissed, which left me broke and abandoned on French soil.

In the process, my first marriage came and went – collateral damage in a typical military lifestyle of combat, booze and birds. Anita and I fell apart in 1990. Five years later, I got together with Sue, who would become my rock. I have two daughters from my first marriage.

After twenty-three years in the army, I'd had enough and the TA unit was being disbanded. At forty, I thought I was heading for the knacker's yard. I'd sweep the streets, drive a bus or deliver the mail – whatever it took. Even then a desk job was never going to be for me. On 8 October 2000, with nearly a quarter of a century of service and a lifetime of travel and adrenalin behind me, I left the army, feeling lucky but uncertain. I didn't have a clue what to do.

I was on eighteen months' notice to close the TA unit and clear the books at the office in East Ham. They still needed someone to turn up, but I was on my own. For six months, I went through the motions, paid, but walking in dead men's shoes.

The game was up. I knew what I wanted to do, but I had no idea how to get there. I would advise current affairs producers on their investigative programmes on a freelance basis, and I would take on any other work between jobs. The problem, as I soon found out, was that I was always between jobs.

In the summer of 2000 I had formed KCM Security with Mike Basson and Kev Sweeney as my partners. I told Sue we would give it until April 2001 to see if it could work. Part of the problem was that Mike and Kev already had other jobs: I was the only person on it full-time.

It had been a call from an ex-regiment mate, Chris Cobb-Smith, at the end of April 2000 while I was still going through the motions with the TA, that had planted this seed.

Chris was safety and security advisor at the BBC. 'Would you like to work as a back-watcher for the BBC at the May Day Riots?' he asked.

'How much wedge?' I replied.

'About £150.'

I didn't hesitate to agree, even though I didn't yet know what a back-watcher was. This was too good to be true. It was a brilliant opportunity to do something different. My job was to protect the camera crews from the anti-capitalist rioters, known bizarrely as The Wombles.

Early the next day, I met Chris and Tony Loughran at the BBC building on the Embankment. (Little did I know that Tony would end up being my boss.) I was assigned to a camera crew whose brief was to follow the parades. Wherever there was trouble, we had to get in among it. Nicholas Witchell was the reporter, and this was his first experience in all his years as a journalist of having a back-watcher. My God did it show.

'We'll be guided by you,' they said to me, 'as long as you understand we have got to get pictures.'

'I'm happy to take you in there,' I explained. 'I'm public-order trained and I'll take you in as far as you can go.'

Their preparation was a joke, but I hadn't been part of the planning. Had there even been any planning – given that I only got the call the night before? They passed me a small rucksack. Inside was a first aid kit, a fire extinguisher and a couple of baseball caps. This was the BBC's riot kit, and there wasn't even enough for our team of four. If anything, it would identify us as undercover police.

I later found out that this all came from a store room at the bottom of the BBC building, which was run by Health and Safety – you got what you could, and you wrote it down in the BBC book. The Beeb were sending people to war zones around the world with a security kit that looked like it had been bought at a jumble sale. Poorly managed, under-resourced and with no accountability, it had disaster written all over it.

But I was buzzing. It was fantastic to be working for the mighty BBC. Me, Craig Summers, with zero education, standing next to Nick Witchell, TV legend. Admittedly, he was your classic ginger-haired public schoolboy, who looked like he would jump a mile if you shouted at him, but he was still the business.

I wanted to go looking for trouble. I was desperate for a call saying it had all kicked off nearby. The truth was that bar a few empty beer cans chucked, it was relatively peaceful.

My military head told me not to switch off. You were always on your guard – we call it sleeping with one eye open. I would check side streets, mentally prepare escape routes, talking through in my mind where we might get blocked in, always listening out for the alarm bell of the slightly intoxicated hitting the streets. I had the same drive and awareness I'd had in Northern Ireland but now it was different. I had to protect not just Witchell but also the cameraman, Tony Dolce. The reporter could voice anything but without the shots, his story had no legs. I recognised that the cameraman was key and bombarded him with questions.

'How do you want to play this?' I asked Tony.

'I will only have one eye on the lens,' he explained. 'But I won't be able to see what's around me.'

'I'll grab hold of you if I have to and pull you back if needs be,' I reassured him.

He told me that was fine and I loved it. Just like Nick, he'd never had a back-watcher before. This is what I was trained for. Now though, I could see a whole new world of job opportunities unfolding before me. I knew I'd love to do this full-time.

For years, there hadn't been any support: the risk they ran was part and parcel of the job. The new duty of care BBC, the Health and Safety culture, and the death of journalist John Schofield in Kosovo in 1995 had clearly begun to define a new era. You couldn't just wander into a war zone any more with the letters B-B-C on the side of your vehicle. The rules of engagement had changed, both in terms of the enemy and of the necessary paperwork dictated by the modern era. I hoped this would be the beginning of something where I would finally get to show my value.

Passing the entrance of 10 Downing Street, we were forced against the railings by the police cordon repelling the demonstrators. They were said to be targeting McDonald's, Gap and Starbucks. The line held firm, which surprised me, pushing the protesters further up the road towards Trafalgar Square. Being penned in really pissed me off. I'd thought that as news crew we could just wander across the line, and I told the cops so. Just as the police baton-charged the rioters, I grabbed Tony's jacket and yanked him close to me.

'We're getting through,' I shouted at one of them.

Somehow, we got pushed against the wall which Tony was filming. I noticed demonstrators climbing onto the roof of McDonald's and pointed them out to him. A Sky cameraman with no back-watcher was knocked to the floor, but we got right into the entrance of the restaurant. And I'd just happened to have looked in that direction, as I tried to either stay one step ahead of the police or move away up the side of the road.

I was on a massive adrenalin rush, and loving the abuse of the great unwashed – mostly students lobbing burgers and beer at us with the odd punch. It was comedy violence, and using a burger as their weapon of choice defined their stupidity. I could more than handle this and I knew it would only go so far. It was nothing to some of the stuff I had seen at war. My military undercover training had taught me that nine times out of ten there was always a way out of a situation and that you should restrain yourself as long as possible. These louts were no threat to us, and within five or six minutes the police were on to them.

'Enough?' I turned to ask Tony.

'Yep, we've got enough,' he replied, and we retreated.

But I felt great. I had kept them safe but, more importantly, I had given them the story, and that gave me the buzz. My soldier's instinct seemed to be exactly in synch with what the journos wanted – where there was danger I would protect them, and where that danger took us was probably the story.

'That was brilliant.' Tony was over the moon, thanking me for pulling him free without knocking his arm holding the camera, which was still running. Nick Witchell thanked me too.

By 21.00, my feet were killing me and the story was dead. A few protesters were out of it and there was still the odd sporadic incident but we were done. I knew I had earned my £150 as we trudged back through Parliament Square, and I really felt part of something as I carried Tony's tripod back to the BBC. When I got home at 02.00, Sue was in bed and I was still buzzing. I knew exactly what I wanted to do and would call Chris Cobb-Smith in the morning. I couldn't wait to get up.

I rang and rang and nobody answered. Nor did anybody from the Beeb call me to say well done. Nothing. I hadn't realised that was how it worked. I was all up for the next job, desperate to know when it was happening, but there was no next job. It was back to the TA and pretending to check the paperwork, playing caretaker. I mostly sat at home, twiddling my thumbs.

Then it happened, out of the blue, nearly a month later. 'I've got something here which I think will be right up your street.' Chris was back on.

'Count me in,' I said without knowing what the job was.

There was no 'you did a really good job last time'. The conversation was short and blunt, typically military on both sides. I needed to get to White City to meet the *Panorama* team immediately. They wanted me to go undercover at Euro 2000 looking for hooligans.

This was what I'd been waiting for. I was a massive football fan and had been involved in a scrap or two myself. My only concern was that I didn't want to bump into anyone I knew. The next day I was straight into town to meet the producer, Tom Giles. On this occasion the brief was simple.

'Can you film undercover?' he asked.

'Yeah,' I replied.

I knew how to work a small DV camera – but even if I didn't, I would have bullshitted. I had to get on the plane and show them what I could do. With just a conversation as short as that it was probably already a done deal, but I didn't know that. I was heading for the Euros on the BBC. I couldn't believe my luck.

I was assigned to work with Tom Giles. We were an unlikely couple – he was your classic BBC type, well educated and from the John Simpson school of journalism. Then there was me, a schoolboy drop-out who'd spent his life in the army. First things first, on any undercover job – what was our cover story?

Before heading out to Holland and Belgium, we decided that we had been at school together and both had military parents based in Germany. I could play that part easily and Tom would just follow suit. I knew from the old days that the key to the other you is keeping it simple. Try to over-complicate who you are, and you're in the shit. We stuck to Craig and Tom – that made sense. I didn't want to start calling him 'Paul' and then shout 'Tom' across a crowded bar. Our real names would do. He knew his football, too, so I wasn't concerned on that front – even though with his bouffant hair he didn't really look like an England fan!

Very quickly, I became comfortable wearing the undercover gear. The camera was a buttonhole in my shirt with wires leading down to a belt underneath. I had the power supply on one side and the camera on the other. A key fob went into my pocket; if I pressed it, a red light would come on and we were filming. Battery life was between one and two hours, and if I needed to change them, I would do so in the toilet behind a closed door. The temptation to keep checking we were rolling never left me.

I couldn't let the gear dominate who I was – the need to stay in character was paramount. If I got in a fight or stood up too quickly, my shirt could show my equipment. In the absolute worst case scenario, I would come clean and say we were working for *Panorama*.

But I knew I could handle myself. I told myself to see it as a normal job, and that meant having full awareness going into any building. Stay close to the doors, never get stuck smack bang in the middle, and always look for exit points. Be aware and keep one eye open. A cursory glance to Tom should be enough to send a message. Mingle with the fans and drink the night away, but only down half the pint. Eye up the flashpoints and join in with the England songs, I told myself. I knew I was an easy casting for the role. Frankly, my two lives had now collided and I wondered why I hadn't done this sooner. I was getting paid for it, I didn't have to justify every expense with a receipt, and I was on tour with the BBC. My biggest fear was letting Tom down. I knew straightaway that this was the life I wanted. I was working undercover for *Panorama* – the flagship news programme on the BBC!

In all we were a team of seven, and it wasn't hard work. Go where the England shirts took you and follow the whiff of alcohol. We did have prior intelligence, of course. You don't need to have followed England at major tournaments to know that we were probably going to be onto a winner. Violence had never been too far away over the years. Specifically, though, we were hunting the Cardiff City Soul Crew; in particular, Annis Abraham.

We knew about Abraham from previous incidents, and we knew he was definitely there. Tom A had also followed over a couple of the known Cardiff and West Ham boys, Shane Weldon and Matthew Marion. Thugs with no chance or intention of getting a ticket in Charleroi had turned up for the ruck. The stadium itself housed only 30,000 – there were at least 40,000 England fans on the street, and you could hear them on every corner, moaning about the fact that they had been on the piss all day long and hadn't got wasted. (The authorities had watered down the beer.) Equally, their musical back catalogue left a lot to be desired. 'No surrender to the IRA', 'Ten German Bombers' and 'Two World Wars and One World Cup' were the particular favourites.

I was soon reminded that if I hadn't been this side of the under-cover filming, I could have been on the other. My mate Wolfy – a Wolves fan, obviously – recognised me in the mêlée.

'What are you doing here?' he asked.

'I'm doing stuff for the BBC,' I openly confessed without thinking about it.

I made my excuses that I had to pick up my ticket and left abruptly. Deep down, I had known I would bump into him and I trusted him. He was a former colleague from the army and no thug at all. But the chance meeting kept me in the zone and prepared mentally to stay in the role. It just planted that seed of doubt that I might run into the old school Inter City West Ham hardcore. I needed to avoid that all costs.

Either way, we had been given the story on a plate. England had been drawn against Germany in this tiny pocket-sized venue. The *Panorama* show was due to air in days. Despite a few minor scuffles, and the striking image of the local police firing the water cannons at drunken English fans, we knew what we were all waiting for. There was no way it wouldn't kick off.

By the evening of the game I was paired with Sam Bagnall. We were a more natural couple. Tom had done a good job in character on the ground, mingling with the fans and singing those awful songs but Sam was a bit more Arsenal and a bit less posh – the casting was perfect. I didn't know how Tom would handle himself in a scrap.

At our meeting to assign new roles, I asked a couple of key questions. I was still new to this and wanted to know how far I could go. I was keen to stay in the role, and if I had to throw a punch, I would. If I could chant and sing, so be it. I was told not to start anything, even if it made us look cowards in the heat of the moment. Join in – yes. Pull out – if needs be. Go with it, but don't be the star of the show. I knew I wouldn't have to wait long, but I had to do it the BBC way, despite my instincts to let it kick off. I'd been told that if nothing happened, nothing happened. We couldn't engineer it. I had no doubts, though. It was England–Germany after all.

Sam and I had hit the streets around 10.30 to get established. Hooligans were predictable and territorial – they would always be attracted to a huge plaza, a water fountain and bars round a square. It was a natural magnet. Throw into the mix some Turks, clearly just there for trouble, and, as I said to Sam, it was an accident waiting to happen. Bare chests, face paint, and the Union Jack draped across the body were the style of the day in searing heat. There was no doubt that alcohol would light the blue touchpaper – regardless of what happened on the pitch.

Three-quarters of an hour before kick-off, you just knew the temperature was rising. I was keeping an eye on the police so I never saw who threw the first punch but it just went mental. The England fans were edging towards the German fans and plastic chairs and pots of beer were raining on the police. Sam and I were about half a row back from the front, war cries of 'Come on, we'll have you' all around us. These weren't the usual diehard England scum – these were the young wannabes wanting to make a name for themselves, keen to prove to the old school that they were hardcore in their first fights on England duty.

The German fans got up and started to move towards us. I was loving it, thinking, 'Come on, let's get the ball rolling and let's get stuck in.' I knew it was going to get tasty.

As the two sides came together, I couldn't locate any of our 'targets'. The police came tearing in and then I spotted the water cannon coming at us. I grabbed Sam and we retreated round the corner. 'We don't want to get hit by that,' I warned him.

Within seconds, the police had cleared the square. I had never seen this technique used before. It was like something out of Mad Max and the police didn't care if they ran anyone over. This was a no-nonsense approach. We made our way away as the fans tore down our street, knowing that the overt crew had the shots with the big camera from the top end of the square. We decided to walk the kilometre or so to the ground.

The fans had to make their way through mesh fencings but just tore them down, battering them with batons. Most of them didn't have tickets. The stupidity of having such a massive game here between two teams with 'previous' couldn't have been more obvious. The police's only response was to go in heavy handed, regardless of legitimacy. Still the songs reigned – despite 'No surrender to the IRA' being completely out of context at an England v Germany game!

By kick off time, we were back in the square to see what was happening. The police and their vans had formed a massive cordon; we retreated to a café further down. When Alan Shearer scored the winner, the place erupted and so did we. But our work was done. The call had come in to get to Brussels. Our information was that the Cardiff boys were heading there.

The fixture list was now irrelevant. England had to play Romania to qualify, and Romania didn't have football hooligans. All roads now led to the Belgium capital. Turkey were playing Belgium the night before England's crunch match – that was now the new flash-point, and *Panorama* was due on air hours after the final whistle of the England game.

We didn't have a great deal to make a show that was anything different to what you had come to expect from England fans. It wasn't really shocking because we had all grown up with it. Everything hinged on Brussels but we were making *Panorama* on the fly with a small amount of panic. We had some footage from Eindhoven, trouble in the square and the stadium at Charleroi, but we didn't have the money shot. Turkey versus Belgium, a throng of England's worst, and the Cardiff fans being spotted in Brussels was our only hope.

I had underestimated Tom and Sam's knowledge, contacts and tip-offs. They were passionate about making the programme and exposing the England hooligans. I hadn't been part of the intelligence about the Cardiff fans prior to the trip. Among their hooligans was actually a current player, Dai Thomas. Let's remember, Wales hadn't even qualified – as usual. These fans were there only to cause trouble.

Caught up in the heat of events, I had made the mistake of thinking the story was dictated by the action on the pitch.

I had a picture of Annis Abraham in my head – something I was able to do through a military technique called Kim's Game, which is used to test your memory to develop a semi-photographic recall.

After just one sighting of his picture, I knew who we were looking for. I had also learned that he was into dodgy nightclubs and young girls, and that he didn't drink. His hangers-on would be surrounding him but he was the one I was looking for.

Buzzing at the thought of making my first show for the BBC, I considered myself an outsider, soaking up all the nervous energy, listening to the jargon but fascinated by the speculation as to whether they could make sixty minutes out of the hours of footage that we had taken. I wanted more of this.

Deep in the Grand Place area of Brussels, we had identified O'Reilly's as the focal point. The England game was not until the next day, so there was no need to go out too early. We left it quite late before pitching up. Our overt camera team was also out filming. We were specifically hunting Abraham. In the corner, a group of England fans were doing lines of coke off the table as I entered.

'Fuck, where's Sam?' I thought.

He was right behind me, filming. We weren't there to make a drugs exposé but it certainly added to the picture. I weighed up in my head what I would do if I found myself at the same table. I decided I would go as far as I could and then withdraw. That was the nature of working undercover.

Outside, someone shouted: 'They've got knives!' England fans were stirring it with the Turks and the Belgium nationals.

My adrenalin rush was on. I couldn't ask Sam if I should join them – that would be too indiscreet. I was slightly reeled in and carried away with the chanting – my ears were ringing with 'No surrender to the IRA' and it was rammed inside. We still had nothing bar the random afternoon scuffle and the odd shot of Abraham walking the streets. I was smart enough to realise the potential of the situation we were in and the need to be patient, but at this point we didn't have a show.

The plain-clothes coppers were standing by, ridiculously obvious in their jeans, lightweight jackets, bum bags worn at the front, cropped hair, and easily visible ear pieces. I wouldn't have been so open myself

– they made it pretty obvious who they were, despite having said that they would keep a low profile until needed. Any football hooligan would have clocked them.

All I could think about was whether Abraham was here.

A mass of England fans charged through the door, the police trying to follow them in. It was smoky; people were jumping. What followed felt like twenty seconds but probably lasted half an hour. Riot police appeared from nowhere. Sam and I tried to force our way to the door – basic instinct, remember the exits. 'They're attacking us,' people were crying. I could see the riot police in body armour appear outside from nowhere. Annis Abraham was round the corner, having been picked up by the overt crew. Sam and I didn't know this.

I shielded Sam so as not to blow our cover when he rang the producers to say it had all gone mental. We had to walk the fine line between staying in character and communicating a message to the guys on the ground. Sam knew that we needed the outside shots and I wanted him to sound as if he was ringing his mates to tell them it was all going nuts at O'Reilly's and we needed back up. As long as he sounded like a thug, it didn't matter, except for the fact that we didn't have an exit strategy. The inside doors were locked and there was nowhere to turn. Tables and chairs were flying everywhere. Much as I loved it, this was the worst-case scenario. How the fuck do we get out of here? Yet the magnet of danger made me want to stay.

Professionally, I was miffed because I hadn't seen it coming and I had been looking for Annis Abraham, not considering the exit strategy. 'Have you got enough?' I asked Sam. 'Do you need any more?'

Sam was fine. He had plenty. The best plan was to leave. Plus, the police weren't taking any chances and I didn't want to declare my hand. I needed to react quickly, and I didn't want to be caught. I could blow the whole thing if I didn't think smart.

The hardcore kept the front of the bar blocked; I was aiming for the side door, just to the right of the café where Annis Abraham was hanging out.

As we were leaving, the police fired tear gas into the bar. We missed it by seconds. I had made the right call to abandon just as the room filled with smoke, leaving most with watering eyes. Of course, the more they rubbed, the itchier they got, as disorientation took over.

Sam and I escaped but there was no Annis. I did spy the overt team behind the police line, which was a great sign. We had been at the heart of the action and I had got Sam out safely. I had taken him as close to the danger as possible without endangering him.

Job done, and well.

I knew we had done as much as we could and the right thing was to disassociate from the scene, avoid arrest and preserve the tapes. Later when I watched them back, they showed our friend from Cardiff arriving at O'Reilly's just seconds too late, filmed coming out of the shop next door, playing the innocent party. The police had also fired a tear gas canister there. Our hunch had been correct.

We handed the footage to a runner to rush back to the Bureau. The show was to air in less than twenty-four hours. I loved it. Out by the skin of our teeth: another few seconds and we could have our kit ripped off and ended up beaten, arrested, or without a programme. I was made up that we had evacuated in time, but knackered too. I went to bed and passed out until eleven the next morning.

Just a few days before, the BBC journalist Gavin Hewitt and I had had a bust-up at breakfast. I had questioned whether we had made the right choice in coming here given that England were playing in Charleroi. I subsequently apologised. 'Don't worry, we're on edge at the moment,' Gavin replied.

We all knew that we didn't have enough material. To top it all, Peter Horrocks, editor of *Panorama*, was flying in to town in the next twenty-four hours. I was confused by the mission, believing in the guys making the show but starting to develop the journalistic instinct that we had been in the wrong place. We had almost retreated.

I awoke proud, thinking this could finally be my big break with the BBC, but my work here was done. At the edit suite, I took it all in, starry-eyed at seeing what it took to put the show together, witnessing first-hand the panic as the clock ticked down, knowing that Gavin Hewitt would still have to dub in an almost live voice-over after the result that night.

England still had to play Romania: the show would follow immediately. I offered my services one more time, but the production manager told me to return to the hotel – they would call if they needed me. I hit the bar and watched the game.

There was nobody in except a solitary drunk American. Suddenly Horrocks turned up. I had never met him before but the timing couldn't have been better. The Yank started taking pictures of us. 'I know who you fucking are,' he slurred.

There was no way he could. I asked him politely to stop taking the pictures, and then I told him the Craig way when he refused. 'I've asked you once, now I'm telling you,' I eyeballed him, flicking the film out of his camera before handing it back to him and calling Hotel Security. To this day, I still don't know who he was or what he was after.

'Thank you,' Peter said. 'You handled that well, and thanks for all you have done at the tournament.'

He had come straight from the edit suite and tensions were running high. I knew that he would remember that, and me, and he had definitely seen my work first-hand in the final edit on *Panorama*. It couldn't have gone better. I was in, I had proved myself, and I could visualise the journey ahead, seeing out my time with the TA and starting straightaway with the Beeb. As I collected my air ticket home from the Brussels Bureau, I knew it was only a matter of time before the phone rang again.

It was now 9 October – officially the flattest day of my life. The week after the Euros I had rung Tom Giles repeatedly. There was no answer. I had done a cracking job, but again they weren't taking my calls. I hadn't expected this a second time. *Panorama* shows came and went as summer rolled into autumn; I would watch the weekly credits looking out for names I knew, like Tom's, and still there was nothing. I would spot 'Tom Giles' on the screen, and think 'I know him' – but I didn't, and every week put more distance between my new dream and my stark reality. I was getting into the role, but the role hadn't been given to me.

This was the day I officially walked out of army headquarters for the last time.

I had entered the unknown. After years of the army being my life, I didn't really know what to expect. I couldn't do a thing myself, and I had no job. Together, Sue and I had money for about six months, but I was worried. I could be a security guard, or retrain, or anything, but essentially I was clueless. Nothing but uncertainty lay ahead.

I rang everyone I knew to tell them about KCM. Our company would do security work for the media. I called Chris Cobb-Smith; Tom Giles told me he would call if anything came up, and I hung on every phone call hoping it was him. I was no businessman and had no idea how to promote the company, and security was a dirty word. People thought I was a bouncer or someone stood outside, marshalling cars. I wanted surveillance and covert work. The bigger security groups were already established, and here we were trying to build a business based on the back of a fag packet.

We were clutching at straws, and going nowhere fast. I had the vision but not the know-how. And then, Tom Giles finally rang.

'Oh fuck, it's Tom.' I froze as my old Nokia flashed up his name.

Back then, not everyone had a mobile, and I had two Toms in my phone. This one was Tom from *Panorama*. I have never answered a phone so carefully, so worried about cutting someone off.

'Hi Craig, it's Tom,' he began. 'Are you happy to go down to Wales and do some undercover filming on your own?'

I couldn't believe it. 'That was Tom from *Panorama*,' I told Sue after he hung up.

I had no idea how much to charge or what the job was. I just felt privileged we had our first job and, best of all, the BBC were trusting me. It was all on me. My work at the Euros had got me moving.

In London, I learned it was more of the same – hooligans. I couldn't wait. I would be mixing with my own. The show on the Euros was called *England's Shame* and later won an award. Tom Anstiss, the producer, wanted more shame and more awards.

They were running a three-part series on hooligans in the UK, Italy, and Argentina. I was heading back to the land of Annis Abraham for more. In my head, I was on the plane to Lazio and River Plate to go undercover. In my bank account I was thinking ching-ching. This was it. Surely, this time, I was in, and it was going to happen.

I was told if it went wrong, it didn't matter. They already had some footage. That sort of watered down my task and I felt a bit used – back to the role of bouncer in among the public schoolboys. I knew my editorial sense was slowly developing, though, and when they told me who I was after, I couldn't get down the M4 quick enough.

My destination was a bar/nightclub called Apollo 2; my company was the Cardiff Soul Crew again. Cardiff City Chairman Sam Hammam was going to be the star of the show! Tom Anstiss met me in a service station outside Cardiff, and a man from Swansea known only as 'The Bear' came along as my cover story. He was the fixer who was going to look after me. This time, I was a massive Wimbledon fan, in awe of Sam Hammam, on leave in Cardiff buying property. Bear was a native, a loveable rogue who knew the bad lads in the city. It was simple and mostly accurate. I didn't foresee any trouble.

I was excited at the thought of Sam the Man being there. What a coup that would be. I loved the idea that Annis Abraham would probably show too. I was also told to look out for two characters called Neil McNamara and Shane Weldon. As I left the car that night, I ran through a mental checklist. Was everything charged and on? Was The Bear going to look after me and play it cool given that I would be the only Englishman in the bar? Could we handle a seat-of-the-pants operation when I was trained as a soldier to recce the joint before any operation?

Inside, I was buzzing that Sam Hammam was coming – and so was the bar. A couple of fans challenged me and I bullshitted them with some Brecon Beacons bollocks but once they realised I wasn't Man U or Chelsea or any threat to Cardiff City, it passed. I'm naturally suspicious and most people aren't. They accepted me.

I became relaxed but not complacent. I was concentrating on the camera – and waiting for Sam. I wasn't entirely sure he would show and I needed a cut-off point to get out before being compromised. Equally, I didn't want to keep asking when he was going to turn up. My over-keenness could blow the whole thing. I didn't want to lose my credibility with Tom by filming some other thug when I should have been filming Sam. I knew I was on trial – they had told me the footage wasn't vital, but Jesus, I knew if I got Sam Hammam that was big drama. The battery was good for two to three hours.

The bar was boiling and smoky – this, too, was before the law changed. Then the stakes were raised. From a side entrance the little man appeared. I thought we would get a good shot but the place was hysterical, bouncing with his arrival. We were close but not close enough.

I retreated to the loo to check the gear, locking the door to make sure nobody could get in. I unzipped the bag and checked the camera, changing the battery because it had been running for some time. But I wasn't alone in the bog. After waiting, I pulled the chain and walked straight past the other two guys in there. I realised on the way back that I was near where Sam had come in and figured that this was the best place to stand. Amazingly, he was announcing that he would lay on coaches for the next away game. Then, as I was attempting to run the tape for 'atmos', Annis Abraham came into the corridor.

'Hello mate, how are you?' Bear said to Annis.

Bear and Annis knew each other? It was my lucky day. Then Bear introduced me.

Annis looked at me as if to say what the hell was I doing here. Thankfully Bear explained the cover story. I couldn't believe I was actually chatting to him.

Then it got even better. Sam Hammam was coming my way and Bear and Annis introduced me to him!

But I wasn't filming. I had turned the thing off. I knew this was the shot I wanted, so I took the risk of stepping back a few steps and hit the key fob to press record and play. Annis and Sam were in shot talking to each other.

Bear and I looked at each other. This was what we had come for. On the way out a couple of Annis's cronies approached us to buy some Cardiff Soul Crew badges. I duly obliged to avoid confrontation. I didn't care. I was desperate to see the film.

As soon as Tom saw us leave the pub, he set off back to the service station and we followed. That Sam Hammam turned up at all was brilliant, and leaving with a well-known hooligan surely condemned him. He hadn't come to preach peace. He was the club owner and he had come out to a bar in the Valleys to meet with convicted hooligans.

I was just relieved that I had got the footage. Sent on a whim, I had delivered. I had been in that pub since 19.30, and by the time I rang Tom Giles to give him the good news it was gone half one in the morning. It had been a nightmare shoot getting so close but it had been worth it – we had a reasonable ten-to-twelve-second recording of Sam Hammam with good sound quality.

I drove home at speed, excited and reliving it all the way. I was home by three but the journey was a blur. I loved my role, mixing it with the scum yet providing the real deal for the BBC Oxbridge elite. I knew I was adding something they didn't have and couldn't ignore again for a third time.

The next day, I rang Tom. And I rang him again. I needed that call. I left voicemail after voicemail and waited for him to call me back. I was now realising that this was the way things worked.

Around half two he finally called. Would I come up to the BBC for a chat? I was convinced I was hired. Finally.

The next day I met him. I couldn't have been more deflated. I had debated whether to turn up smart or casual but it didn't matter one iota. For goodness sake, I would have worked for free. The chat lasted just ten minutes and I got the usual. 'If anything crops up, I'll give you a call,' he told me.

I was devastated. It was another smack in the stomach I didn't need. I'd gone from hero to zero overnight, and this time I felt it was the end of the line. I rang Chris Cobb-Smith, who said that was the just the way it went – it would always be fits and starts. You were only as good as your next job, often forgotten about in the interim. I begged Tom to see if there were any vacancies in *Panorama* for people like me. He told me straight – they normally used APs (Assistant Producers) on six-month contracts. Ad-hoc was all it was ever going to be.

Chris told me that night in the BBC Club that I needed to look at other avenues like Amnesty International. My dreams temporarily on hold, I thought this was the way I would have to go. It might still be an in-road.

By Christmas, I'd had a good look at my life. Nothing was happening and I was worried that I was wasting my time. I was also eating heavily into my army money. Chris got me an invite to a security exhibition at the Charing Cross Hotel in London to meet some people and hand out some business cards. Again, nothing. The furthest I got was meeting Mal McGowan, whose company Pilgrims had just taken over the Hostile Environments Course at the BBC. Later, I would come to know it only too well, but for now, it was just another brick wall.

By February 2001, I was really depressed about the whole thing – getting used to civilian life also took its toll. Despite the money running out, I had made a long-standing promise to take my daughters on holiday to Los Angeles.

Just before we were due to pack, the phone rang out of the blue. It was Chris Cobb-Smith. 'I want to go freelance,' he began. 'I don't want to be tied to a particular job. Are you interested in taking over from me?'

It was the last thing I was expecting. Uncharacteristically, I stalled him and rang Sue. As desperate as I was for the gig, I didn't want to seem too keen. I also called Mike and Kev, who backed me 100 per cent. They knew the business was going nowhere fast, and we had always had an understanding that if something permanent came up, I would have to take it.

This was it – finally, some nine months after holding Nicholas Witchell's hand at the May Day riots, I could get a foot in the door. If I ballsed it up, this would surely be my last chance gone. I had never applied for anything in my life, let alone online. I'd just gone from one army posting to another and now here I was desperately trying to follow the application on the screen, with pages of notes all laid out around me at home. I had to give it everything.

My dial-up connection failed me. Back in those days, any online form was a race against time before the screen froze, and we lost this one more than once. Sue told me to leave it for the night and come back the next day, but I had to get it done there and then. By midnight I had finally pressed send. Then it was a waiting game, until an envelope with those three famous letters on the front dropped onto the mat. I froze; when I read the contents it got worse. I'd thought I would just go in for another chat and the deal would be done. Instead I had been summoned to a board interview at exactly the time we would be in the States.

I was panicking more than I ever had in any war zone. Sue made me ring the number to explain, and I was able to reschedule so we would return from America on the Saturday and I would interview on the Monday.

When we landed back at Heathrow, I flicked on my mobile – there was a message from Tom Giles. Would I go to Cardiff tomorrow for the Worthington Cup Final – Liverpool v Birmingham – for a whiff of my old mates from the Soul Crew?

I'd had four seats to myself on the plane back so I wasn't jet-lagged. I told Sue that, interview or no interview, I had to go. I was still a freelancer, and who knew how Monday would pan out? If I blew the board, I still had an in with Tom. I was totally buzzing again, both at the prospect of more work with the Cardiff lot and at the real possibilities that Monday could lead to. My brief was to traipse around the bars and see how their fans reacted to the Liverpool and Birmingham fans, given that this was one of the first major matches to be held outside Wembley while the new stadium was being built.

The mission was a no-go though. The rain wrecked it, there was no sign of Annis, and trouble was minimal. I wondered why I had bothered, but it was work. This was the downside – the stuff you don't see on *Panorama*, when there are no BAFTAs because there was no footage.

My mind was on the interview all the way home, of course, racing with questions I would probably be asked. I got through the door at half one in the morning, wet and knackered, and the night wasn't much better. The disappointment of not getting the money shot for once had given me a reality check, and my head was spinning through every hour.

I was confident of my own knowledge, but not of my suit, nor the BBC process. I had no idea how to behave and I looked like someone who'd been demobbed in 1958. Some people look fantastic in suits and others look like a bag of shite. I was the latter. I was so uncomfortable about my first real job interview.

In the morning, I drove to Slough and took the Reading train to Paddington. I was in town within half an hour – ridiculously early. Chris was going to meet me beforehand to give me the lowdown on the job.

Stupidly, just as I got off the tube at White City to meet him, I got soaked in a downpour, and now looked even worse. My suit was in ruins, looking as if it had been screwed up in a bag and then put on. What a dickhead I was – I was in such a hurry to get there, I had made a schoolboy error. Seconds later the skies cleared.

Chris reassured me, telling me not to worry about the suit. 'Don't worry, the job is yours,' he told me. 'They'll ask you a couple of scenario questions – take your time and be confident.' Then he left me in the foyer and I was on my own. In the toilets, I looked in the mirror, sorted my suit out and had a good word with myself. I knew I could I do this if my nerves didn't muck it up.

Tony Loughran led me up to the board. He was giving me that 'You'll be fine. I want you on board' look. I felt the valve on the pressure cooker being released ever so gently. Also present were Bob Forster – ex-RAF but now head of Safety. Tony was the senior security advisor and alongside him were Harry Muir, a health and safety advisor, and Jenny Baxter, the stand-in Foreign News editor.

Harry hit me with some questions about journalists carrying respirators and nuclear biological germ warfare. I could handle that no problem. Tony asked me about my medical training and how I would react in a war zone scenario if there was an accident. Again, that was right up my street. He quizzed me on my priorities – safety first or getting the pictures?

'We're in the business of getting pictures.' I told them what they wanted to hear. It was also the way I had begun to think during my previous engagements on *Panorama* duty. That work had stood me in good stead, despite the irregularity of it. Crucially, too, I was showing them that the ex-soldier was learning to think like a programme maker.

It felt like I was in there no time at all. They grilled me for just under an hour. The fact that it flew by told me I had done well. I had put the suit behind me and my knowledge on the table and was mixing it with my own. In fact, I felt they had a bit of a simplistic attitude to security but being interviewed by ex-military definitely put me on a level footing. I left thinking one thought. I had got that job. (I found out afterwards that Jenny wanted a female to do the job. I don't think she wanted an ex-squaddie coming in. The previous applicant had been a woman.) I rang Sue to say that it had gone well – the inside info from Chris had calmed me. Unless I had totally misread it, I knew the job was mine.

Two days later, they rang. I would start on 5 March 2001. All my frustrations and uncertainties were laid to rest; the four individual jobs I had been given since last May had shown me the way, and my badgering of Chris and Tom had finally paid off. Little did I know that the weekend that I was due to start, the IRA would decide to bomb Television Centre.

OFF WITH A BLAST

Seven people were injured when the Real IRA detonated in front of TC at half past midnight on the weekend of the 3 and 4 March. The building would have been less populated than at any other point in the week. They hadn't wanted to kill anyone; it was simply a warning in response to a *Panorama* special naming certain individuals. What a welcome to the BBC.

I was up early on the Monday as a big adrenalin rush kicked in. I hadn't been interested in working for any other networks – for me, it was all about the BBC. Not only did I have the job I chased for months but suddenly on day one, when I was meant to be sitting down to a Health and Safety induction, I had a chance to show my worth instantly. Yes, in the new era, courses and form-filling were rife, but I knew this was tasty. Ireland had been my patch four years previously, and now they were on our very own doorstep the day I started work. I was flashing back to Armagh. There had been no phone call to *Panorama* or the BBC, even though the IRA usually like to take credit, but we knew and I knew.

Tony and Chris met me at the door – except it wasn't the one I had walked through for my interview. That had been blown off. I entered through the side and within an hour we were marching over to *Panorama* to brief and be debriefed. I was desperate to get started and to bump into Tom Giles again.

Straightaway, I was assigned to talk to the wife of reporter John Ware, teaching her about number recognition systems, and how to spot changes to her car – a mark here or there, and the boot might have been tampered with. Always check under the vehicle, too, without being obvious about it. I told her to look regularly and to go to the police with anything unusual. There was no point checking it only the next day. Ireland had taught me to look for something like a small Tupperware box with a tilt switch attached. When you drive off – well, you don't. You get blown into the sky.

This wasn't the first day that the department had had in mind for me but I loved it and stayed for twelve hours. They'd wanted someone slightly below my skill set who was more into Health and Safety, rather than an individual who could develop the security side, but on day one I saw opportunity and have never looked back. I began to carve out the job for myself. The IRA's attempt to blow up the BBC actually triggered my most significant career move yet, saving me from a life of paperwork and thrusting me into the heart of the action.

When I finally got home, Sue could see I'd had the time of my life. I told her about everyone I'd met and everything I'd done and when I finished I was already watching my mobile, hoping for it to ring to call me back in. I was loving it. My journalistic taste buds had been tickled and I knew the BBC needed me in security. They had done an average job patching up the building after the bomb with some guard rails set up outside and some half decent measures to screen the thousands of people coming and going. They had just about got their shit together but it was clear that security at the BBC could never be the same again. I was already in pole position to help shape that.

I gave everyone I could my number to put myself about, and told them I was there 24/7. By Friday, the week had become a joyous blur – I felt like I had always been there and had a key role to play. By the time we treated ourselves to a takeaway and put our feet up for the weekend, Monday couldn't come quick enough. Honestly, I have never been happier. I knew if I didn't balls this up, KCM was history, but who cared? It was already dead and buried before it had got off the ground. I now worked for the BBC.

Then came the classic BBC nonsense. By Tuesday of the next week Bob Forster had me down for that Health and Safety course, which rendered me a zombie for two hours and left me cursing under my breath. I needed a NEBOSH qualification, whatever that was, to tick the boxes. That bit of paper would make me a Health and Safety god. Jesus.

Next followed the crushing blow – he dropped into the conversation that I was not to assist Current Affairs in any covert camera work. That was not in my job remit. He was trying to pigeonhole me after my flying start last week. I hadn't been there a fortnight and was desperate not to lose the job, but I was not happy. I took it in silence, but the second thoughts I was having dominated my mind. I wanted to walk, but the experiences of the past year told me that was foolish. I had craved this so badly. I would sit it out and network, make friends with everyone in news, and annoy the shit out of Tom Giles. I needed to get back out in the field but for now politics had left me desk-bound The first two weeks couldn't have been more contrasting. I was rock bottom.

FRIENDLY FIRE

Within a fortnight, all that turned out to be bullshit. I was a plane to Macedonia and then Israel.

First, Malcolm Downing, the senior desk editor, asked me to fly 50,000 Deutsche Marks to the producer in Skopje. I rang Sue immediately and left the same afternoon. Talk about a U-turn. Malcolm said he would talk to Bob, and Tony Loughran told me to leave as soon as possible. The left hand didn't know what the right was doing but suddenly I was back in the game.

Sue asked me if it was safe and so begun what would become a familiar routine of me palming her off nonchalantly – over the years she would only ever watch the news if she knew I was heading there. This was the first time I had ever been a courier, and out here the BBC credit card would get you nowhere. If you needed fuel, hotels, fixers or bribes, cash was the only currency that counted.

Crucially, I was trusted. One man standing in my way had been overridden by the immediacy of the demands of news, and that was just the beginning: over the years, I flew to Jenin in Israel, Pakistan, Turkey, Jordan, Kenya, Brussels, Borneo and even Peru to lay the groundwork for a series on planet Earth!

I was quickly learning who to hang out with to fulfil my dreams. But of course, the stakes were suddenly raised on 11 September 2001. Everything changed overnight. The world was at war with Osama bin Laden and I now had a front-row seat.

When the planes flew into the Twin Towers, I was in Paris being courted by a ballistics company. I had seen a French reporter in Israel wearing a special type of flak jacket that I knew we would need going forward. This was my new life, being wined and dined on the Champs-Élysées, living it up on the BBC, but ultimately 9/11 was the moment which would define the next decade of newsgathering for all journalists and also for myself. Just like the IRA bomb, for those in the field, bad news was good news.

As I raced to get home, my journalist colleagues were trying to get to the States, eventually hiring a 747 together with ITV and flying to Canada, before tearing down through North America in a hire car. Certain teams had already been deployed to Pakistan without my knowledge and I got straight on the phone to Tony to tell him I had to get there. I was told that a freelancer had to go – I was needed in London as the link between News and the teams on the ground – but that was bollocks. They were trying to fit a square peg in a round hole. I didn't get further than delivering kit to Stansted.

In place of myself I had to send an old mate, Tony Rippon, but I made sure he only stayed a week and a half! Then I called him home, having blagged it to the news team that they needed more kit, more sleeping bags, and more meals. Sooner rather than later, I was on that plane to Islamabad.

This was to be the first time I met John Simpson. Over the next decade we would be close to inseparable on such trips. I then got summoned home – they didn't want me out there more than two weeks. We were all simply waiting to get into Afghanistan. We had only just met, but as I flew back to do bloody paperwork, John told me it was ridiculous: someone with my experience, which he had not been used to having in tow previously, had to stay with him on the ground.

A decade of Health and Safety was getting underway at the same time that the world changed forever. Apparently, it was more important for me to complete the paperwork on sitting upright on a

BBC chair than it was to penetrate a border by nightfall as guns and missiles rained supreme all around.

When I returned, Tony told me that Bob wanted me back. It wasn't my role to chaperone John as he famously 'liberated Kabul'. I had to fill in the forms and tick the boxes back at base. As the new era dawned in the West, I had to fight the internal war too. The world was watching America and her allies. The War on Terror had begun.

†

Over a year later, in February 2003, I went into work in London as usual, but with an extra spring in my step. I knew from my days in the army when it was all kicking off and it was obvious from the headlines that the US and the Brits were going to invade Iraq. This was what I was here for.

The phones had been ringing off the hook but all I had been able to do was prepare equipment – the Beeb were nervous about sending ex-military personnel in before hostilities had broken out. Then Tom Giles called and Malcolm Downing came to see me. Jim Muir, the Tehran correspondent, was crossing the border as we were talking; Stuart Hughes was out there on his first trip to do radio; and John had newspaper columns to write, a book deal in the bag, and needed to file for *Panorama*. Fred Scott, an American was on board as cameraman ... would I go as the security advisor?

I didn't need asking twice. Within a day, I was on the plane. I told Sue that my return depended on Mr Bush! In fact it was a done deal: by the end of that meeting Dave Bristow at the travel desk had already booked the tickets and Oggy Boytchev had come over to introduce himself as the producer. There was no doubt at all that we were leaving and it couldn't come soon enough. I had grabbed together what I could from the BBC Safety Store – Sat Phones, GPS, sleeping bags, duvet jackets, body armour, helmet and rations. If I thought I needed it, it was in. However, I had gone to work that morning knowing that tension was in the air but unaware that within twenty-four hours, I would be gone for two months. Our planning was shit. But I loved it.

We flew to Turkey, then on to Adana in the south, before taking a 21-hour coach journey to the Northern Iraq border. You couldn't fly into Iraq, and the key meeting place for all foreign journalists was on the Salopi border. Although time consuming, this was the fastest, safest route in. When we got there, we still didn't have a BBC coach, and we were kicked off the CNN one – tempers were running high. It took thirty-six hours in all to get from the border to Arbil in the north, Iraq's fourth largest city. During that time, one of our fixers, Dragan Petrovic, heard from Belgrade that he had become a dad. John had promised to get him on this trip after working with him in the Balkans, and Dragan needed the money. He should have been at home, especially as for the next five weeks we did fuck all.

John was getting frustrated waiting for the war to start, and he was convinced we were in the wrong location. We had nowhere to go, having been given only a four-day visa. We ignored its expiry date and decided to sit it out for the duration.

In the weeks up to 19 March, our days would be spent planning, doing the odd bit of local reconnaissance, and generally batting away all the local fixers and car dealers who had got wind that the BBC were camped in the Tower Hotel. Word was out that the great John Simpson was in town. This meant money to the locals. Eventually we forked out an extortionate $3,500 a month for a Hyundai and a Toyota. We also seemed to have acquired a fixer caller Russa and a freelance stills photographer, Abdullah, who had great contacts with the local Peshmerga and – much to my irritation – had wormed his way onto the team. I knew he thought John was his meal ticket (and I mean that literally). Not only would the BBC's World Affairs editor probably be on the scent of the story, there would be three fine meals a day – and Abdullah was always first to clean his plate. Risgar, the manager of the hotel, couldn't do enough for us either, even offering me a pistol to take on the road, which I declined.

I learned that he was cutting deals with FOX TV, too. Clearly, this was a big payday all round.

By night, we would chew the fat, sing some songs and Fred would start up the card school – John the Ace Simpson and Craig the Shark Summers fighting to the death over the jackpot prize ... of tooth-picks! We were that bored. To make it worse, Fred had just had a little baby and had spent only twelve hours at home in months. He hadn't even heard her cry. That was the price we all paid just to get the story.

But there was no story. All John could think about was getting to Baghdad but we had no way in yet. He had knocked on my door one night to express his concerns that we simply did not have enough or the correct equipment for the locals we had taken on. This appalled him, and rightly so, but that's often the deal when you leave at a moment's notice. I did my best to scrounge around for extra supplies.

On the night of the 19th the Americans fired Tomahawk missiles into Baghdad. Finally, we were in business – and a good job too, because Bob Forster had already tried to get me home once. I briefed our locals to tell their families our plans and ordered everyone to pack a bag with spare kit so we could move as and when. I also checked the vehicles for road-worthiness. Word was reaching us that morale was low in the Iraqi army; the streets were quiet and shops were beginning to get boarded up. The war had well and truly started. But it wasn't until the first ten days of April when we tasted the horrors of conflict ourselves and, in our hunt to get the story, became the very story itself.

†

By 2 April, Stuart Hughes had been in Iraq for two months. As the front line between the Kurdish-controlled North and the Central and Southern Territories held by Saddam Hussein began to crumble, Stuart, Kaveh Golestan his cameraman, and a local Kurdish soldier were on the road gathering material near the oil-rich city of Kirkuk.

As American bombs poured out of the sky, Stuart and Jim Muir stopped at a checkpoint to get some knowledge of the best vantage point for footage of the Yanks attacking the frontline in the distance. The local Kurdish Peshmerga guide told them it was safe to proceed to another track, 100 metres on the right, turning left to a second route near an abandoned Iraqi military position. They should pull over there to avoid being 'crested' (visible on the other side of the ridge). Jim was nervous about stopping off-road and parked his left-hand drive at an angle.

Kaveh had sat next to Jim in the front; in the back Stuart was on the right, Rabeen, a fixer, was in the middle, and the local Peshmerga sat on the left. He was the first to exit.

Stuart was next to get out. With one step, his right foot set off the first mine. Jim threw himself down next to the driver's door, believing they were taking incoming fire. On hearing the first detonation from the rear, Kaveh ran around to the front of the vehicle for cover. He threw himself onto two mines, and was gone. Killed instantly.

Rabeen was the only one left inside the vehicle. He had also thought it was a mortar attack, but quickly realised there was no distinctive whistling sound so it must be a mine strike. Then he heard Stuart crying out from the rear right – but he could also see Stuart's legs. Ahead, he saw another body covered in dirt. In the moment of impact, he thought it was a dead Iraqi, only understanding it was Kaveh a few moments later when Jim called out he was going to rescue him.

Rabeen urged him not to risk further injury but Jim insisted. It was too late. There was no pulse.

The local Peshmerga fired his rifle to attract attention. Rabeen pulled Stuart into the vehicle over the bags in the cargo area behind the back seat. Jim dragged Kaveh to the vehicle and rested his body across Rabeen, revealing extensive abdominal and lower-leg injuries. By now there were twenty or thirty locals out on the track. Jim put his foot down, heading for the nearby hospital about five minutes away.

At this point, my phone rang. It was Quill Lawrence, who worked for Boston the World, a radio outfit affiliated to the BBC. Quill was one of the first on the scene. 'Look, there's been a bad accident,' he began. 'I don't know how many are dead. They are on the road to Kifri and I can't get hold of Jim.'

I was two hours away, having dinner with Tom Giles and John Simpson. By the end of the call, I had upped and left. Together with Oggy, I drove like a mad man towards Sulaymaniyah, in the northeast of the country, all the time talking to Quill on the phone.

He had pulled a blinder. He had spoken to a US Forces medical unit based just outside the city. Plans were underway to get the guys moved from the local facility, and an escort vehicle was on its way. He also confirmed that Kaveh was dead.

Stuart had been given a pain-killing injection and an antibiotic, with a stop at another hospital to administer glucose liquids. We met them in Sulaymaniyah. At the American base, the facilities were the business. I explained to the surgeon who Stuart was, then they asked everyone else to leave. I was to stay to facilitate his evacuation, and for support, while they operated. He was gone for hours – the drugs knocked him for six. I watched from the corner while they un-bandaged and took pictures of the remains of his foot.

'It's fifty–fifty whether he keeps his leg,' I was told by American captain Jeff Joyce. 'We'll clean it up but that's as far as we'll go. We're making arrangements to get him out on a helicopter to Germany or Cyprus. We'd like you to sit with him.'

They offered me a sleeping bag as I had no kit. It was going to be a night on the floor for me.

'How are you feeling?' I asked Stuart.

'A bit groggy,' he mumbled back. 'How's my leg?'

'It'll be fine mate,' I lied. 'Don't worry, it's still there; you'll be playing football for Wales soon.'

I thought this was the best thing to say even though I knew otherwise. There was no point stressing him any further. He had asked me if anyone had spoken to his parents and I said Oggy was through to London and they now knew. Moments later, Stuart was out for the count again. I went to check back in with Jeff, who told me London were all over it but Stuart's family wanted to talk to me on the Sat Phone. They didn't know me from Adam but I assured them he would be on his way tomorrow and was in good hands, and returned to sit with Stuart, rolled up in my sleeping bag ...

He was in and out of sleep, and by 05.00 the Yanks were in anyway to move him. It was time for me to leave and for him to make that long journey home. My job was done and someone else would take it from here, and that was how I saw it. Nothing like this choked me – I was more concerned about getting back to Arbil. I had seen too much of war and life to get emotional. Stuart faced a long road ahead, but tomorrow was another day for me. That's just how I was, and how I learned to deal with tragic incidents like this. I had done my part and had no personal responsibility to his section – that wasn't my style. It would be months before I would see him again.

As I said goodbye, I had one last question to ask. 'What were you wearing on your feet?'

'Sandals,' he replied.

I'd feared he would say that. 'How many times have I told you? Why weren't you wearing boots?' But now wasn't the time to criticise. I had said it before and I would say it again hundreds and hundreds of times over the years.

This was Stuart's first big gig and even though the locals believed that these mines dated from the Iran–Iraq War of the 1970s, and the terrain was now lush and green, our guys had all learned about off-road driving into places like this on the BBC Hostile Environment Course.

I hated to say it. This was an unfortunate accident; it might not have made a difference, but we both looked at each other knowingly. Stuart shouldn't have been in sandals.

†

'How's things?' they asked when they saw me enter the restaurant.

I had hitched a long, precarious lift back to Arbil. I needed my single bed in this pokey little hotel, my feet dangling over the end of it. I was that exhausted I didn't care.

'I am fucking knackered,' I told the boys, before filling them in on Stuart's progress. And then we left it. That's what we did. I told them what I knew and we moved on. A small amount of sympathy, followed by a relevant dose of information, topped off with the next briefing. It's just how it was.

By the next morning, 4 April, Stuart was hardly mentioned. We had a war to cover and Simpson was itching to cover it. Even knocking on the door of sixty, he still had it, and couldn't wait to get cracking. The word was that fighting had increased and, again, John was worried we weren't near the story. Rageh Omaar was looking like a star in Baghdad. That had been John in 1991, and he wanted it to be John in 2003. He was desperate to find a way out of here but even with that mindset, there was no way he would be embedded. That, to John, said control and censorship. He wanted to roam, hunt down and sniff out the story that nobody else had. That's why he was John Simpson.

The next day we found ourselves twenty kilometres east of Al Qasr. One of our tip-offs had come good and we found ourselves spending the night with American Special Forces. I had wandered over discreetly to introduce myself as one of their own and see if they would mind if we took some general shots. Clearly, if they were here, there was a story, as if their laser finders on the jeeps didn't give it away.

We shook hands and they were cool, so long as we didn't film them or specify location. I assured them that we wouldn't. I could have sold them down the river of course, but you don't want to get a reputation for that – you would never be allowed in again. They told me that they'd lost count of the number of times they had been here. I offered them my Sat Phone so they could call home – against their operational procedure. We shared kebabs and talked squaddie shit all night. I loved every second. As we swapped parachuting tales, for the first time since I had crossed the line from soldier to undercover beef for the BBC, I crossed it back again. I was totally at home and slightly jealous, as brilliant as my new life was. Twenty years of memories of sleeping rough under the stars, staking out the enemy and nailing good over evil came flooding back as I was mixing it with America's finest. Despite the flea-bitten blankets and the odd bang in the sky, I could still cut it, and I still loved it.

Curiously, it wasn't for John. The BBC drivers had taken him back to the hotel, around forty minutes away. His news radar told him there wasn't a story here, and he wanted to head back as he didn't have his medicine for his kidney stones. We would hook up again in the morning, and I told him to be prepared – get kit for forty-eight hours and get ready.

†

Sunday 6 April 2003.

None of us will forget this day.

John was back in the village early. I'd had the best night ever. Over in Tehran, Jim Muir had flown in for Kaveh's funeral. Yes, we were sorry for him, but no, we hardly mentioned it. We had work to do and needed to crack on, and in the cutthroat world of news and war, it was the BBC's job to send representatives. We had work to do and John wanted 'colour pieces'. We were five hours from Baghdad.

We were heading to a village called Hawler when Abdullah called me over while John was doing a live two-way back to London. He had heard from Commander Nariman, who had been leaking info to us. The town of Dibarjan had fallen. This meant an about-turn and saying farewell to the Special Forces. It's brutal to say it, but I was sadder at this than at the thought of Kaveh's funeral. No disrespect but that's the military fraternity.

We turned on our heels and chased the story, passing discarded uniforms and blown-up trucks on the way. The evidence had been clear and General Nariman's previous information had been accurate up to this point. I drove – and fast too. I always drove. It was a poor excuse for a road. Dust, tarmac, potholes and bumps all the way made the Highways Agency look good. Vast expanses of plain flanked us on either side.

Of course, as seemed the way in these parts, I couldn't know for sure if Nariman was talking to everyone. We hoped this was our story and not everyone's but you could never know until you got there. Sadly, we never did. As we pulled up at the agreed checkpoint, the Peshmerga troops were everywhere – finding Nariman was like searching for a needle in a haystack. Abdullah, Fred and John went off to look, only to learn that a distinguished Iraqi major had been captured; and then John, being John, was pushing for an interview.

'No film, no film, no film,' the Peshmerga were saying.

Fred returned to our vehicle and urged me to go undercover and film on my mini DV camera at this small pen in a tiny holding by the side of the road. It was like a scene from the Middle Ages – peasants waiting to be slaughtered. I told Kameron, our translator, not to move while I checked the shot. Kam was nervous – we were starting to attract attention, even though it was hard to get close enough, and we were filming covertly. The film never got used because of what would follow, but its significance lies in the conversation I then had with Kameron.

While John was coercing Nariman for the big interview, Kameron told me had been offered a job as a Special Forces translator. He had seen his moment and gone for it, claiming he had been offered double. Oggy let me manage the fixers, drivers and translators: I told Kameron it was the wrong moment, and that as soon as the Yanks moved on, he would be forgotten. I had promised him a bonus when we got to Baghdad but this irritated me. I laid it on the line bluntly. We would always be able to find another fixer. His timing was poor.

As we were about to push off with a bad atmosphere still lingering, two land cruisers pegged it past.

'That's Waji Barzani,' Abdullah said.

Barzani was the son of the Kurdish president! Unbelievably, the US Special Forces were in tow, and we all knew we had to follow. I had heard his name but knew no more. The fact that the SF were travelling with him was more than a giveaway as to his importance. Nariman and Dibarjan – despite the latter being a major crossroads to Mosel, Kirkuk, and Southern Iraq – were no longer the story. When I spotted the SF, my boys and I knew it was our lucky day – sort of.

We passed through three checkpoints in pursuit, at the last, avoiding buried mines in a huge pile of earth. We didn't want to suffer the same fate as Stuart on the day Kaveh was being buried.

The convoy turned out to be twelve vehicles in total. This was big drama. We stayed about 100 metres to the rear. At this third checkpoint, it just looked like mounds of earth and blockades up ahead, yet there was lush green on the side. We had sufficient time to catch up and we could always spy the tail of the last car through the dust; plus we had walkie-talkies to communicate between the cars. We put Kameron in with John in case there were any problems. Ultimately that decision condemned him, but it was the right thing to do from an operational point of view.

As we drove back up a mound to our penultimate checkpoint, we came to a grinding halt. There was now a long convoy ahead and behind us.

'I think we should put our flak jackets on.' I don't know why I radioed everyone but my sixth sense for danger had kicked in, and I had no idea what lay beyond the next ridge. I could hear noise in the distance. There was no way any of us were walking blindly into an ambush.

The convoy, now some twenty cars long, stopped again safely near a T-junction. The road bent up the brow of a hill – potential danger lurked round every corner. We were caught in the valley. Barzani's car, hitting tarmac for the first time, had floored it through the middle of the pack. To the right stood a tank, Roughneck 91. This was a relic from the original Gulf War, a stark abandoned reminder two decades on of what had gone before, its barrel pointing down defeated.

I ordered our three vehicles through. John, Fred and Kameron got out to talk to the SF guys to see what the hell Barzani was doing out here. Kameron made for Barzani himself. My concern was the vehicles. Seeing plumes of smoke over the summit of the hill, there was clearly a contact further up the road – I had to make sure all the trucks were turned round to face the way we had come. We couldn't be staring at the danger.

Fred shouted at me to get the tripod out of the back of the Land Cruiser just after I had turned the first car round. To my right was a local Peshmerga; adjacent to me Tom's phone rang. It was his birthday and his mum had called from the UK.

'That's the sound of freedom,' he told her, holding the phone to the planes in the sky. It was a stupid time to take a call unless it was for work – and we were about to go live. For a second he was caught in the moment, his guard down, and he couldn't know how his words would resonate forever.

Still concerned to turn the cars around, I looked through the side window of the Land Cruiser.

And then I spotted it.

It wasn't the sound of freedom at all. And it was coming towards us. I knew that distinctive red nose and grey body. I could see it falling through the air,

We were dealing in split seconds here – each of us powerless, no time for fear past my initial 'Oh fuck', not a second to protect myself. Then it hit.

The lights went out.

The next thing I knew, I was picking myself up off the floor, but the Peshmerga villager to my right was gone. In front of me, I saw an arm, then I heard his body shrieking for a few seconds. It didn't last long. He died before my very eyes.

I had taken a blow to the head – my left hand and right arm were bleeding from the almighty blast. I couldn't account for any of the team at this point. With the shock I had hit the deck. Robotically, I picked myself up again. I'd been out for seconds. Did I actually hear the noise or had the shockwaves sent me reeling into blackout? I don't know, but even the echo of the aftermath was louder than fuck. Did I see the bomb? Yes, for that nanosecond. What made me look in that direction? I don't know. Years of training which hones into instinct or a stroke of luck? Pass.

Thank God I was still alive. I knew immediately what had happened.

It was 1982, and I was back in San Carlos Bay. That was over so quickly, too. I heard the air-raid sirens from our ships and two to three seconds later the Argentines dropped their bombs on us.

I knew that sound. This time, I didn't have those two to three seconds.

Special Forces on the ground had described the target. Less than a kilometre away, we had been charging towards Iraqi tanks engaging with 173rd Airborne. We had been about to wander into that. From the sky the target had become the T-junction, the mass of vehicles and the abandoned Iraqi tank. The pilot had simply got it wrong.

I dove to the side of the bank to my left and lay there. I found Tom with another Peshmerga gibbering away, blood running down his head from an intake of shrapnel. I kept asking if he was OK but he just stared at me, glazed in shock.

Tom's mum had heard it all.

I screamed at him as he ran down the bank towards another small sand bank. He had to hit the deck now because most planes on attack come round twice.

I grabbed Tom's phone because mine was in the car. I had to tell London. 'There's been an own goal.' I had known straightaway. 'The Americans have dropped a bomb on us. Tom, Giles and I are fine. I've gotta go. I'll give you an update when I know more.'

I hung up. There was still no sign of John and the others. I had to get to work. I got up and ran to the vehicles, searching each for bodies. The impact had been less than twenty metres from our vehicle – it was like a scene from a movie, except this was very real. There were bodies everywhere – the flames and the ammunition within them stunk. Some people were burned to a crisp; others were still alive but heading that way. I've seen plenty of bombs and bodies over the years, but that stench never leaves you.

'They're fucking dead,' I told myself. But I stayed calm and level-headed. Surely, there was no way in the world that I could find John, Fred, Dragan and Kameron alive. If that were true, so be it. I wasn't thinking emotionally or as an undercover reporter. In my military head, and as BBC security advisor, I had to account for them in whatever state I discovered them. I would take it one step at a time.

As I was sorting through the vehicles, I realised I was heading back the way we came. This was the wrong thing to do. If I was going to find them, the impact was behind me on the right – that's where the American SF jeeps had been. 'Check every body,' I told myself repeatedly. 'Account for everything.' I wasn't looking to save other lives or bury bodies. I was employed to protect John Simpson and I had no idea where he was. I began to call out for Fred. I was probably shouting too loudly because of the blast to the head. Who knew what perception of sound everyone still alive now had?

Still there was nothing. And then, in a moment as surreal as Tom's mum tasting the sound of freedom while wishing him birthday greetings, three heads popped up comically from behind the bank. They were safe, and in one piece.

'It's an American own goal,' I shouted at them.

John was livid. 'It's coming back' he shouted. 'I saw the fucking bomb. I saw the fucking bomb.'

Fred had a gash to his head; John had lost a trouser leg so he was full length on one side and wearing shorts on the other, with shrapnel hanging out of him; Dragan had a bad cut to the ankle. They were all sufficiently OK for now to continue. There was no sign of Kameron. Nobody had seen him.

'Have you called your friends off?' John shouted to the Americans. I had never witnessed him like this before. 'The world has a right to know what you know,' he told our 'friends'.

'Stay here, John,' I ordered. 'And stay together. Here's my phone. Call London and do what you have to do. I've got to find Kameron.'

I don't know if finding John meant the show had to go on or not. If he had been dead, I would still have looked for Kameron but it gave us all renewed purpose. I could hear John shouting to Fred to 'shoot this'. He was straight back into work mode and, my God, he knew as we all did that this was one of the biggest stories of the war. As soon as we'd established we were all fine, we were in our element. I didn't give two hoots about Abdullah – he wasn't part of my remit. I was concerned for Kameron, but the story was unravelling before us. As I would do many times in the future, I walked that line between story first and danger second.

'I'm doing a piece to camera,' John told Tom Giles, what felt like seconds later. 'Fucking morons,' he cursed the Yanks before miking up.

At the same time, I found Kameron lying on the bank. The American medics were running down with trauma packs on their back, helping whoever they could.

'Come over here,' I shouted to them, but it wasn't looking good. His foot had been completely sliced off and blood was pouring out of his leg. He, too, made that gurgling sound that I had come to associate with death.

Some of the medics went towards John and the guys but he was already live on the Sat Phone to Maxine Mawhinney on News 24.

The medic told me to apply two tourniquets on Kameron's legs above the wound to stop the blood loss – that surprised me. Only one leg was injured but he wanted both doing. I assumed he was more medically qualified than I was so went ahead and made it tight. I then got out my knife to cut Kameron's shirt but I couldn't see any wound. Still he carried on fading and gurgling.

'Have you ever put a Given Set in?' the medic asked me.

This was a saline drip, and all I had to do was to get a vein up and slide a cannula in. The medic had already made one up.

'I can't get a vein,' I shouted over to Tom.

Kameron's veins had collapsed. I knew he wasn't going to make it.

He was convulsing. The grumblings were getting louder. I asked Tom to sit with him as I had with Stuart. I told him to talk to Kameron and just keep him company but I knew I couldn't do any more and I had to start to clear the area. Our vehicles were now on fire.

That had to be sorted immediately but at the back of my mind was our conversation earlier about the money, and for a moment, I felt bad that he would die alone. My rare compassion was not for another victim of war – I just wish my last conversation of substance with him had been different. Crucially, even though his leg had borne the brunt of it, Kameron was one of the few in the car without a flak jacket. We didn't have enough to go around. That was the mistake. It was the sandals all over again.

As we loaded Kam onto the vehicle, I knew he was gone.

†

'This is a really bad own goal by the Americans,' John was live and just in earshot. He was raging inside, but as cool as a cucumber when the red light was on.

(Weeks back, we had offered to give our co-ordinates to The Pentagon but they simply weren't interested. It would be nice to think this wouldn't have happened if we'd been embedded, but then we wouldn't have been chasing Barzani across Iraq.)

Just then, someone spotted a body in the back of one of our enflamed vehicles. That awoke something inside me to save the story, let alone the body. I ran to my car to discover it was a sleeping bag wedged against the back window, but I had to rescue the remaining broadcast equipment. There was no point at all us being here if the videophone and all the footage were going up in smoke.

I managed to get the hatch open but it was like a furnace in there. I climbed inside to cut the rope to free the two spare jerrycans. I ran to John, threw them just to the right of the camera, then turned and went back to the other vehicles through the flames. Fred shouted to me to save his gear.

All the cars were burning now – the third one looked seconds away from explosion as I grabbed our personal bags along with John's diaries, notebooks and fucking Tilley hat. It was like a barbecue out of control but the smell was horrendous – nothing is more ghastly than the smell of burning fuel and smouldering flesh combined. I blocked it out of my mind and concentrated on the vehicle. All our lives were in those trucks – my focus was now totally on preserving the story and not human life. The guys I was concerned about were safe; the gear was not.

John was raging again when he finished the live. 'There's gotta be a fucking inquest into that,' he yelled to everyone and no one. 'Was that OK?' he turned to Tom. John had been better than OK. He was at his best, flicking an internal switch from anger and disgust to smooth calm.

It had been a disgraceful error. Forty-five had been injured, sixteen lives lost. The Americans were worried there was more incoming and wanted to evacuate.

Some of the gear was damaged. Most importantly, John's Tilley hat now had a hole in it. Some twenty-five minutes later, my concern was still the vehicles. Despite that toxic mix of fuel and flames, I could see one of the Peshmerga guys trying to steal the third vehicle; the other two were burned to shreds.

'Fuck off – this is our vehicle!' I screamed at him.

In the back, he had placed his weapon along with some ammo. I found a hand on one of the seats. I told John to stay with the vehicle as I began to move everything into this car, piling stuff on the roof and clearing the glass from the seats. I had no windscreen left.

By now, all the traffic was coming towards us – the rest of the media had got wind of the story and were piling in our direction. All we wanted to do was leave, heading back down to the original checkpoint.

'What about Abdullah?' John asked.

We agreed to have one last look.

Checking under the vehicles and charred corpses in this scene of devastation, we found nothing except the truth. He hadn't even bothered to stick around. That was the final straw for me with him. If he wasn't my responsibility before, he certainly wasn't now. It was time to go. In every sense. Even for battle-hardened souls like Fred and me, it had taken its toll.

'That's it, I'm off,' the American announced through the dust and wind in the front of the Land Cruiser. But he meant off and out of the country. It was time for him to get back to California to see his little baby. This was just the wake-up call he needed to get off the adrenalin rush and back to the real world.

'Yeah, that was a close call,' I agreed.

It all showed what a difference a day could make, and indeed a week. On the same day that Kaveh was being buried, we nearly met the same fate. Just a few hours ago we had been buddying up with the very guys who called in the airstrike – and I'd been reminiscing about old times with them. The SF had told me none of theirs had died but I don't believe that to be true. I saw them towing away a Land Rover in which I knew one of their men had gone down. Meanwhile Waji Barzani was helicoptered out of there to hospital. His brother fell into a coma.

Despite his war fatigue, Fred continued to film out of the glassless window, the camera always on his knee. But he understood now and he meant it – it was time to go and see his baby. He had come straight from a month in India. All he knew professionally was putting his life on the line for the story – but when it became this real, he'd had enough. And even though I was the ex-military guy, the tough man in all this, we both knew it was an epic event to walk away from. It's not every day John Simpson wipes blood from a TV camera lens minutes after a 1,000 lb bomb has fallen a few yards away from you, dropped by an F14 on your own side, tearing across the sky at close to 500 mph. For now, enough was enough.

Oggy met us at a checkpoint ninety minutes down the road. He told us Abdullah was on the way to the hospital with shrapnel in his neck and thigh. He asked us if we were OK to carry on driving, but we knew we had to complete. He also told us that Kameron had died. It was only what I'd expected.

By 16.00 we were back in Arbil. Word had spread that a BBC team had been bombed. I was shattered by the time I unloaded the gear into the hotel lobby – there was nothing left in the tank – but the warmth in the locals' hearts was genuine. It was one of those surreal moments where people still have compassion, even when there's a war on and you have to put yourself first.

Someone sorted a car to take Fred to the UN medical facility at Ankawa on the other side of Arbil – his head badly needed dressing. As I saw him off, I sat down outside the hotel with another security guy called Steve Musson to talk it through and I realised just how fucking lucky I had been. I wasn't in delayed shock; I didn't get emotional; yet this was the closest in all my scrapes that I had come to meeting my maker.

Suddenly I found a conscience and thought the right thing was to go the hospital to see Abdullah. It was chaos. Waji was in there too and the locals knew it. For once, our hotel manager played a blinder and got me straight through to the doctor, who checked me over. I really wasn't sure if my hearing was still in one piece. Thankfully, I was given the all clear.

Oggy was already there and took me to Abdullah's room but nothing had changed. He had nurses swooning all over him and he lay there playing the hero. There was a small amount of shrapnel and the odd bandage but, my God, he was still alive – unlike poor Kameron. When he saw us, he turned into a terminally ill patient going for an Oscar. To rub it in, I passed dead Peshmergas on trolleys on the way out. That was the true level of the mess that the blue on blue had caused. I had done the decent thing – and that was it. I hoped I never saw him again.

There was still work to be done amid all this. I hadn't even called home, although London had rung Sue. She knew the score. We were up against it – two hours from doing a live into the Six – all of us traumatised but in denial and Fred a whizz kid on the edit but desperate to get out of there. We worked our bollocks off on autopilot and John went live on the roof at the top of the bulletin.

Again, the legend was at his best at the end of a day nobody will forget. Afterwards, we hit the bar and I broke my golden rule of never drinking on tour. We downed a beer and raised a glass to our late friend Kameron. Earlier we had also been to see his mother. 'God gave us Kameron and now he took him back,' John put it beautifully. Kameron had been the main breadwinner for the family, yet they didn't really know the danger he was putting himself into – they thought he was a translator for the papers. He had told John he had wanted to work for us out of friendship and adventure – the wailing at the family home told us they'd had no idea he was risking life and limb.

You can only grieve so long in this game. There was no word from Jim in Tehran either. We were so knackered and insular ourselves that we'd barely spared a thought for Kaveh that day. It was extraordinary that all this had happened at the same moment he was laid to rest.

I finally spoke to Sue and, of course, she was worse than me. My girls had been told as well. As we hit the sack that night, there was indecision and uncertainty over whether we should come or go. We decided to sleep on it.

In the morning, we revisited the bomb site for *Simpson's World* on BBC World. We spent half an hour walking round the scene. John asked me for my thoughts as the camera was rolling. I loved it just like the first time back in the bar at Charleroi. I was now well and truly bitten by the TV bug.

But you could see the crater and the scorch marks in the earth. The blood from the bandages where Kam had died was still there. Things like this happen, as sad as it was. In my head I wasn't carrying the same baggage as the day before but I still knew it was time to go home. A translator called Huwer approached us and said that, with all eyes on Baghdad, he could take John and Tom to Kifri. John was adamant that he wanted to continue and told me to go home. Fred was already on his way and Dragan too wanted to see his baby for the first time.

I was split – my responsibility was to John but he had ordered me back. I also had to look out for Fred and Dragan. Ultimately, I took my lead from John: if he said go, then go I would.

On 11 April, we were driving home, overland to the border and on via Istanbul. It had been the right call to go. On the 9th, the Yanks staged the money shot of the toppling of Saddam's statue. John hadn't made it in time for the fall of Baghdad but, my goodness, in chasing the story he found himself at the heart of it. As for me, what I was asked to do next couldn't have been more extreme.

HELLS ANGELS

A couple of months later, I was on the plane to Boston. This trip was like no other – a welcome break from paperwork and numerous trips back to Baghdad to set up the Bureau there. In that short time, Iraq had changed so much it bore no resemblance to the country that had taken Kaveh and Stuart out and nearly did for John and me.

My old friend Sam Bagnall had called. 'Would you like to infiltrate the world of the Hells Angels?'

What? Too bloody right; you couldn't get me out there quick enough. Sam had already got some undercover stuff in the can: would I like to go to the legendary annual event that Hells Angels from all around the world fly into? I was heading for the World Run in Laconia, New Hampshire. My mission was simple: were they all long-haired, drug-dealing, gun-touting individuals? This was right up my street. Whatever covert pieces I could get would be the icing on the cake after Sam had got access to a former American cop who'd been working undercover as a Hells Angel for the previous two years. We had also sent an overt crew into the media scrum for general views of Laconia and bog standard interviews with the local police – but this stuff was ten a penny, and all the international news crews had the same footage.

Jason Gwynne, the producer whom I had worked with on the Sam Hammam show, was also coming with me. He trusted me, knew

I could handle myself, and of course my bald head on a good day could persuade you that I was borderline Hells Angel.

'What do you know about Hells Angels?' Jase asked.

'They ride bikes and have leather jackets and wear their colours on their back,' I stereotyped.

'Do you know how they get the colours on their backs?'

'Well, I know you become a "prospect" before you become a Hells Angel. You wear your "chapter" on the back of your jacket, but you don't have the Hells Angels wing.'

If there was a test to pass, I had walked it. Most people didn't know this much. I felt like I had been given a bonus when Jason confirmed the trip. My wife Sue just laughed.

It was becoming a great year for me in terms of making a name for myself at the BBC and I was absolutely loving it. Bob Forster was still around but Caroline Neil, the Head of High Risk who had worked undercover herself, was a breath of fresh of air. She told me this was a great gig, I had to go, and she would sign it off. Too right, it was; I was off to get pissed for the BBC.

I had found out just a week before that I was heading to Laconia with around a thousand international angels of the hellish variety. In that seven days, all I could see were Hells Angels – any sign of a bike or long hair or leather jacket and I was honing in on them. Now I was going to be in their midst, that was all I thought about. I had no idea where Laconia was but there was no stopping me. This jolly had Craig Summers written all over it.

At the top of my thought process was one thing – I was being paid to work, drink and film all weekend with a bunch of bikers all day and night. This was going to be brilliant, and hey, if we got a story, too, happy days! I was living a dream that people would have paid millions for, acting a role out for the cameras. My military and TV worlds had merged – I needed a cover story, commonly known as my 'legend'.

I googled what you needed to become the perfect Hells Angel. I soon realised that I couldn't pretend to be something I wasn't – there was no point trying to penetrate that close-knit family. I didn't invent some chapter that could trip me up. I was into bikes and had heard about The Run – that was as close as I would get to pretending to be one of their gang.

Instead, I was on leave from Iraq, had touched down in Boston, and was on a road trip with my old mate Jason, who had never been to the States before. I would talk about all the Yanks I had met in the Gulf and they would lap that up. I kept to the basic rule of the false ID – stick to something you know, and keep it simple. I could talk army bollocks all day long and have them eating out of my big military hand. If only they knew that their own fucking idiots had dropped a bomb on me just a few months before.

In real terms, the Boston leg was true, followed on by a nightmare drive down to Laconia in really shit bad weather and a stop at your typical small American motel. (My appetite for the BBC credit card hadn't waned, but I needed to stay somewhere right for the role.) We had caned the beers on the flight over, and Jason told me he loved the cover story. If he was filming, he knew I could do the talking and engage an audience without suspicion on my two favourite subjects – war and myself!

By the Saturday morning, we were good to go. Just outside Laconia, we had to get to 65 Fillmore Road. This was the massive Hells Angels' house – all their meetings took place here. It was where the action was, but it was no go. The fraternity had put a barrier across the road. I could see the huge trees and the clubhouse, bar and log cabins behind it down this dead-end road. We weren't getting in there and there was no point trying to slip in. I'd leave them to discuss their drugs and guns and whatever else.

Police and media were all over the town – the locals feared gang warfare. The truth was the opposite. It wasn't that kind of event; it was more a huge stag party over three days talking bikes. It didn't get more interesting than that.

I dressed in t-shirt, jeans, jacket and Timberland boots – as casual as you could get in what was lumberjack country. In my t-shirt was a camera – Jason and I would split the day and film half each.

Our first port of call was Tower Hill Tavern at Weirs Beach. I didn't rush in to get my weekend bender underway. I would say I wasn't actually holding court at the bar before 11.00, but it was close! Jason, too, was a reasonable drinker – and that was the only essential qualification for the part. There was no point standing there holding a lager shandy among all these hairy-arsed Hells Angels and all their birds with their tits hanging out when the AC/DC came on. The only way to get involved was to drink.

By 15.00 it was heaving. We were in for the long haul. I was glad we'd got in early to stake out our position at the bar, rarely leaving the counter (although the piss breaks came more frequently), always establishing our stories by laying it on heavy with the staff so they could vouch for us if it all kicked off later.

For much of the time, I got chatting to some Argies. I was gobsmacked they had come all the way from Buenos Aires. How stupid of me. It became clear to me very early doors – this was the World Cup Final for Hells Angels! They were loving it though, as I was; talking bikes was a piece of piss. They asked me about Iraq and I hammed it up a bit. I didn't bring up the Falklands but it was at the back of my mind and, deep down, I was doing the maths to see if I could still live the lie that I had been serving then as well as now, even though I actually had been there for real in 1982. The voice in my head was urging caution. You never knew who you were talking to, and I didn't want to get carried away. What if I was so tanked up that I deemed myself so perfect in the role that I bullshitted my way into some story, and one of their relatives had been killed living General Galtieri's dream, and they suddenly placed me at the scene of the crime? Fucking hell. I loved this gig, but have a word with yourself, son.

Around half three, I knew we had struck gold. Into the bar walked a new bunch of Hells Angels. The only way you could tell one lot from the other was that chapter on the back. These guys said 'Windsor'.

The only banter we had to deflect was to explain why we were there: having got in position early with the bar staff meant that they could often finish our story for us. We loved spotting the various groups – Germans, Danes, Argies, Brits. This was it big time and it was starting to get rowdy.

'All right, guys, you from England?' the Windsor lot asked us.

And out we trotted the cover story again.

'Cool,' they said. 'What was it like in Iraq?'

I knew I had them. In one sentence I had turned them around, moving from suspicion to getting to the heart of what they were about – talk of war and guns – and they loved it. All their tough-guy posturing counted for nothing but respect to us when they found out we were the real deal, making them look like pantomime horses. Except, of course, we weren't! To win them over further, I asked a couple of dumb questions. I knew obviously they didn't have their bikes with them, but asking about them when Harleys came up in the conversation helped me throw the spotlight of respect back in their direction. They loved meeting real heroes and having their own egos stroked when I sought every drop of information about their pride and joy, but these guys were pussies.

All I was thinking was the bigger the bike, the smaller the cock; and, of course, was Jason rolling? He didn't let me down. We were a great double act – me talking the sweetest of all cover stories and feigning naivety in their presence; Jason getting everything in an eight to ten hour filming session. Occasionally we would have a team meeting in the bogs, changing the battery behind a locked door in case anyone tried to kick it in. Sometimes Jason would go on his own – my only concern was a pissed-up angel stumbling in through the door but I felt Jason could handle himself and I would just let the beer keep on coming.

'Is it true what they say about the Hells Angels?' I asked one of these pissheads.

'Nah, it's all rubbish,' he replied.

'I'm sure I read about the Windsor Hells Angels; didn't someone get shot?' I went in for the kill.

'That was years ago,' they dismissed it.

Clearly it had happened – and I hadn't been told to specifically target any particular chapter. I loved showing my innocence to them but in the same breath letting on that I had a small amount of knowledge. They loved the sound of their own voices as much as I did mine! When I asked them if they had security cameras in their own clubhouses, they wouldn't shut up. They were eating out of my hand. I quizzed them on guns and I went for them on drugs – they told me they could get coke anytime anywhere in the UK.

'Did you kill any fucking Ragheads in Iraq?' they were thriving now.

'Yeah, a couple,' I lied.

They started asking me about the weapons I was using. I just turned it around back on them.

'You carry guns don't you?' I goaded.

'It's illegal innit? Hahaha.' one of them gave the game away.

I knew none of these had never even been in a fight let alone a war zone. I was something they dreamed of being. The beers were flowing; I was bigging myself up, bragging about my Iraq money and getting the rounds in.

Then the Yanks started joining in. 'So you killed some sand niggers? Brilliant!'

They might have come for bikes, but I'd stolen the show. Even if Norman bloody Schwarzkopf had walked in, I knew exactly what I was talking about.

Jason and I did have a quick conference. We were well on the way to Smashedville, and we couldn't blow it now, so we decided to knock off the booze a bit. Well, just a small bit. It was rammed, smoky, and the lights were going down. People were coming rather than going;

leather was the outfit of the hour. If you suffered from claustrophobia, you'd be dead. The fog of marijuana wafted across the bar through the flashing disco lights – it was like a 1960s dance hall.

By around six, the Windsors had gone, replaced by a gang from Sacramento. Jason felt we had enough. The only way to get anything new was to leave and head for another bar. At eleven, the police turned up. Their concern was about not disturbing the neighbours – never mind that the whole bar was stoned and as pissed as a fart. As they dragged a few of them out, we were licking our lips, thinking they were going to throw everyone out and the Angels were going to kick off. We were waiting on pepper spray, cuffs and tear gas, but it never came.

One of the coppers tried to move us on until I fed him the Iraq bullshit. The policeman bought the whole thing too, telling us how he wanted to sign up and hunt bin Laden. I had him in my pocket as well. It gave the mob the chance to flee back to the clubhouse. Suddenly the streets were empty. Jason and I realised that we were fucked in every sense of the word. Pissed, but with no chance of getting back to the motel. There wasn't a cab in sight.

I pulled rank, so to speak. 'We've been drinking all day. I don't mean to be rude but is there any chance you can give us a lift back? I've just come back from Iraq. You know what it's like.' I said.

He clearly didn't. He paused for a moment, then said he couldn't – that was against the rules.

Once again I played the Iraq card. Jesus – I knew my other identities better than I did myself! Let's face it, I had been in Iraq and was bombed there, but there's a fine line between telling that story and making up a whole heap of shit that you were breathing down bin Laden's neck in the Tora Bora caves.

He hesitated, then saw the hero in me and told us to jump in the back. He drove us like royalty the five or six miles back to the motel! If I had pushed it, I think I could have got an out-rider or one of those dicks talking into his lapel – they totally respected the whole war thing. As for me, I just loved what a ridiculously good actor I was.

Back at the motel, we heard a kerfuffle.

'You fucking bastards.'

'What the hell was that?' I said to Jase.

Not all the Angels had gone to the notorious clubhouse. I couldn't believe my luck – half of them had rocked up at Crossroads! We dashed for our kit and made for the balcony. It was all kicking off outside.

We pegged it into the car park and headed towards our vehicle. The plan was to do a 360, lurk in the bush round the back, drop Jason off and hit the record button. It didn't matter how pissed we were. I re-entered the car park sheepishly and texted Jason to find me.

Ultimately, the footage was too dark – you could just about make out three or four thugs having a go at these other Angels, but it was mostly shadows as the lighting was poor.

Then the cops turned up. Fucking brilliant. If it had been the same guy who had dropped us earlier, then that would have been the icing on the cake. Either way, we had nailed them on the piss, scrapping and bragging about their guns and the coke.

Job done – though I was all up for another day on the piss with the heavies! In fact, the overt crew told me we had enough footage. I wasn't needed any more. What a weekend.

At the airport, I was getting ready to chill my way home in Business Class when, to my disbelief, I saw half the Windsor Chapter in all their gear preparing to board. If it was anyone I spoke to yesterday – and fuck, I was so pissed, how would I know – my cover story wouldn't have held. At least I wasn't wearing any equipment. It would be professional suicide to try to take the covert cameras in the hand luggage.

I managed to avoid them. I knew they would be in cattle class. I think that underlines how important it was for Craig Summers always to fly in style at the BBC's expense!

And for what? We had flown to the other side of the globe for what was eventually just forty-five seconds of footage. I flipping loved it and, more to the point, I felt natural in the part! Who wouldn't? I had been on the ultimate boys' weekend, and I wanted it to kick off. The truth is that nine times out of ten, undercover stuff is pretty tedious – but you always have to be on your game for that winning shot.

When I saw the show, I was really disappointed by how little they had used. In this business, I was learning fast, you were only as good as your next hit. My ego was crying out for the glory, and any great *Panorama* with my name high in the credits meant that I removed one more ankle chain from the desk marked Health and Safety and strolled over to the office marked Undercover. I was desperate to be as important as Simpson, and I would always go the extra mile to get there for the BBC.

I don't mind admitting that, on this occasion, I got carried away in the part. I love spending other people's money doing a job but, equally, if I had sat there on lemonade all day, nobody would have talked to me. The only way to get involved was to become them – I had no problem with that. I wanted to see them get their guns out, or start lining up the coke, but it was sufficient that they bragged about it on camera. I described it to Sue as a stag weekend. There was no need to file report after report when we got back. Jason and I had a quick debrief and that was all. If anything, though I didn't know it at the time, the whole weekend would make a mockery of what followed.

TSUNAMI

My stock had remained high after Friendly Fire – I was entered for a Rory Peck Award and the *Panorama* show on Iraq won a Royal Television Society Award. John and Tom had travelled to Washington and amazingly got access to a female pilot from the crew who had dropped the bomb on us. We were able to confirm that the Special Forces had called in the strike.

Since then Tony Loughran had quit the Beeb and Bob Forster began to leave me alone. Caroline Neil called the shots and I felt that she was the one to protect me. She understood that needs must and she knew how ops worked. It was the beginning of the BBC's formation of a proper High Risk Team. Finally I was moving from safety to security.

I had been back to Iraq several times and Afghanistan, too – indeed my last trip prior to Boxing Day 2004 was as late as 9 December. When I returned, I was whittling down the time to Christmas. We were done for the year at the office, and I hated all that bullshit anyway. I couldn't wait for the next mission.

Such is the random nature of breaking news, even I was taken aback to wake up on Boxing Day and find that disaster of the highest order had devastated one of the most beautiful places in the world. Instantly, I was transfixed by the story and alive to the possibilities. I didn't move on 26 December. As with Friendly Fire, it was like a movie but very real indeed, watching those waves leap out of the ocean, knocking houses and vehicles for six. I flicked from the Beeb to Sky to ITN and back again like a junkie. I watched swimming pools being swamped, the water climbing up the balconies of hotels towards people who couldn't imagine they were in danger. It didn't matter how tough you were; you couldn't not have feelings. But through it all I was weighing up the possibilities.

One report in particular kicked me into action. I saw John Irvine on ITV, holidaying in Thailand, on the beach with the sea going out only for him to grab his kids seconds later as it charged back in. That was it. I need watch no more. I had to get out there.

This wasn't the usual Craig Summers cup of tea, and I wasn't sure they would send me. They saw me as a bombs, bullets and bastard kind of guy. It wasn't a war zone or football thugs on the piss – this was natural disaster on a biblical scale. I rang the planning desk. My old mate Malcolm Downing was working the Christmas period and we had a first-class relationship. Of course, because it was Christmas, I knew we had a skeleton staff. I told him straight – I was happy to deploy as soon as possible – and I told Sue the same. I even packed my bag. Malcolm gave me what he could. At this point they didn't really know what was going on and he would call if I was needed.

'I'm ready to go; it's not a problem.' I put the phone down, sketching out my next adventure. This was going to be massive. Malcolm was right though. Nobody knew how big at this stage. I also phoned Paul Greeves. 'We should be out there – it's right up our street and it calls for a military operation,' I pitched.

I had to get on that plane, and years of being on standby for military ops that might or might not happen told me only I could be the logistics guy at a moment's notice.

'I'll be in touch,' he flat-batted me back. 'We should be across it as a team.'

It was clear that it was part of the world that nobody really knew much about – and it had happened at a time when the world had gone to sleep. I know this would cost us four or five days. Most people didn't even know what a tsunami was. I was so thick that if I hadn't been presented with a Japanese flag at the Hong Kong Sevens earlier that year by a team called Tsunami, I wouldn't have known either!

Once again, I waited for the phone to ring and, once again, the silence was deafening. The fact that I don't like Christmas – Sue calls me Scrooge – made it worse. Normally I would have gone to the football if West Ham were playing at home but, even though they were only at Fulham, I abstained. My mind was working overtime – and not to my pleasure. I could see the reporter Andrew Harding working out of Singapore, filing by videophone. I knew, as well, that the Delhi Bureau would handle Sri Lanka. I saw Jonathan Head, the Tokyo correspondent, and it was clear we were pulling in everyone on that side of the world. I was glued to the net and the rolling news; Sue was watching repeats of *Noel's Christmas Presents*. I was chuffed we were there but felt the moment slipping away.

Most of the Beeb had eyes on Phuket in Thailand – that's where the majority of Brits had homes or had chosen to holiday. In the early stages we were largely dependent on mobile phone footage. I soon learned that Ben Brown had flown out with Duncan Stone on camera. My phone never rang. I had it by my bed permanently switched on. At five in the morning, I would still be checking to see if the office had called. The story was leaving me behind.

Frustrated, I gave up watching the TV news and hit the gym, resolved that if nobody had called me after my workout, I would ring again. I knew that they would need help with the stories, food on the go, and that sickness was a problem. They had no logistics hub.

'I know you want to go, Craig,' Malcolm told me when I finally got through. 'I know we need to organise equipment, food and tents. Let me establish what's going on and I will call you.' Same again. I didn't see why there was a delay. 'When can you go?' he asked.

'Now,' I answered.

He told me he would do his utmost to get it sorted. For the first time, I thought I might be going. I rang my old mate George Booth at the Outdoor Adventure Shop – we had served together, of course, like all my old mates. I asked when he was next open. He told me tomorrow. That was 28 December. I said I would come the next day, but heard nothing from work for the next forty-eight hours. My stuff was laid out at home ready to go. I took myself to the gym again to fill the time. I didn't ring Paul Greeves.

God, I wanted to, but I didn't want to piss him off. I had played my hand, and I couldn't overplay it. I distanced myself from the news. I knew the story was drying up. I could see that they were doing live feeds now, and that they were coming off dishes not videophones. I also spotted Rachel Harvey from the BBC in Jakarta out in Thailand and Sri Lanka – that told me the infrastructure was in place. Once again, my moment was passing.

By the time I made my token visit down the M3 to Poole in Dorset to see George I had almost given up. Of course, as was always the way, I was twenty minutes from the shop when the phone rang. It was Paul.

'Newsgathering want you to fly to Banda Aceh in Indonesia to assist with the setup – 45,000 lives have been wiped out.'

'Yep, no problem,' was all I could think of to say.

I was on the plane.

'You fly at 18.15,' he finished the call.

Bloody hell. I rang Sue immediately – she was tearful. This wasn't like me heading to a war zone. It was Christmas and everyone had seen it on the news. It had cut right through. She changed her shift there and then to get home and get me back to the airport. I was driving faster and faster to get to the shop and straight back out to London. I marched round the store like a machine, bought X, Y and Z and apologised to George. Within half an hour, I was back on the road home.

My phone that never rang was now doing so off the hook. Even my flights changed – there had been two available via Singapore and I was offered £5,500 on BA or £3,500 on Singapore Airlines. On this occasion, I didn't fly with the world's favourite airline.

I was now due out at 21.00, but had to hit Heathrow by 18.15 to meet the supplies. We needed what we call 'grab and go bags' (enough supplies for a couple of days) plus tents, showers, and water purification. That was your classic disaster pack and, God, we didn't know how many we would need.

At home, I had grabbed everything I'd previously laid out – I always packed for two weeks and made the rest up. Just after I finished, there was a knock at the door. The BBC had gone from apathy to overdrive in hours. It was a courier with a massive bag of stuff.

'I thought I was picking this up at the airport,' I told him.

'You are; this is another one,' he replied.

It had all gone nuts. I took a moment to have a peaceful bath, mindful that I might not shower again for weeks. Then, Sue drove me to Terminal Three in silence. Deep down she didn't believe I was actually going. I did my usual trick of laying out an incentive on our return. I talked up a trip to our place in Spain. I never gave a second thought to whether that would come off or not.

There were two huge bags waiting for me – we really had gone from shoddy to hyperactive. Check-in was hectic, and I was never one to linger. I went straight to the Virgin Gold Card Lounge. That's the benefit of having your wife work for the airline. It was New Year's Eve. On the flight, I was out like a light for seven hours. The next thing I knew I was through Singapore and checking into the Mandarin Hotel in Jakarta. I went straight to the bar for a beer.

The world's media had concentrated on Thailand for the past week – that was where the first footage had come from, and John Irvine had turned the spotlight onto that coastline. Everybody had missed the real story – there were actually 250,000 dead and unreported on in a little place called Banda Aceh, which was where I had to get to.

'Can I get on that flight?' I asked Jason from Associated Press, who had been looking after things for us as the attention shifted countries. The answer was no.

I had no idea where I was going, what I would find when I got there or what I was going to do. I just knew I had to get there yesterday. There was only one flight a day to Banda Aceh and most of it was filled with aid and aid workers. To get it, I had to get to Medan, some 600 kilometres adrift. That was the only flight I would be getting in the morning.

When I arrived there, a freelance producer from Sydney by the name of Paul picked me up, drove me to the hotel and briefed me. He had been there since 30 December, acting as our Logistics Coordinator; the fact that we were relying on a guy from Oz should tell you how stretched we had become, how slow we'd been, and how far away from the story we still were as fallout from the tsunami entered its second week. If I thought the images I'd seen up to now were bad, Paul told me, then I needed to prepare myself. The worst was yet to come.

At the Garuda Plaza Hotel, he warned that I had missed today's flight to Banda Aceh and I couldn't go anyway unless I had a Blue Card to travel.

'Can we drive?' I asked.

'No,' he told me, condemning me to another day twiddling our thumbs.

I was concerned that everybody would be packing up by the time I had made it out here. Far from it – it was a cat-fight to get on this one plane a day. I rammed every possible idea at Paul to get the maximum information for what lay ahead – I even asked if we could get there by boat now that the waters had receded. I needed to know how the hell I could get a vehicle of supplies in there ready for when the main team arrived. I still had a nagging worry, as you do in places like this, that the plane would take off without me.

It was warm, humid, and I had been on the road for three days. In that time, I had slept for just seven hours total. This was only the beginning. Like the soldier I still was, I unpacked my kit then packed it again. I knew I had to be ready to move at a moment's notice –

always expect nothing to happen, then for it all to kick off in seconds. Inactivity followed by panic was the order of the day.

Because of the time difference, it was impossible even now to get my head down. Calls were coming in from London and around the globe at any given moment. Paul Greeves – I learned – was on his way out behind me. I got the word to set up an operations base in Medan and to work with Paul when he got there, organising convoys of supplies in; to brief new arrivals as teams changed over; and to create the hub – you had to go through Medan to get the story. We definitely needed to do this – Australian Paul was inundated with requests that it wasn't his job to deal with. The sooner London Paul got there, the better.

On 2 January, I was first to check in at the airport – this was now Day Nine. Everybody wanted to make that 09.00 flight – I don't think it mattered if you were booked on or not. It was chaos. Of course, there was no sign of the flight being called and nobody was saying anything. As I sat around waiting, wondering, I couldn't believe what I saw next. I hadn't been told about it.

Coming towards me from across Departures was a friendly face I knew only too well. Straight in from Bangkok, onto Jakarta and down to Medan, it was the BBC's Ben Brown. I asked him how things had been in Thailand – very grim was all he would say. They had now realised that the story was moving on. Something had triggered with the reporter Rachel Harvey, who was based near the epicentre; she knew that what she was watching on the TV didn't ring true. It was down to her that all roads now led to Banda Aceh, though of course they didn't – every route in bar this solitary flight was blocked.

I was pleased to see Ben and his cameraman Duncan but he looked worse than I did. When I first spotted him, I didn't know him at all. He looked like a bedraggled man dragging a suitcase across the airport. Of course, he had no paperwork either, nor did he know he needed any. Ben would have got the flight anyway and argued the toss at the other end. He would tell them the world needed to see this story. As we were delayed, Aussie Paul took him back into the city to the Press Centre to get him accredited. He was back within the hour and the flight was still waiting to go.

We knew little of Banda Aceh – it was heavily Muslim and a good diving place. That was it. It would, from this moment on, forever remain in the history books.

I could barely imagine what lay ahead as Ben painted the picture of Thailand, full of makeshift morgues, each with bodies piled high, all bloated through their intake of water. Beaches had been washed away. Both Ben and his cameraman Duncan in all their years had never seen anything like it. We now knew that was nothing compared to what was coming.

At 12.25, we finally boarded in torrential rain and thunder. Air Garuda had one of the worst safety records on the planet – so bad they weren't even allowed over UK airspace. The flight only lasted forty-five minutes – around me were journalists, aid workers and locals trying to find their families. It was the approach to landing that shocked us all.

About twenty minutes out, there was a surge to the windows and everybody grabbed their cameras. The West Coast was gone – washed away, flattened and devastated. Picture the white cliffs of Dover, which you can probably visualise in detail even if you have never been. Now, imagine them gone. That's what we were looking at. Heaven only knew what we would find on the ground.

When we landed, it took us two hours to gather all our gear and get away. We drove straight to the military airport to meet Jeremy Hillman; he was now based in Asia, knew the patch inside out, and had been on the first plane into Banda Aceh. It was a thirty-minute drive to what would become the BBC house.

I had never seen anything like it. I had witnessed ethnic cleansing and mass burial in Bosnia. This was on a scale a million times worse. Duncan had no choice but to film through the windscreen. Those who had survived and the poorly equipped authorities hadn't been able to get started even over a week on. By the side of the road, we saw mass graves and bodies after bodies. Even for someone like me, who had seen it all in war, this was no way to go.

The team put their masks on. There weren't enough to go around, so I went without. To my right, I saw an open pit and a massive tipper truck tilting up with its back open. Bodies were flying out into the graves. It smelt of death and decay; every time, you would smell the bodies first before seeing them as you got closer. It stunk in a way death had never reeked to me before – so different from that burning flesh and fuel in Iraq. These were abandoned souls and it was beyond humane, but there was nothing anyone could do – they were simply left to rot. You would just be getting used to the tilting truck when an army vehicle would pull up with more bodies. It never stopped. It reminded me of those black and white movies where Nazis, or those whom they ordered to do so, loaded bodies into pits.

Ben looked horrified – and he had already seen a week of this. I told him all I knew. The only way to rid yourself of the smell was to take it in. It was easy to trot out stuff like 'apocalypse of biblical proportions', but this really was monumental. From locals burning fires in their doorways to keep warm, to nearby bridges with dozens of boats rammed up against them, and bodies just floating in the water: this was new territory for even the most battle-hardened.

I had to crack on though, as sterile as that sounds – Paul Greeves and I had attempted to send that convoy off from Medan as a tester to see if it would get through the sodden landscape in what we knew was bandit country, even at a time like this. We'd packed twenty cases of water and food because we had to be self-sufficient and healthy amid the carnage – if one vehicle made it through that would be a success. We had told Peter Leng to meet us at the big mosque in Banda Aceh. Neither of us knew this place but we figured it was the only prominent landmark that anyone would still recognise. It could, however, represent a danger, given that people flock to religion in moments like this.

As night fell around 17.00, we set off on the main route into town. It was cold and eerie, with just the little fires offering light and warmth. Darkness brings suspicion on both sides; we had to get in and out as quickly as possible. Having already attracted the unwelcome attention of two guys on motorbikes carrying AK-47s, who knew what was round the next corner?

Thankfully, the convoy had made it.

At 03.30, we hit the sack. The time difference for the Ten meant this was going to be the norm. We were up at the crack of dawn to hire a boat to take us to the open sea. It was horrific. Every time we approached a bridge, there were bodies on the bank. I had to take pictures as part of the job. Dead bodies don't bother me: they can't hurt me once they're gone. I just got on with it.

It was body after body after body, each with breasts swollen to breaking point, eyeballs popping and tongues hanging out, and in the rubble of the destroyed buildings, more of the same – often semi-clothed, always swarming with flies. The heat of the mid-morning sun made things worse – more flies and more stench. As I proceeded like an emotionless machine, people were trying to clean up the houses and shops that remained. Haunted spirits got on with the soulless task of attempting everyday life, even though there was little to live for. These people would never forget: they would see reminders forever on every corner until their number was up, too. It was different for me coming in with a job to do – I would soon be out of here on the way back to Baghdad and new adventures. As we shot footage of Indonesian sailors cleaning one of the islands, you knew that they would play that film in their head from now until the end of time.

I was called back to the house – Peter Leng had summoned me and sent a bike to pick me up. After it dropped me on the bank, I walked back to the first bridge we had passed. Crossing it on foot for the first time at the mouth of the river, I had needed a mask. The sheer volume and horrific condition of the corpses, plus the fact that they were still there after well over a week, would have troubled even the most resilient. When I picture it now, I can still smell it.

Peter was panicking because a satellite dish was coming in and someone needed to fetch it safely. I also had to organise more food for more conveys to come in. We needed to get the house into shape. We couldn't make the schoolboy error of falling ill because of our hygiene.

I set up a chalkboard with everybody's locations and numbers. I stuck a massive sign saying 'Take One, Replace One' over the bottled water in the fridge, and bollocked the guys constantly about the overflowing bog out the back. I also hired a local guard, a couple of fixers/drivers and a chef/cleaner – Eva, whose husband had perished in the tsunami. She needed the money but never spoke of what had gone on. She had now assumed the role of provider in her family. Every night when she left, we gave her food to take away. Yet she was probably the lucky one, if you can call it that, falling on her feet by working for us.

I also renegotiated the contract for the house with the owners – the story might not be going to change, but we wouldn't be leaving here any time soon. Equally, some mornings between 05.00 and 07.00, just after finishing for the Ten, we would still get the odd aftershock. There were eleven of us sharing what was no more than a building off the back of a flower shop. I paid up until 15 January.

By 4 January, things were getting better but only marginally so. Vehicles were now getting through regularly from Medan to Banda Aceh. I was sending back daily food lists. The convoy was also getting quicker – generally we would see it a day and a half after it had set out. On Indonesian TV there had been only sporadic coverage. We had no sense of the vast numbers of New Year holidaymakers, who, I later learned, had flown back without passports and in just their t-shirts and shorts. The world's media now understood that Banda Aceh was where the story was – but look at how much time had passed.

The Indonesian army were starting to get their act together, even though one whole barracks had been completely wiped out. Muslim law regarding burials had long since been overlooked – the army was 'hoovering up' bodies and dumping them en masse in an airport hangar. More and more people were now on the streets but, everywhere you went, there was still the constant sound of wailing as individuals learned their fate. Photos of missing relatives hung off walls, holding out the most remote of hopes. By now those looking for loved ones were way past the last chance saloon, and as more prayers went daily unanswered, some sense of reality was returning – except for one thing that suddenly dawned on me.

There were no pets.

As if they'd been using that sixth sense that you sometimes hear of, where animals are tuned into weather patterns and seismic movements, there wasn't a dog or cat in the street. That was unusual for these parts. I only realised this when a cat appeared near the BBC house. I immediately took it under my wing and named it Tsunami. This little ginger and white thing had come into our lives – but unbeknown to me, Ben Brown hated cats!

'Get that fucking thing off the table,' he yelled, after I had let it trough down a load of tuna.

'Come on, Ben, it survived the tsunami,' I replied.

It was a rare moment to break the stress and fatigue. So amused was I at this arrival in our lives, I decided to wash the bugger, covering it in shower gel. Then, borrowing one of the girls' hairdryers, I entertained myself by drying it off and styling it.

Perhaps this was a sign that the story was moving on. There were only so many times you could hire a boat, watch the clean-up, go to a makeshift morgue and file accordingly. Every day we went out looking for that one success story – an act of goodwill or an overcoming all the odds moment. That's what you did in Newsgathering in the days after a natural disaster. Deep down, we knew anyone trapped was dead. The story was over, but we were still here, mainly because it had taken so long to break in the first place. In the modern era, it really is unheard of for word to get out so slowly: that was the Banda Aceh story.

In the Central Business District of Meulaboh, we found a lone official fishing bodies out of the water with a rope and a stick. One by one, she pulled them out and checked their pockets for any chance of ID, and then she catalogued them on a clipboard. It was a thankless task but she told me that within a fortnight of the tsunami, the infrastructure was returning. She spoke a little English to us and it hit me what a big job this was for one individual. If she couldn't identify someone, she just wrote down 'Body One – unidentified' and carried on to the next one. I didn't enquire if she had lost anybody herself.

There was something about the clipboard that struck me. We had got used to seeing piles of bodies rather than seeing them as individuals. The fact that she was cataloguing them made it very personal. She couldn't have possibly known on the night of our Christmas Day that she would be doing this come the New Year.

Nor could I have foreseen what I awoke to on the morning of 7 January.

✝

It was a rest day – the struggle to get here, the long hours, the time zone and its demands, plus the unprecedented intensity of what lay around us had left each of us knackered. I still rose early – that had become my new body clock.

I went to the kitchen area and, as I had done every day, replenished the fridge with water. Two noises hit me straightaway.

First was the silence – I couldn't hear our fixers and drivers on the doorstep because today was a day off. I had got used to waking up to their chatter. That air of peace paved the way for the next sound. It was all I could hear; as I got closer to the source it became louder. It was a buzzing sound.

I opened the front door. The sun was rising; nobody else was up. Swarms of flies hit me in the face and surged through the doorway. Flies had become the norm since we got here, but now there were millions, and I had no idea why.

Then I looked down and saw it.

Dead and naked, lying on cardboard, a baby boy had been left for us. He looked between one and two years old, his eyes closed and his black hair matted in the aftermath. There were no other obvious identifying marks.

'Who the fuck has dumped that there?' was my first thought. I was disbelieving at the discovery rather than emotional at the find. Then I thought how tragic it was.

There had to be a reason for this. This wasn't random or down to chance – someone had specifically left this baby at what they knew to be the BBC house. They were either beyond their last resort and thought there was something we could do, which was wrong because we couldn't help (it was just a baby with no ID and no trail to trace its family) or they still didn't understand the way this story had gone round the world and wanted this child to resonate around the globe. Ultimately, in the big scheme of things, this was just another body. It wasn't in my instinct to get attached to the story.

I don't know why the baby boy had been dumped before first light for me to find this morning. I have no idea where the body had been since Boxing Day – most people had died on impact; many had been in their beds. It seemed odd and desperate but equally considered and deliberate. Was I wrong to think it was calculated or had I misunderstood a grief-stricken parent on the point of breakdown?

It didn't matter. I picked it up with my bare hands, and looked around. Nobody was watching. I walked over to the rubbish which night after night would pile high in the streets waiting for the authorities to burn the next day by the side of the roads to stave off the threat of rats. Removing some cardboard from the tip, I covered the baby with it.

'What's that, Craig?' I heard a voice say. It was Bob, the Australian paramedic who was staying next door to us. I walked towards him. He didn't need me to answer. 'What are you going to do?' he asked.

My response was instant, and came from the mouth of a soldier in the zone and on autopilot. My sole priority was to protect the BBC crew from infection.

'I'm going to burn it,' I answered.

'That's the best thing to do.'

There was no way I was going to leave the baby in a bag for some-one else to pick up later, and there was no other way – where could we put it? Bob went to get some petrol from the jerrycan, while I hastily made an opening in the rubbish and grabbed a box that we had used to store water. I placed the box in the centre of all the other stuff we had chucked out and laid the baby down. When Bob came back, I soaked the lot in petrol, then set fire to it.

As I stood back, smoke and intense flames burned among card-board, disused toilet rolls and food containers – a putrid, charred smell everywhere, more than if it had just been the daily rubbish burn. We moved upwind of the smell to avoid it. It was out in ten minutes. Bob and I bagged up the rubbish, bits of wood and plastic still smouldering. I didn't look to see the remains of the baby; both our heads looking down while shovelling. Nothing was said. We just got on with it. We may have left a skull on the floor – I can't recall. I just wanted it done. Bob thought the boy had already been dead for two to three days.

I saw Peter Leng standing at the door. I had no choice but to come clean. I told him we had to keep this to ourselves – I didn't want anyone else to find out.

'I wondered what all the flies were,' he replied. 'How do you feel about it?'

'It's a sad situation, but I am surprised someone has dumped it on our doorstep,' I answered bluntly.

Only years later did Peter confess that he had told a couple of people – he also said he was grateful and couldn't have done the same thing. Peter and Bob may have looked at it differently but I was in operational mode. In the same way that I'd lied to Stuart Hughes about playing for Wales, and that we gave little thought to Kaveh's funeral on the day that the Americans bombed us, any emotions were saved for later. Right now, I was working and this was the job I had to do. If they were still alive, I couldn't give the parents that closure because there were no clues on the baby. I didn't know how it had got here but I felt sure it was orphaned and deliberately dumped. I couldn't change its fate. I did what I had to do. There were no alternatives but to cremate the baby. It was the most humane thing to do, before it became riddled with maggots and was left to rot in the street. I couldn't put a sign up outside the house saying 'One ex-baby here – please knock'. If the parents hadn't died, why would they dump it?

I pride myself in my work; nobody got sick on that trip. Nobody even came close to diarrhoea and I knew that I had done my job keeping everyone healthy. I ran a tight ship, ensuring everyone always washed their hands with wet wipes. The baby was an obstacle to their health; the next day it would be a blocked toilet. I hadn't known it was coming but I had to deal with it, and I would do the same again. Perhaps I could have taken a second opinion but the soldier in me stood up and made a decision. The rules of war applied here. What I mean by that is that the rules of war constantly re-define themselves as horrors unfold before you and you make split-second decisions. There was no textbook or BBC course for something like this.

Emotionally, too, while everyone else in that house had seen more than enough, they didn't need to see this. My duty was to make sure they never knew. I didn't think it was a story for Ben – we had filmed nothing but bodies, and even though it wasn't my place to editorialise on this occasion, I just couldn't see that this was something we would report on, even if every day was now becoming the same journalistically. Ben wouldn't be able to trace the baby. Lottery odds were better. I made that call and I stand by it today. Other than Peter, nobody who woke in that house that morning would ever know.

It was done. I had stuff to be getting on with. So did Bob. We agreed to catch up later. I washed my hands and put the kettle on. As one by one the team came down, I carried on as though nothing had happened.

'Thanks for your help with that business this morning,' I said to Bob later. We both agreed that it stayed between us. My only wavering concerned whether to tell our fixer Ivan to see if I had offended local custom. I chose not to. In the end we had been as busy as normal, as I went out filming with Andrew Harding then did the cooking in the evening. It might have helped, I don't know. I was able to move on very quickly.

It was after midnight in Banda Aceh before I rang Sue. She was the only person I ever discussed it with in detail. I stood alone in the street on the Sat Phone – nobody could see me in the pitch black. 'How's things?' I asked. 'Been busy at work?'

Over the years, I had perfected the small talk call home that normally began with functional stuff about the mail and ended abruptly with me making an excuse to go. Sometimes she would say she had seen Ben or John on the news and ask if I was with them. Beyond that, she didn't take much notice, and left me to it. She knew my addiction to the next story and war zone would never leave me. It was just one of those unspoken things. Only I really got what happened in my job and she would let me get on with it. Then I would be home again.

Among all those minutes and all those miles spent talking crap from various places around the world, I will never forget this call. 'I had to do something I have never done before,' I began.

'What did you do?' she replied.

And I told her.

There was nothing. Seconds of silence felt like minutes. 'Are you still there?' I asked. She was taking it all in. I knew I had to tell her.

I didn't need to confide in her – I wanted to tell her. I always did. Craig the rock didn't need a rock himself but she was my soul mate. There was no way I wouldn't.

'How do you feel?' she asked.

'It had to be done. Pretty normal day though, really. Not a lot happening.' Then I changed the subject back to the post.

'Any idea when you're coming home?' she asked.

I had already made plans. My replacement was arriving imminently and we would be home for 11 January. Ivan, the fixer, had already asked me if we would ever return and I replied that we would see what would happen – that was the way my life was panning out. No longer the top story on the Ten, we'd been living in a shithole for the best part of two weeks. My only wash had been when we got caught in a monsoon and I took the shower gel outside and stripped down to my boxers. For our hardship, the Beeb offered us a £250 bonus – fuck all after the tax. At least Paul Greeves said 'job well done'.

Plus, I had to return to Baghdad a week later to re-unite with John Simpson – the Iraqi elections were calling.

KATE

Paul Greeves was back on the phone. 'We need you to fly to Nairobi to carry out an investigation.'

Kate Peyton was dead.

I had gone straight from Indonesia to the Gulf. In the process we made a special trip to Kameron's family to present them with our Royal Television Society Award for the Friendly Fire programme. Now, a senior BBC producer had been gunned down in one of the most lawless spots in the world.

In 2005, the Transitional Government of Somalia was at the helm. Kate and Peter Greste, a former freelancer from Kenya who had spent much of his career in the region, were sent to cover their return to power. There was talk that it was a trip Kate hadn't wanted to make.

I had first met her in Johannesburg in 2001; we had been in Israel together, too, and I had last seen her back in South Africa at the end of 2003 while I carried out a security review. Of medium height with brown mousy hair, she was a rarity in this business – very easy going, kind and happy to help; quite caring in the strange selfish world of the media. We had nothing in common.

In 2003 she had met a cameraman and they were trying to adopt an African girl together. She was her usual self, told me how happy she was, but there was an undercurrent that made me think something wasn't quite right. I later found out that her position in the Bureau was up and she was worried her life was about to fall apart

– she didn't want to have to return to England. Her decision to go to Somalia turned out to be fatal.

This was all I knew before I flew out – my colleague John Glendinning had carried out the risk assessment. There had been a specific threat to Western journalists but nothing direct to any individual organisation. Even though this was one of the most dangerous places in the world, one with links to al Qaeda, where aid workers can suddenly disappear off the radar and the local law of silence tends to prevail, we knew people at home wanted to see the story. Prior to the trip, we would do the maximum amount of groundwork possible through the vast networks of contacts and fixers around the world. The BBC had a Somali service in Nairobi. They would be as prepared as for any trip to any part of the world. Everyone knew danger was part of the job.

Kate, Peter and our fixer Aulad Hussain had landed in the Somali capital on the morning of 9 February. She would be dead by the evening.

Touching off the African Express flight from Nairobi, Aulad took them straight to the Shamu Hotel for a briefing lunch with an AP photographer, Karel Prinsloo. He explained that they had been following the government for the past fortnight without incident, bar one moment where a burst of .50 calibre was fired close to officials and the press. After lunch, they visited an internet café, with eight gunmen as an escort.

By early afternoon, Kate and Peter had decided to go to the Sahafi Hotel, where the government was holding court at a press conference. In tow, they had two 'technicals' – armoured vehicles, one of which was equipped with a 50-calibre machine gun. The place was rammed with security people. Nobody paid much attention to the BBC.

Peter told me later that it was a really relaxed atmosphere. In a place like this, you can never get too comfy, and because of the huge number of vehicles and guards milling round, the hotel compound was rammed. That, unfortunately, left Kate and Peter exposed.

At 14.05, they left the compound. Their driver couldn't access the hotel. On this moment alone hung Kate's life.

Kate had her back to the street as they waited for their car; Peter was facing the building. Suddenly one single shot rang out. Kate fell against the vehicle, moaning. Peter pulled her round to the passenger side, opened the passenger door and laid her down on the back seat. She had been a stationary target.

That's all he could remember initially – like all these things it had happened so fast. They had been parked under a palm tree at the perimeter walls – the two technicals were on either side and the government cars were either side of the BBC and the technicals. Kate had her headscarf on, covering her face. At the moment she reached for the passenger door one car drove past and opened fire. Logistically, it was a horrible mess. That BBC car should have been in the compound, and Kate and Peter needed to be on the move. She didn't stand a chance.

Within fifteen minutes, Kate was at the hospital. One of the technicals had raced off after a dark Sedan, which the locals had fingered as the getaway vehicle. By the time they got there all they found in it was a pistol, an AK-47 and a copy of the Koran. It seemed a random shooting. Kate was talking all the way to the Red Cross Hospital at Medina. Pete said she was very responsive. When they got there, he rang Kate's Bureau Chief, Milton Nkosi. They needed a Medevac fast. Kate was well enough to converse. Pete needed to know as much as he could.

'Am I going to die?' she asked him. 'Get me to Johannesburg.' To me, that question now had an all-too-familiar ring to it.

Between 14.30 and 14.40, Kate was taken straight to surgery. There was little Peter could do at this point except call Malcolm Downing on the desk in London, while the medical teams prepared to operate, scouring the building for blood supplies. They were so low on donors that by 15.30, the stock of O Negative was empty. They had spent the previous three-quarters of an hour asking everyone in the hospital. There were three possible matches.

During surgery, one of the doctors carried out the now imperative transfusion. These guys knew what they were doing – if anybody saw gunshot wounds as their bread and butter, it was the medics in this part of the world. There was also an English nurse, Rachel Byers, in attendance. By 15.40, Kate was stabilising. At 16.00, Peter was told that Kate was in no danger – her spleen had been removed, she had minor damage to the liver and the bullet had been extracted. Shortly after that, her vital signs were improving and she was breathing on her own.

Rachel had advised that Kate should not be moved before the morning unless a full medical team was present. That was a problem in itself because there was no night strip to land on. The plane would have to land early the next morning.

Suddenly, her condition worsened and she needed to be moved there and then. She was fading but Peter had left, rightly believing that this was the time to go as things had become considerably better than initially feared.

Back at the hotel, Ajaf the security manager told him everything he knew about the vehicle, and crucially that he believed it to be owned by a man named Afgi whose organisation had been involved in a couple of incidents over the past few months in the Horn of Africa. These included a grenade attack and rifle shots at a radio station; a journalist had also been beaten and tortured. This car had history, and word about the attack had spread fast.

Peter went upstairs to pack all the equipment together while Karel sat with Kate at the hospital. Kate's shooting clearly meant it was time to go, just as Fred Scott and Dragan had done before. That short trip back to the hotel was one Peter would regret forever. He'd hardly got started when his phone rang. 'Get back to the hospital urgently.' It was Karel.

Kate died at 20.25. Paul asked me if I would be prepared to go in to help recover Kate. I said yes, but it looked like it wasn't going to happen, as Milton would surely get there before us for this sad duty.

Then we left at 10.00 the next day.

All I knew at this stage was that what had happened was very unfortunate. She was a good journo, and she died doing the job she loved, but the cloud hanging over the trip she felt she had to make would now linger forever. I needed to know more about that, too.

Consequently, as well as bringing the body back, I knew there would be questions asked internally, as many within the Corporation as on the street in which she was killed. Did she have a right to say no to this mission? What effect would this death have on every trip from now on? As matters stood now, hindsight told us that Kate's personal plans meant nothing when life was taken away from you. I did feel considerable sympathy as we landed in Nairobi, but equally I was getting into the zone, well aware that what I reported back would be enshrined in BBC Health and Safety policy forever and probably be part of evidence at any future inquest or court proceedings back home. That was what my job was all about and for that reason alone, despite feeling genuine warmth and respect for Kate, I adopted my usual robotic attitude.

London were dealing with Kate's family. It wasn't my place to put in a call. Apart from Paul ringing me to say we were going, the only person I'd spoken to was John Glendinning. He sent me over the watertight risk assessment that he had done on Mogadishu before Kate had left South Africa. This was proper, thorough professional security work from John – none of the nonsense that wasted so much of our time. This was what we were hired to do, and if Kate's death served any purpose it should be to remind us of just that.

I had to speak to as many people as possible, but in reality there weren't that many and in a place like this the key players would inevitably have gone to ground. Definitely on my radar were Karel and Rachel but my first port of call after landing in the Kenyan capital on the night of 10 February was Milton Nkosi's bedroom in the Norfolk Hotel.

I had to wake him. He had endured the day from hell, flying in from South Africa and getting into Mogadishu – unbeknown to me, he had already recovered Kate's body.

'Fuck, what am I gonna do?' I thought. That was my job, and I was desperate to get into Somalia to smell the scent of crime and to eyeball the liars. Paul Greeves and I could see that the operation was ahead of us already. We had no choice but to sleep on it and make a plan the next morning.

At breakfast, we decided to split up the roster of potential witnesses. We definitely needed the surgeon's account of how Kate could just have slipped away when it was looking like she would make it. My instinct already told me that if she had been shot in the UK, she might have pulled through.

Her partner Roger had now turned up, too, along with the little girl the two of them had been hoping to adopt. I didn't really get to know him but he bore the look of a Congolese guy who had seen this all too many times before.

The extraction of Kate's body turned out to be a key moment in what we would learn and what we could take back as fact. It was determined that there was no need for us to return to Mogadishu. We would conduct all our enquiries by phone from Nairobi.

I was told it was too dangerous to go back in and that we would put others at risk. Danger was what I did and I had to get in there. I would deal with any consequences after the event. It was simply bullshit to conduct an investigation into one of your own down the phone. I needed to get to that hotel compound, walk that street where Kate had been felled, and see the vehicles involved. Then I needed to get face to face with Ajaf in the hotel. To say this was unsatisfying was an understatement. In effect, I was an on-duty policeman reduced to taking statements.

Rachel confirmed everything I already knew, and highlighted the aftercare issue, reminding me that many of these surgeons had trained up to fifteen years ago and in a place like this had little chance to update their skills. She talked me calmly through the night – she had no connection with Kate. She told me like a nurse and without emotion. I knew that, like me, she had been here before.

I conducted four interviews but I felt I was just ticking the boxes. I wasn't solving it or understanding it; I was simply going through the motions. This wasn't my kind of work or my forte. Not going into Mogadishu made the process harder.

Karel handed me some pictures and that was as good as it got. But I needed to be there in Somalia so we'd be better prepared the next time this happened. One of the most important aspects of my job was to show the journos what we had learned from previous trips anywhere in the world – I couldn't do my job if I was unable to sketch out the position of the vehicle to the compound, making the point that they had to get inside at all costs and, failing that, highlighting the angle of the passenger seats to the street. Not going meant potential exposure for any of our teams around the globe in the future. The basic errors were totting up – sandals, no flak jackets, and entering a vehicle from the open road outside the building you were visiting.

I learned the most from Kirsten from NGO (Non-Governmental Organisation) Security Service. She had the greatest insight into the local political terrain and was the only person who could offer knowledge on who had pulled the trigger. There were three simple but different theories.

Had there been a threat to the Head of the BBC Somali Service, a known opponent to the Transitional Government? Kate may have taken the bullet on their behalf. Kirsten also thought it could be part of a simple vehicle contract dispute. That wasn't uncommon in local gang warfare, nor was it as random as it sounded. The BBC had been offered the gunman's vehicle before Kate's shooting but had said they didn't need it. That could be enough to set anybody off. If we took Ajaf at his word, this car already had a track record in the underworld. Ultimately, the vehicle behind Kate's death could have been the one our guys were driving and might already have had a blood-stained past. The actual owner of the car brought the paperwork to the hotel and confirmed that three men had hired it, assuring him nothing would happen to it.

Disappointingly, theory number three was simply that the gunmen were bored. The vehicle had been hanging around since midday looking at targets and Kate was just in the wrong place at the wrong time. They were always going to take someone out – Kate was their opportunity. Doors close very quickly in these parts; witnesses, weapons and vehicles disappear. Crime goes unsolved. How depressing to think the killers could just have got pissed off waiting.

Both the government and the security team had investigations underway. We would learn very little at that point. My gut said that Kate wasn't the target – the Transitional Government was in their sights. She was the first to exit, and I share the boredom theory. If the guys had parked in the compound, Kate would be alive today.

I called Aulad, the fixer. He told me nothing new. In fact, he said that he felt everything was fine; the threat level had been the usual – it was just a normal day in Mogadishu. He described the Shafi Hotel as a safe place, well equipped with good internet, larger than the other hotels. Many dignitaries stayed there. Interesting, but little help if I couldn't get to see it. He did fill me in on the vehicles. This, I needed to know. The cars had been parked four to five feet from the gates. There had been the solitary shot. Panic ensued and, amid the shouting and screaming, one of the technicals shouted, 'That car – it shot her.' He told me a doctor and a woman gave blood for Kate in the hospital, which I knew already, and that Ajoos had driven Peter and himself back to the hospital after Karel rang. They then gathered up Kate's clothes and headed for Dayniile Airport, at that time controlled by one of the drug warlords. Aulad had been told that Kate wasn't a target – her shooting was an attempt to destabilise the Transitional Government.

I then rang Ajoos, who had been employed by AP as one of their technical staff. He had been asked by the BBC fixer Daood to pick up

Kate and Peter from the airport. It was dangerous territory, just a strip some 110 kilometres away used mainly by aid workers. It was Ajoos who had taken them to meet Karel at the hotel for lunch. He was pretty vague, said very little, but did confirm there were two conflicting stories: either weapons and the Koran had been found in the car, or indeed nothing had!

My nose was twitching. I needed to put my boots on the ground. I was in the wrong city and the wrong country and this confirmed it. I didn't know who was telling the truth, who was covering up, or indeed if I was wasting my time. I liaised with Hamish, the head of UN security in Mogadishu, who was working on the history of the car and digging through his local contacts to see if the police had pulled in anyone. There was nothing.

It was a total waste of time – I was chasing shadows. In the narrowest of modern worlds, with GPS, the internet, CCTV, this was one of the last places where anyone could disappear at a moment's notice; there was no government and whoever had the most guns and cash would be in control.

Paul Greeves and I got together to piece together the day. We were both banging our heads against a brick wall. Everything about this trip was wrong and I hated it. I didn't operate like this. It was one dead end after another, bar piecing together how Kate had died. We knew a bit more than when we left the UK but essentially, after twenty-four hours, we were driving down a road with no headlights on, our first report little more than a checklist.

These were the principal questions:

Had we sorted everything before she left? Was it all signed off? Was the operation to BBC standard? If she had been wearing body armour, would she have survived?

The last point is key. Wearing a flak jacket would have made her a target, and the threat at the time didn't warrant that. We do provide covert body armour and could have done so but hadn't advised it in the planning. This was a grey area.

That evening Paul and I learned that Kate's post mortem would be done the following day and her body would be released to fly back that evening. I wasn't allowed to go to see her. Someone from the BBC should have gone out of respect – she had died in the line of duty. In this part of the world, there was also a pretty good chance that not everything would add up. Rachel had been present through the entire operation and she told us that there was a small bullet hole. If Kate had been gunned down with an AK-47 or a 7.62, the shot would have gone straight through and there would have been a massive exit wound. There wasn't. It was a nine millimetre bullet that killed her.

I saw no point in staying. I could have sat around on the BBC's cash eating the finest steaks five star but I wanted out. I immediately offered to take Kate home. Paul had never known Kate. It should be me to take here back to the UK. I was done.

This wasn't the first time I had taken the dead home to be buried. In 1985, I had been on exercise in Belize when one of my best mates, Mick Small, had been killed in a bad road accident. In total, I flew five bodies back to the UK.

Flying back was the easy bit. I boarded with a hard-nosed soldier's mentality. The bodies were in a metal case in the hold and I couldn't reverse their fate. Nor can you sit next to them, obviously. I had been on a six-month tour and selfishly, all I could think about was that I would get two weeks' leave at home. Every soldier looked death in the eye. It sat on all of our shoulders. I was conditioned to deal with it way before any of my BBC life. Every soldier would have seen it as the same – a fortnight's leave and thank God it wasn't me. But the truth was that Mick's wife was pregnant at the time, and that was bloody awful.

In Belize City, everything had shut for the weekend – I had flown the five bodies in body bags in a helicopter into BC and they had been left in a refrigerated food truck until the Monday because there were no morgue facilities at the weekend.

In reality, then, there was little for me to do for Kate. In London, we had a 'Repatriating a Body' document – people inside the Beeb knew how to get the dead home. They had been here before and had prepared for it on many occasions. I was surprised that it was all taken care of for me. In the eyes of the world, I was flying with her out of respect, but I would never see Kate's body again.

Before the flight, I rang Ajoos, who filled me in on the two investigations. Something didn't ring true, though. I felt he was a major player in the whole story, and the only way I could find out if he knew anything more, anything sinister, was to be in the same room as him. Attempting to do so from Nairobi didn't help.

Then I called Sue to say I was on the way. 'I'm bringing Kate's body back,' I told her matter-of-factly.

'That's really sad.' She had become used to bad news: wherever I called from, it was probably because there were dead people there. She was relieved when I told her I wasn't going into Mogadishu, even though that's where my heart was. As usual, I kept my conversation to the minimum.

I still made no contact with Kate's family. I wasn't one for small talk and I didn't know them well enough. Someone else would make that call. Sarah Ward-Lilley at Newsgathering had rung to thank me. In reality, I had done bugger all.

The operation to get Kate's coffin home was military-like, discreet and under the radar. If you were a passenger watching bags being loaded, you wouldn't have seen Kate being transferred on the plane. Plus, it was a night flight – nobody would ever know. Probably only the captain and I knew the horror of what lay beneath. There was nothing I could do and nobody to meet; nor could I bring her back to life. The British Consul and the BA staff took care of everything. I checked in and boarded. That was all. Symbolically, I was on the plane as a gesture, but it didn't matter if I was on the flight at all. All I really could think without being disrespectful to Kate was: have a drink, next stop London. I don't say that inhumanely. Years in the job had taught me that to do the job well, you remove yourself from it.

As I landed at Heathrow, BBC legend Fergal Keane texted me to say he had said a prayer for both of us. I loved Fergal to bits but to me that was bollocks. I didn't need any prayers. I had been an actor. Not even that – more an extra, fulfilling the goodwill gesture of someone being on the same flight home as Kate. I could see through my role even if no one else could. The truth of the matter is that the real drama was yet to come.

†

I didn't go to the funeral two weeks later; I went to Spain on holiday instead. If I had been home, I would have made the effort but the world and his dog were there. When you get to my age, all you do is bury the dead, and I hate running into all the hypocrites at funerals who sing your praises when all your life they've slagged you off. It just isn't my scene.

For Kate's family, it would never end. They had to wait until November 2008 for the inquest. Charles, Kate's brother, claims that her boss didn't even give a statement to the Corporation until three years after, and he accuses them of being evasive and vindictive.

I had to send every email to do with the trip to the lawyer, even if the mail just said 'thanks'. John Glendinning's risk assessment was the Corporation's saving grace. Personally, I hadn't been waiting on the verdict. Life went on and a lot had gone on in three years. As much of a grievance as I knew Kate's family felt, I think I only glanced at it in the paper. The coroner, Peter Dean, recorded a verdict of 'unlawful killing'. He also sent the BBC a letter urging them to learn lessons from the inquest – while Helen Boaden, the Director of News gave an interview to the BBC website claiming that the coroner had made it clear that 'the BBC did not put Kate under any pressure'.

Unbelievably, as recently as 2010 Rebecca Peyton took a stage show telling Kate's story to the Edinburgh Festival. For the BBC, life went on. Hindsight is a great thing: the question of body armour came up time and time again. For Western journalists, Somalia was up there with Afghanistan and Iraq in 2005. I felt that not wearing covert body armour was probably the right thing, though it should definitely have been available.

After Kate's death, any mission deploying to Mogadishu had to be cleared by the High Risk Team in London in consultation with senior BBC management. If you were working with UN troops, you now had to wear overt body armour; if you were working independently, covert body armour would suffice. Of course, we were in a dangerous business and journalists always had the sixth sense to take more and more risks. There was no way that what happened to Kate would not happen again. We would inevitably be back in similar territory soon.

I didn't have long to wait.

HOOLIGANS

'**C**ome on, Tom. After Japan 2002 there's going to be an appetite for it, and it is Germany, mate.' I was touting for business, itching to get out there.

'If it is it going to be the same as 2000, we're not sure,' came the reply.

But I knew. Only the proper fans had made the trip out to Asia; for this World Cup, 170,000 supporters were expected – 3,500 of them on the banned list. If I was still with the old West Ham boys, I would have been planning this from the moment the final whistle was blown last time around. A country with a Nazi past as backdrop, which itself had a clash with Poland on the horizon, meant this was going to be the hooligan faction in its element.

The Germans were desperate to make a statement to the world about their new unified country. The spotlight was on them across the globe, but internally they were digging deep, too – their coach, the legendary Jürgen Klinsmann, regularly jetted in from California. Nobody fancied them. On their own doorstep, and on so many levels, they had everything to prove.

I had heard that internally it was Jeff Wilkinson who would make the call – I didn't hesitate to email for a meeting. Typical BBC – no reply! Finally, he called, and I was in there the next day. 'I'm not sure how this is going to work,' he began. He explained that Simon Boazman was on board.

I had to think on my feet. 'We need two undercover teams – one restricts you.' I couldn't not be on the greatest jolly yet, could I?

Budget was an issue. I even offered my own kit to save on costs or, to put it another way, to get me on the plane. News were giving me grief, though – I was meant to be working for them, sorting the security on the ground. I bullshitted them, telling them that Current Affairs had summoned me specifically to go undercover. I did them the courtesy of sorting their back-watchers with the brief that they were to avoid contact with me because I was there as a fan as my cover story but they all knew I was feathering my cap. Nearly six years into the job, that cap was pretty well feathered by now!

But this was my territory. I didn't need a brief – I had to just get stuck in and if that meant joining in with the popular hit 'I'd rather be a Paki than a Kraut', then I would play that role. Euro 2000 seemed like yesterday, and the old ICF West Ham days never leave you. For some hooligans, this was the first trip; I would be the guy to look up to, a veteran of the thug element. In fact, at Heathrow on the way out, I was given a 'red card' by the authorities – they briefly took my passport for looking like a thug. They actually were stupid enough to issue physical reds. I was warned that I was going overseas, and that these were the rules, blah blah blah, and that I had to behave myself. Gimmickry had come into policing.

Yes – I would be on my guard for slippery old customers. If there was a square they would be there; if there was an Irish bar that would be the meet. They were all creatures of habit who couldn't resist a good punch-up, and the famine of Asia 2002 meant this would undoubtedly be a feast.

And guess what? Before a ball had even been kicked at the tournament opener, it had all started. Germany, you may recall, hosted Costa Rica in Frankfurt for the opening match. Once again, all roads led to O'Reilly's – this time opposite the main railway station. We were pitched up in a hotel five minutes away with the commentator John Motson. He told me England couldn't win the tournament.

That meant it definitely would kick off. More importantly, it saved me from a stat attack from a man who couldn't use an iron but could tell you who played left back for Nigeria in a B international in 1976. Bring it on.

It was scorching hot – trouble was in the air. It was going to be a long day.

The overt crew had the long lens on the bar. I was out with Simon, filming through the buttons on a specially made-up shirt. My Ralph Lauren shorts were specifically doctored so I could slip my hand in to record. If necessary, we could pop back to the hotel and change roles. It would be a welcome break from these dickheads.

We had checked each other down – Simon was carrying the spares, and he stuck the lead to my lens onto my shirt with gaffer tape. We did the crucial dummy run, to see if I was shooting too high. To get the perfect angle at head height, I had to lean back or bend down – and that looked ridiculous. It was a good job we'd gone through the basics first.

Our phones were off – only coppers or journos made prolonged calls in this environment. By 11.00, we were in the bar. On our approach, we toured all the side streets, planning our exit strategy for later. I had learned from last time around with the tear gas. This time, it would be through cafés and sex shops. For the role, I was in familiar territory.

The early signs were there: a few England 'fans' were already tying flags to the railings; face paint was everywhere; footie tops were off; and buying and selling was well underway. I already knew that if we were offered tickets, I would decline, joking that I was here for the trouble. This time we were tracking the Huddersfield posse – but at this point we only knew that they were on their way.

Seeing O'Reilly's was comforting – here we go again, I thought. Same bar, different country. I wasn't worried one bit. I knew how this would end. What happened next was what always happened next.

Around 13.00, it was as though someone had scooped up around 150 England fans and dropped them in the bar within the space of a few seconds. It was game on.

We took our cue to exit to the street with our beers. As a pair, Simon and I were looking good – as two people, we would attract another pair, and we were natural allies. He was bigging it up for the North London massive – Spurs all the way.

Outside, the traffic was at a standstill. You could feel it rumbling. An open-top car with some bird waving a Brazilian flag in the front passed by slowly, and you could see exactly what was going to happen seconds before it did. 'Who the fucking hell are you?' some of our twats yelled.

The Burnley, Carlisle and, yes, the Huddersfield fans, were caught on camera bragging that they had never had a chance to mix it with the big boys! Well, support a team that might get into Europe other than for a holiday, then.

The heavens opened up on this vehicle, drenching the Latin girl. A group to my right threw their beer over her; one yanked the flag from her hand. They were jumping – despicable animals. Everyone tossed their beer in. I stopped myself from joining in.

At the same time, a German walked past, in between the adjacent railing and the road. I don't know if it was one of the small-town lot but he got smacked in the face, chased out of town and kicked on the floor. It was definitely let's-get-it-on time and, for him, it was because he was German. Some decent supporters tried to usher the poor, defenceless fan away only to receive abuse from their own.

'Who the fuck are you? We're England!' St George screamed at St George.

Pathetic.

And we hadn't even played yet. Unwittingly, England had created a no-man's land. You walked through at your peril. The police were watching from the station, and I had one eye on them watching us. England had dominated O'Reilly's at the sides, the front and the inside – the whole of the bar was rammed across that road, and all the racist bigotry was airing in song. 'The only thing I want to do is slice a Muslim's head off,' one thug said on film.

I knew instantly that would make the cut. After a long period of chasing shadows in the undercover game, that gave me an adrenalin surge. I knew we were winning. Capturing hooligans or fans without tickets, bragging that they wanted to 'get stuck into those Nazis' was the only motivation I needed. This was typical football thuggery – nothing but cowardice at the heart of their argument. Shove them in front of al Qaeda and we would soon see.

At one point they turned on each other. 'If it had been a Greek or a Paki, fair do, but one of your own,' I picked up on camera. Brilliant footage, but disgusting, too.

All around, the England fans' bottle was on the increase – in every sense. The lower the booze in the pint glass, the higher their bravado in their ego. Just like in 2000, the weapons of choice were glasses and chairs, and now it wasn't England versus Brazil; this was Churchill versus Hitler – the Germans had turned up.

England surged. Jason and Nick were on one side of the road; Simon and I were on the other. Huddersfield, Wolves and – bloody hell! – Accrington Stanley were all giving it some as the police moved in from one of the side roads, battering everyone with sticks. Nick and Jase shadowed the Huddersfield thugs, while we moved towards the fight. The riot police even went for the Germans – this was a red rag to a bull. Taunting the home nation was a doddle after that.

Their undercover guys looked amateur, though. The British police were among them, but you could see the wires hanging from the spotters' ears. They fitted the classic Nazi ideal – blond-haired, blue-eyed boys in classic German shirts, shorts and boots with a bum bag round their waist – but were borderline effeminate. None of them tried to mingle or disguise themselves as fans. This was their tactic and I think this is a legacy from the war and a divided Germany: they didn't want the pictures of violence on German soil radiating around the world, so they stood there being obvious with radios in their pockets. Even if it had been nearly sixty years since the war, everyone would draw the same conclusion, and they just didn't realise that the England fans wouldn't give two hoots about a family-friendly Fanfest where everyone could mingle. It might have been their united showcase to the world, putting their transformation from brutal murderers to supremely socially tolerant economic heavyweights behind them, but that very background also propelled the worst of England to an international podium.

So keen were they to impress that prior to the tournament, the world's media had been invited to an open day with the German police. They emphasised tolerance, and a 'We will talk them down' mentality was the ethos of the moment. If only they knew that 2006 was the same thing as 1944 for a generation of thugs who lived off their grandparents' stories. It was almost as if the Germans had had a few bad years in the 1940s, and were actually now a decent lot; while back then we had hidden behind a gentlemanly facade and stood up to them, but what was happening now was the true norm for England.

'Two world wars, one World Cup,' they sang, as if their choice of tune justified all their actions. Idiots.

I warned Simon it would be tricky – he would watch for the cops, and I would get involved. As missions went, this was on a plate. All I had to do was stay close: they couldn't help but brag, on camera, of course. Some Hells Angels – them again – complained like soft shites to the German police that one German gang had been staring at them for an hour. We were all asked to leave.

'You fucking want it or not?' they screeched into the lens.

'Yeah,' came the reply.

A Peterborough supporter confessed he was on the banned list. One fan, Ian, whom I would meet again, told me on film that he was Chelsea until he died. He had flown into Dublin and then onto Germany – he couldn't believe how easy it was, despite his ban. We put our club loyalties aside to bond! 'Come on, we can do these cunts. We're England!' And he meant it. On any other day, his Chelsea would meet my West Ham in a dark alley and get it on but not now, not when there was a war against the old enemy to be fought. 'Let's do the English Old Bill – the Germans won't stick up for them,' he declared.

What a twat. Did he even know there was a tournament on? I made sure we exchanged mobile numbers – that meant I was for real. Anybody with anything to hide would bullshit their way out of doing that.

Next, I ran into a guy called Frank who organised fights. That was what he did. He latched onto me because I was a Hammer, telling me that Frankfurt were coming to Upton Park and could we arrange a scrap. Would I like to come to 'The Shop' after the tournament to meet the owners and stock up on sadomasochistic gear and hooligan clothing? You couldn't make it up. A pissed-up fight was one thing; an industry born out of violence another. It didn't shock me; I just laughed. How the fuck did you get so off-track in life?

Normally, the thugs love a lens, but they were so pissed and violent that one of them attacked our 6ft 4in. cameraman Jonathan from behind, sending his equipment flying off his shoulder.

'You fucking people are scum. You're an Englishman, cameraman. You're betraying us,' reasoned the pisshead.

Jon recovered to catch a guy in an England shirt who had been hit with the pepper spray from the German police, leaving him separated from his own son, a mere teenager. This guy was caught up in it and was in no way a thug. As indiscriminate as the England aggression was, so were the actions of die polizei. The English disease, as *Panorama* later called it, was still rife twenty years after Heysel. If you were from the land of the Union Jack and you travelled the world watching the national team, something in your blood drove you overnight into chanting racist songs, verbally abusing innocent bystanders and then turning on yourselves once the beer had kicked in.

I was happy to live the role, but glad that my new career made me see through what I could have become. Yes, I snarled and sang the songs and, yes, Simon told me to be careful on the tapes for fear of over-encouraging the mob mentality, but I knew that I had to be credible. That meant that the double-edged sword that would take you right up to the front line to get the money shot induced everyone to follow: at this point, I would remember what I was doing and pull the charge back. At one point, I nearly got ram-raided.

My old mate Steve had turned up. I had been at school with his brother Paul, but Steve was now a stills photographer and we had seen each other on our respective world tours. He ran across the bar to me shouting 'Craig, Craig ...'

He was so pleased to see me that he jumped on me. 'Are you working for the—'

I interrupted him. I grabbed him, hugged him and nearly fucking strangled him. He tightened up, almost rigid in shock. 'I'm working undercover,' I smothered him. Ushering him straight to the bar, I told him to shut the fuck up.

If he had blurted out 'BBC', we would have been in the shit, but I nailed him just in time. He was a big bloke, and very loud. He really could have blown this for us. Simon gave me the eyes to check everything was fine and Steve got the game too – realising it was time to get out, he made his excuses and left. He rang me the next day to apologise, not that he needed to. That was the curve ball I'd feared but he had read me like an old pro.

Occasionally it was hard, but to be the best, undercover in a football hooligan scenario, you had to ride that wave with radar eyes and walk that line – the one that meant everyone followed and looked up to you. Then you had to throw the Christians to the lions and get the hell out of there.

When we got to Stuttgart, I too became a Christian.

✝

25 June 2006. England v Ecuador.

The national team had been at their most brilliantly average, scraping to victory against Paraguay in Frankfurt and then on to

Nuremburg to play Trinidad and Tobago, before drawing with Sweden in Cologne. Like you, I can't remember the results, except that we made the last sixteen, but I can't forget that many of the fans went on a cultural visit to the balcony where Hitler had delivered his big speeches, to soak in a real sense of history and show their sensitivity to the past.

Did they, bollocks!

We filmed the last of the racist bastards giving the Hitler salute, somehow lost in a moment of National Front bigotry, summoning from history the most odious character of the modern era, and breaking contemporary German law in the process by waving swastikas and making mock Nazi salutes.

'My granddad killed your granddad,' they chanted melodically.

Proud to be English – they claimed, but who would be proud of that, so far from the moral high ground that we took when good old Britain entered other people's wars. If their granddads had killed in the name of freedom, they failed to recognise that they were pissing that liberty up the wall, and trampling all over their ancestors' graves. 'Five German bombers in the air,' they entertained in almost choral proportions.

Yeah right. Wankers, the lot of them, some even as young as ten – nothing but aggression and racism in their tone. Even it was just the one per cent of the fans, the figure was way too high.

Much as I loved being here, it was same shit, different day – scorching heat, get your kit on, lager it up, and follow like-minded hooligans, with sporadic scuffles the order of the day. We had arrived in Stuttgart three days early. It was clear this was where it would next kick off, and we needed to get our bearings in advance. We had filmed Ronald Kirsch undercover – an acquaintance of our old mate Annis. Organising scraps was his game.

Against Trinidad, there was no whiff of tension – the fans wouldn't lower themselves to that against such relative no-hopers – and against Sweden, it was the ultimate wide boy porn fantasy. There was no trouble here – all the English just wanted to nail the blonde Swedish birds. Plus, there was that added notion that Sven might come good. Finally the Emperor's New Clothes might come off and reveal the genius he'd been threatening us all with since we walloped Germany 5–1 in their own backyard all those years ago!

Alas, no. It was hard to hate him, and everyone knew he was going. In many ways he had become a bit English himself, meaning that come another England versus Sweden game, there was no point wasting any hostility. Instead, we enjoyed the sheer comedic potential of our manager singing both national anthems on the touchline, knowing that what lay ahead might be more tasty. In fact the Germany versus Poland fixture was more of an obvious flashpoint.

At the last sixteen, Stuttgart was built for the thug. The Germans had tried to lay on a big party atmosphere for the English. At one point, they had described our fans as the best in the world. Those Germans, and their sense of humour, hey? The square was as always the focal point – another hot day was looming and these huge buildings towered above the traditional magnet for England fans. I must have counted, at best, a dozen Ecuador fans. The booze was flowing from ten in the morning and the Germans were great hosts – sadly, our lads had different agendas for a party.

Predictably, the fans were burned to a crisp, shirts off and no sun tan lotion on, standing on the steps with twenty pints of lager inside them, wanting to fight the world. Apparently there was a match on. This is a snapshot of the English hooligan abroad. The Germans were out, too, even though it wasn't their gig. It was, after all, their country, not that it felt like that.

And then it started. We were standing around chatting, Simon on the covert camera so I could pretend to get pissed, when a German girl wearing the national scarf walked past the steps and the massive Greek-style pillars where the world had gathered. The enclosed atmosphere said trouble was on the horizon. England were chanting the usual bullshit – anger in the air.

They approached the German bird and someone threw a pint pot at her, so her knight in shining armour tried to have a go back at the English lout. The next thing I knew, a load of German passers-by who had nothing to do with football didn't so much get caught up in it as they positively joined in. Again, the weapon of mass destruction emerged – the plastic chairs were brought out ready for another night's hurling. Caught up in the middle of this, a young Turk got punched in the face right under Simon's covert camera. Another thug took his picture – then the English scum smashed his specs and drenched him in beer. His face was bloodied. The hooligans were cheering, spitting and pissing on the German flag.

This was a revenge attack for all the incidents when Leeds fans had been stabbed at the hands of Galatasaray, even though week in week out, all this lot hated Leeds. We were left on the steps, caught up in a cordon of German riot police.

'We need to get out of here, mate,' I said to Simon. 'We're gonna get caught up in this.'

At the back, the coppers were circling. I spotted our very own Richard Bilton and his cameraman Nick Woolley. I knew we were going to get busted. I tried to exit through the guys at the top of the square. I gave my colleagues the eye, telling them not to say anything. Their back-watcher, Bunny Coleman, could see the shit we were in – he tried to create a sideshow so we could get out but I had that sinking feeling that we had been trapped. Caught up in the filming, I had made a schoolboy error. I hadn't been looking for an escape route. We were there to film, and had got right to the heart of it, but now the riot police stormed in, grabbing everyone regardless of guilt. I knew we were done.

As the oldest-looking guys, it also seemed to the cops that we were the ringleaders. We were fucked. They came for me first. In seconds, I had plasticuffs on me. I was dragged along the street to their van, the first to be thrown in. All around us, either in the know or working on journalistic instinct, the snappers were having a field day. The overt BBC crew were also there! To their credit, they put their gear down and didn't shoot me being thrown in, not that it mattered. We looked like the ringleaders. I didn't resist – just for the drama and authenticity of it all.

Inside, it was a completely sealed unit with two benched seats, one either side, and a grilled unit in the corner. Next came a West Brom fan, followed by a Man U thug and a Southampton piece of shit. Simon was still outside.

'Where you from? What's gonna happen?' they asked me. They were giddy at their arrest, looking up to me as the leader. Inside, I was pissing myself. I was in a small amount of shit and didn't really know how this would play out, nor if I would have to play the BBC card. But, I also knew I'd been granted access that I would have craved if it was pre-planned. My concern was that I had two spare batteries and two spare tapes on me. That was my only weakness.

Bang. The door opened. Simon was next into the van. 'Everything OK?' I asked.

'Yeah yeah,' he replied, a massive grin on his face.

'Everything still working?' I coded.

'Yeah, yeah,' he nodded.

I told the other thickheads that he'd had a kick in the nuts and thankfully his meat and two veg were in order. They bought the whole thing. 'What's gonna happen now?' they asked me.

'Nothing much. They'll take us down the nick and then let us go tomorrow morning.' I was playing the hard man who had been nicked a thousand times before.

It must have been fifty degrees in there. We were dripping with sweat. Then the door flew open again. The next one in was still singing 'Engerland, Engerland' as he was thrown in. Don't you show some humility at the moment of arrest rather than breaking into song? 'You fucking German cunts, I'll have you, we'll fucking have you. We're fucking Millwall. You've never fucked with Millwall,' he put it at his most eloquent best. Who couldn't be prouder? 'We've fucking done 'em!' he shouted

There were just six of us in the back and two belonged to the BBC! He was nineteen, both in stone and age, wearing just his shorts.

'Yeah, I'm from West Ham and we fucking hate you, so shut the fuck up,' I snarled at him.

At this point, the pissed-up Millwall yob got up to confront me, just as the driver pulled off. It was probably 6 by 4 in there and the copper put his foot down, which left Millwall so wasted that he fell to the floor, spewing up all over the van. 'Get me up, get me up,' he whined like a baby as we all moved our legs out of the way. There wasn't much room in the first place but now you couldn't move for puke, most of which he was now rolling around in. 'I need a piss, I need a piss,' he shouted. That would be the next lovely stench coming our way.

The West Brom fan had managed to get his hands round the front – god knows how. He still had his plasticuffs on.

'Pull my shorts down, pull my shorts down. I need to have a piss,' Millwall roared.

'You're not having a fucking piss in here,' I pulled rank.

'I'm not fucking doing that,' said the Brummie.

Then he delivered his ultimate death sentence. 'You don't know who I fucking am,' he screamed. 'I'm fucking Millwall and I was one of the boys who killed that bloke outside the fucking station.'

Jesus, what a dickhead, but bingo, and Simon was filming. What a stupid thing to say – a live confession of an unsolved stabbing. That's what we were here for. If I had thought about it, I really would have tried to get nicked before, and worked the show from the inside. The van was clearly where crooks put their medals on the table. I was, after all, the first to be arrested, just as I'd been warned at Heathrow – I stood out as a father figure-cum-ringleader, twice the age of many of the new breed of thugs. The downside to that tactic, though, was having to show your BBC hand. It wasn't something that had even come up in discussion, because Simon and I backed ourselves as experienced operators – it wasn't even a consideration.

Then Millwall pissed himself. We had no choice but to lift our feet again, while he found it hysterical ... for about two seconds – then the joke was on him.

The driver slammed on the brake, sending Fatboy flying from the back all through the piss and the vomit to the front of the van down the middle area between us all, and back again to the rear of the van.

Outside stood the camp. This was a specially constructed detention centre, fenced off from the main police station just for the World Cup hooligans – or, as most people called them, the English. Simon and I gave each other the look – now wasn't the time to say we were under-cover. To do so at anything other than the last possible minute meant that we were failures in our field. We were along for the ride now, and had to stay in character, safe in the knowledge that we had done nothing. We would get what we could until our gear was seized, and then whip out our press cards. My only concern was that I wasn't sure if we were getting head shots or filming somewhere near the midriff.

There was an inevitable pause before the doors opened. Fatboy from Millwall was left on his own. Getting out without slipping in the piss and the chunder was hard enough for us.

Dozens of English fans were already lined up outside. I just thought this was Colditz all over again, and I was waiting for *The Great Escape* to pipe up. I scanned the line to see if there was anyone I knew, or anyone I knew I had filmed. This was not the time to be recognised.

Amid the shouting and ranting, I had a quiet word with Simon. 'Stay together, and let's choose our moment to show them our hand,' I said calmly.

He told me he still had all the kit. We were almost definitely still rolling.

The Germans ran a tight ship – this time, some three weeks into the tournament, they were ready. We had been quickly outflanked by German police, cutting us off from everything, breaking into the cordon and nabbing the perceived ringleaders. I clearly looked the part. We were playing it by ear, drunk enough to play drunk but sober enough to be aware. Drinking ten or so pints a day had become routine.

I tried to take charge to show the lads that Craig Summers had been here before. 'Don't play with the plasticuffs,' I told them. 'That's what they're there for. The more you struggle with them, the more they tighten. Stay calm and see what happens.'

It would help if Simon and I weren't forced to separate.

We were marshalled into a hut. It was like joining the military a quarter of a century ago.

'Stand next to him, stand next to him,' they bellowed. 'Name – do you have any identification?' It fulfilled a classic German stereotype.

There was a row of German officers stood in front of us. Behind them, one of the Old Bill was observing. I knew this was now the moment.

'Can I have a word?' I said to the bobby.

'Why, what's the problem?' he replied. I got the sense that his presence there was just a pacifier to any racial tension that might spill over.

'Can I have a quiet word?' I asked again. I had one eye on Simon and the other on the two guys putting all the personal stuff into bags.

'What is it?' he said standing right under my nose.

'We work for the BBC,' I declared. I explained how we were undercover filming and had got caught up in it; our friendly copper leant over to the German who was dealing with me and whispered in his ear.

Two more thugs were sent to a cell, and he stopped anyone else coming into the room.

'Look, I've got a covert camera, spare batteries, and loads of other bits and pieces in our pockets,' I explained.

'Take the camera kit off and put everything else in this bag now,' he ordered. He took the lot, including our press cards. And then processed us as hooligans.

We were sent outside again to re-join the queue together, waiting to be escorted to rows and rows of cells. 'Engerland, Engerland, Engerland,' was all I could hear. Doors were slamming all around us. The yob element still hadn't got the message.

I was thrown into one cell, Simon into another. Everybody had to take their shoes off. I knew it was a waiting game – I had to trust the English copper. I was confident that I hadn't been sold down the Rhine here. In the cell were two others from the van and two more thugs. Still they sung. I sat there on the wooden bench.

'There's no point ranting and raving,' I told them. 'It ain't gonna get you anywhere.'

And they saw sense and shut the fuck up. That didn't last long. The door flung open. My worst nightmare. It was Millwall.

'All right West Ham, all right.' He was in my face. 'Engerland, Engerland, you fucking German bastards you can't keep me. You fucking German cunts, you can't keep me. I'm Millwall, I'm hard.' He was banging on the door. No, not again. I knew someone would knock him out in a minute.

'Listen, you wanker, sit down and shut up,' I glared at him. 'You stink of piss and you stink of sick. Sit the fuck down and shut the fuck up.'

As I was giving him the dressing-down, two massive German coppers stormed our cell, slammed me up against the wall, whacked the plasticuffs back on me, dragged me out, and banged the door shut.

'Stay with it West Ham, we're England.' Millwall was back on his high horse.

I would have pissed myself if I'd been watching, but I was in it. This was me, hard man Summers being dragged out. I'd thought I was sorted but I wasn't sure now.

I didn't panic but I double-checked my memory. Did I chuck beer on anyone in the square? Did I throw a chair or go for anyone? They didn't hold back in roughing me up, frogmarching me down the corridor. There was no gently-out-you-come; the cuffs were dead tight and my arms were up against my back.

'Leave him alone, you German cunts,' the new arrivals shouted. 'He's English.'

I was taken to an interrogation room. Then, it all became clear. I could see the English policeman sitting there.

'Release the plasticuffs,' he said when he saw me. This was a game. 'I'm really sorry about that but if you are an undercover BBC reporter then I don't want to blow your cover,' he explained.

'You know what, mate?' I replied. 'That was absolutely brilliant.'

I loved that. I was on the inside with the best access possible and now I had got my own country's police force playing the part, too. There was still some work to be done, though.

'I'm going to be dead straight now,' he levelled. 'The head of Stuttgart police is going through all the footage in the square and if I see you or your mate doing anything untoward then you are nicked as a football hooligan.'

I couldn't be sure of what was on the CCTV. The jury was still out.

Next thing, the door flung open. It was Simon, and they went through exactly the same drill. I loved it, but I knew we were still in for a bit.

'Unfortunately, you've got two choices here,' he went on. 'I can put you back in with the others and then I can pull you out and put you in a cell by yourselves. I don't know how long this is going to take, if you can bear with me.' Then the plasticuffs went back on. There was playing the part and playing the fucking part.

So, the head of Stuttgart police was now trawling his own network looking for Simon and me. If he was that bloody good, why didn't he just seize all our footage – we had a live confession of a stabbing on the tapes. That was a start.

I was thrown back in the cell.

'What happened, mate, what happened?' My cellmates couldn't wait to see me.

'They fucking interviewed me,' I egged them on. 'They reckon they've got me on film punching some Kraut.'

'Fucking brilliant.' Millwall was loving it, kicking the door with his bare feet. 'We're English, we've fucking done them,' he shouted.

From the tiniest of cells, they were off again. 'Ten German Bombers' was out once more, and everyone was joining in. Then came 'I'd rather be a Paki than a Kraut'. As much as I loved the gig, I didn't want a night of this.

Three long hours later, almost when I had given up, the door flew open again. Here came the heavies once more. Ridiculously, Millwall, thinking he had sobered up, tried to grab onto me to keep me in the cell. The Germans palmed him away, sending him falling on his arse. The door slammed once more – this time I was on the right side of it. There was nobody in the corridor. Except the British cop.

'Here's a bottle of water,' he offered. 'I'm putting you in a cell down the corridor. Your mate will be with you in a minute.'

'Can we have our phones?' I asked.

'I'll see what I can do.' He seemed to be roaming free on German soil.

By the time Simon turned up, he had his mobile, which was a sure sign that they believed us. Why would you give comms to someone you were holding? The signal wasn't great but we got hold of Jeff back at base by text. He already knew – News had told him, because the overt team had seen us going in. We texted back to tell them not to charge in with a BBC card because I felt we would be out soon.

After an hour or so more, the British cop came in to say they had cleared the footage and returned all our stuff to us. 'I can't let you go at the moment,' he said. 'We've so much going on, I can't get you into town.'

I told him we were happy to walk, knowing we would be picked up, but he asked us to wait, possibly until 06.00.

After he had gone, we inspected the bag. The twat had lied. None of our tapes had been removed from it, let alone dubbed off. Yes, it was brilliant that there was an English copper there because a

German might have just treated us as one of the mob but equally he had done nothing. The Germans could all speak the lingo but you couldn't know that they could read your tone. Like me, he was loving living the part.

At 05.30, he was back. There was nobody around. 'I've got you guys a vehicle.' He showed us a caged dog van and apologised. 'That's about it, I'm afraid.'

We couldn't care less. Nobody saw us leave and I think that's the reason why we went at that time. He could have been a right dick and confiscated everything but I felt he played a blinder. We were dropped at the train station, and both Simon and I looked at each other and chuckled.

'I'm fucking knackered,' I said.

'So am I,' my mate replied.

I phoned Jeff and told him we were on our way and going to hit the sack; I also rang home and Sue told me I was a bit too old for all this. She was probably right.

Who knows whatever became of Millwall? This was as close as I would ever come to walking the line and crossing it – where I nearly blew a mission for being too good at it. It was the dream job, and my worlds had merged. Asked to be an undercover reporter at a major football tournament that the world was watching, I myself was uncovered, watched by my own camera crew! I was never in any risk, but I couldn't live anything other than dangerously.

And of course, a few days later, England slumped out of the tournament as they always did.

Motty had been right after all – his opening words in the match against Portugal among his best and among his final as a commentator on England at major tournaments. 'The gateway to a World Cup semi-final or to World Cup oblivion.'

Oblivion it was. Except, of course, for those who had gained notoriety through our footage. Praised as the best fans in the world, we were now once again dubbed the 'English disease' – a culture of excess taken beyond the level of acceptable behaviour. One Sunday newspaper had reported at the time that two undercover BBC reporters had been arrested. There was no shame in that, and the obvious conclusions to draw are either that the British cop took cash to leak the story (given that he played a blinder, I dismiss that), or that among the mob were other undercover reporters too.

What if Millwall worked for the *News of the World*? What if all six of us in the van had been press? How stupid would that be? I doubt very much that anyone other than our own recognised us being thrown into the van.

The best was yet to come. When the *Panorama* show aired, my phone bleeped into action. It was August, well over a month after our pathetic exit. The show had been massively re-jigged. I had given them over 130 hour-long tapes.

'You bastard. You fucking stitched me up,' it read. 'I'll fucking have you.' It was Ian, the Chelsea fan.

'Hahaha, some you win, some you lose,' I replied.

'If you ever come to Chelsea, I know who you are and I'll make sure we do you,' he bragged.

I felt the chances of bumping into him were slim. 'Bring it on,' I bashed into my phone.

I laughed when he sent me his final text, and it just made me even more determined. Where there was danger, there was a story and where there was a story, I was drawn to it.

'You're dead.'

I never heard from him again.

HARRY'S GAME

Had the Corporation learned the lessons from what happened to Kate, or was that all about box-ticking? It was true that if you sent individuals into the most dangerous places in the world, some of them wouldn't come back, however thorough your risk assessments were – that was the lottery of life and the Achilles' heel of journalism. To get to the heart of the story, sometimes you become it – the wrong person in the wrong place at the wrong time.

On 14 March 2007 the call came for me to get my backside out of Baghdad and into Jerusalem. Alan Johnston, our correspondent, had been kidnapped. I knew instantly at the start of the conversation that the words 'Alan' and 'kidnapped' were coming – my military sixth sense had already tuned in.

My mind rewound to the previous Christmas – Alan and I had shot a video diary on the whole security situation in Gaza. He was never blasé about what was a very real threat, but he was also well respected by each of the factions in the region. The Beeb were shitting themselves – this could be Kate Take Two but much more prolonged. There was no bringing Kate back. Who knew how long Alan would be missing? Every day would be a reminder. Nobody in our industry had ever forgotten how long John McCarthy had been gone for.

When the videos came through of Alan in a suicide bomber's vest, even I thought the game was up and he would be the next body I would bring home. We were definitely in a different era now, and the BBC no longer had a protective coat around it. If anything, the reverse was true: such an organisation was a magnet for nutters around the world, for whom the price of death was the ticket to paradise. In this case, Muslim extremists with links to al Qaeda, led by a local bully, Mumtaz Durmush, were pulling the trigger. Except they didn't.

A second video came and on 18 June a deadline passed. I felt that was the key moment. The more demands you issued, the more ultimately came and went. Every time that happened, you left them with fewer cards to play. The BBC decided that no correspondents would live in Gaza from now on, and armoured cars would be the vehicle of choice. Again, just like Mogadishu, any stories in the region had to be cleared by the head of Newsgathering and the High Risk Team. The John Simpson days of barging into places saying, 'I'm from the BBC', were fading fast – unless, of course, you were John himself! There had been too many rude awakenings in recent years.

Alan was released on Wednesday 4 July, some 114 days after he was kidnapped. 200,000 people had signed an online petition. Hamas, with whom the BBC had kept up a dialogue, had played a crucial role. I had only spent three weeks out there: very soon, it had become clear that nothing was moving fast. I didn't negotiate Alan's exit, nor did I hang around for the circus of vigils that followed as the world and his wife wanted to be seen with him. I had already been called home to play Harry's Game.

'We've got a breakfast meeting tomorrow with Paul and Dom,' Newsgathering had said.

Paul and Dom made their living sniffing out stories around the world and pitching them to major broadcasters. Craig Oliver, the News editor of the Ten, was also coming; Sangita Myska was mooted as the presenter. I was asked to suss out whether these guys were genuine and if the story had legs – we were going to buy children in Bulgaria.

My first instinct was no. I felt these two were a fly-by-night crew who wanted a quick hit and a fast buck. I sat there and said nothing. Then Craig asked me what I thought.

'Sangita going in is wrong. She needs to be part of a couple. Sangita buying a baby in the underworld doesn't look right. I need to play her husband,' I said, shocking them. I felt Sangita thought I was trying to block it, but they just hadn't thought it through. 'I will be the elder husband, who has married a young Indian girl totally against the rules. I've got fingers in pies everywhere but I'm a bit of a dodgy East End car dealer. Obviously I had a bit of a record.'

Inside I was rubbing my hands at the story, and I wanted a starring role. I didn't really think Sangita was the right casting and I knew somebody would ask us why we hadn't done this legitimately in the UK. Paul agreed that was perfect – and he knew the type of characters we were likely to be dealing with. Our plan was hatched – I appeared to be the only one who had thought it through, when actually, prior to the meeting, I hadn't really thought about it all.

We gave Paul and Dom a week to come back with something concrete. In the meantime I began to cost up the trip. We would need an initial recce from Paul and Dom, then Sangita and I would fly out. It came in way over budget, but we farmed the idea out to radio, News 24 and the Ten, and shared costs. We were given a green light – subject to Paul and Dom doing the groundwork.

This was like nothing I had done before. I couldn't wait to get started. What a story to tell your grandchildren – assuming I could get the right price for them in Bulgaria!

Paul and Dom were back a week later, now with specific targets to aim for. I told them it was the time to introduce me into the story – make sure you drop my name frequently into the conversation, keep this mythical figure alive, the dodgy East End car dealer who was coming in to buy. Our plan was to take it to the wire, and then go to the authorities.

By 16 June, Dom was in Sofia, working his underworld network, putting the word out that they were looking to buy a baby. They were well connected in the world of the shady and could be a bit slippery themselves. It was how you survived in that kind of world, and, of course, how they got this and other stories. A couple of days later, they set up shop in Varna, the third-largest city in the country, right on the Bulgarian Black Sea. It was here that they came across Harry.

He had been the first to take the bait. They met him at the petrol station adjacent to Varna's central bus depot. Harry drove them south to his favourite resort at Kamchia Beach, to a soundtrack of his favourite Gangsta Rap. 'Pump my Pussy' was his personal favourite.

It was safe here – the tourists didn't get out this way. Nor, clearly, did any serious musicians. In fact, he had laid his whole lifestyle on the table to the boys, wining and dining them, offering girls for company – not just any girls, 'no dogs', just pretty ones. Then he drove Dom and Paul through 'Sexy Forest' – £10 a time for a quick shag in the woods. What's more, he seemed to be on first name terms with them all, pointing out his favourites lined up by the street. Either he knew them, or he had the controlling stake in the business. He confirmed the latter.

The lads said he was relaxed and happy – and clearly trusting – but they felt he wasn't the main player. Someone was controlling him. He couldn't wait for me to get over there. 'I think it's best if we get the baby and all the paperworks complete,' he had confided. 'That way gonna be no problem getting the baby out. I have my connections with the orphan house, the manager and the politicians. We can make this very quickly. Maximum three months. We'll pay for all the paperworks to be like official documents. It will happen quickly. I believe in action not only talking.'

Added to this openness, astonishing so early in the piece, he had girls in his empire on the way to France, Belgium and Spain. He also had a team in Germany laundering some of the finest counterfeit cash we'd ever seen, guaranteed to fool over-the-counter checking devices. He wanted to lure Paul into taking this business into the Subcontinent, specifically India. I was clearly London's meanest gangster, not to be messed with. He was a pimp and a trafficker. The underworld had sprung to life.

Paul rang back to London to say we were on. I needed to get out there as soon as – Sangita would come later. Craig Oliver agreed, much to my delight. Alison Ford, the Home News editor said it was a great idea. I was to leave the next day.

Sangita was slightly edgy. I got the distinct impression that she felt this guy from security was taking over. I assured her that this was the right way to operate – there was no way your dodgy East End gangster would take his young Indian wife out on the first meet. This was boys' stuff and no place for the bird. Reluctantly, she saw it my way.

We all agreed that we would film our second meet – never film the first and never put too much on the table at the initial get-together. That was only about establishing trust and authenticity, and you couldn't ever know who or what they would bring with them. If they gave us dynamite on day one, we would simply go over it again next time when we would be rolling. It was better to lose anything on the first night, rather than nearer the kill. I also told Paul that when I got off the plane, I expected the works. I only travelled in style and what I said went – I was at all times playing the Big Time Charlie.

When I landed in Varna, we were straight into character. Paul was a better actor than I had imagined! We couldn't know if Harry's people had eyes on the airport. Once I was through immigration, they took my bag off me like I was royalty and escorted me to the waiting car. There was no back-slapping 'Hello, mate'; I was the boss at all times and should be addressed accordingly. In the car, Paul got in the front as the muscle; Dom sat next to me in the back. They had both notionally been on my payroll, shifting dodgy motors.

'This is the boss,' Paul told the driver. And they kept it up all the way into the five-star Kempinski Hotel, checking me in and taking my stuff up to the room. Only behind closed doors did we drop our guard.

'Right, what's the score?' I asked.

'Harry's well excited, and we're going to meet him tonight. He wants to meet you,' Paul replied.

We re-confirmed there would be no filming, but gave ourselves the option of getting the gear later. We would meet in our reception, on home turf at 21.00. That way we were in control.

Paul was to ring to check he was on time. Dom told me that Harry normally came alone, turning up in his black Audi, all the rap music blasting out of the speakers. We would probably hear him before we saw him. I started to get into the zone, picturing this small-time crook and working out my questions in my head.

At half nine, Harry rang. I had deliberately commandeered a specific table in the reception, myself at the head, flanked on either side by Paul and Dom.

'Hang on a minute, Harry,' Paul said pretending to half cover the phone. 'Boss, Boss, Harry's gonna be late – half an hour,' he went straight into the role.

'You tell him from me, I haven't got all fucking day. I haven't flown all the way over here to be messed around. If he's not here in half an hour, then we may as well not bother.' I made sure I was loud enough. First impressions would count.

'Harry, Harry, Boss not happy,' Paul went back on the phone.

He had heard it all. 'I'm just dealing with a problem,' Harry replied.

We hung up. 'That was excellent,' Paul said. 'That's exactly what we need and that will keep him on his toes and he will come here to impress.'

One–nil.

I ordered a large G and T and sent Dom to the bar, indicating that next time he went I would produce a massive wad of euros to show Harry the player I was.

After ten, Harry arrived.

Around 5ft 11, he was stocky, muscular and had clearly worked out. I could tell it was him straightaway but I was disappointed. I was excepting 6ft 4, twenty stone and a monster. I knew, though, I would have him eating out of my hand before we had even been introduced.

Paul and Harry shook hands first.

'Harry, this is the boss.' Paul gestured towards me.

I handed Dom 2,000 euros in fifties. I could see Harry's eyes light up. This was going to be a piece of piss. He started asking me little questions, mostly on cars, and I knocked him back with tales of Rolls and Porsches. I told him I didn't rate Audis, just to wind him up. He said he recognised my London accent and knew I was genuine East End from his favourite film *Snatch*. I was one of the characters in it! It left me no choice but to compliment him on his average English.

He was either going to be the Real McCoy or a fucking idiot, and the only way to find out was to get into the role and mix it with him. I lived that part way too easily. My wife Sue always said I was such a good liar and she could never tell.

After half an hour of this bullshit, Harry wanted to move – he said the bar was boring. I didn't read it that way. Moving location was an obvious move to first base – there was a deal to be done. I hadn't put any scouts out around the hotel. I believed he had come alone, but I will never know. In the confines of a five star and with three of us against him, I was happy to hand him the control that I had sought when we had pitched up at the bar.

Agreeing with Paul and Dom, I didn't think he was the big cheese either. I had clocked him as some middleman. We might have to deal with someone else higher up, or might never meet them. Someone was definitely pulling his strings. That would be how these things normally panned out. Harry either trusted us or saw pound signs. Regardless, Harry's Game had begun.

He drove us to the Timbuktu Restaurant – he wanted to eat but I think it was part of the process in checking us out, moving us into various locations, making sure we were real too.

In the car, Harry was relaxed. His body language indicated trust – he was laughing with us.

'This isn't fucking music,' I bantered with him. 'Come on mate, turn it down.'

'Boss not happy, Harry,' Paul would chip in.

The pussy was being pumped again, and it showed no signs of relenting.

I started talking cars with him again, taking the piss out of his Audi, throwing him the odd carrot now and then. 'If everything goes well, we might be able to do a bit of business together,' I teased him. With all dodgy people, one bent deal could lead to another, whatever you had come looking for initially. I knew he was eating out of my hand.

Then he pulled up by a car park. He was checking us again. Two muscular blokes were waiting for us. 'They work for me,' Harry told us.

'You're not sussing us out are you, Harry?' I made him feel like he was in control.

'Nah, nah, if Paul tells me you are the boss man, then you are the boss,' he joked.

At the restaurant, I made sure I sat right next to the little weasel, with Dom and Paul opposite, my shrimp and salad nothing more than a prop to open him up. I was a fat bastard, I didn't eat salad and it didn't take long.

He was lining me up for bigger things and repeat visits. He promised me that a Formula One racetrack was going to be built locally – this would be an economic boom for the pair of us.

'If you can do this for me, I will show you my appreciation. It's very important to me,' I bullshitted.

'I am the same,' he replied. 'Craig, I will do this for you.'

I was talking bollocks of course. Since that very first day working with Nick Witchell, the story was all I cared about.

'Have you been to England?' I asked him.

'No, Ireland,' he explained.

'What have you been doing in Ireland?' I probed, knowing I was opening up his little trade routes.

'A bit of business. I've got a few vans over there, moving stuff around ... just stuff.'

He spoke like a crook. They always referred to stuff. His wife, from whom he was separating, also lived there. Or so he said. He told me he had already got the ball rolling. His man in Turkey had fixed the orphan house. Those words alone told me that, at this speed, this was a regular operation. 'My man in Turkey' for fuck's sake – that's a different country and he'd only met Paul and Dom the other day. Clearly, I was just another customer.

'Do you like the ladies?' he asked.

'Course I do. What bloke doesn't?'

We were moving on fast. When the crooks start taking you to their clubs, it's game on.

'The boss's wife is very beautiful, Harry.' Paul kept the story on track.

'Yeah, yeah, we'll just go have some drinks and watch some nice women dance,' he protested.

'Yeah, I'm having some of that. What goes on tour stays on tour,' I joked.

We walked round the corner from the restaurant onto the main drag. I thought three of us were too many to be going into some seedy unknown nightclub. While Harry was chatting up his bouncer mate on the door, I told Paul to make his excuses and get back to the hotel and stick by the phone in case anything kicked off. Dom confirmed that he wasn't tired and was definitely up for girls! Even though I was on Harry's turf, I felt comfortable. The boys had bigged me up so much that all he wanted to do was impress, probably by now already dreaming of ditching that Audi for a Porsche.

'Come on, Harry, that's a bit insulting,' I complained as the bouncers patted us down on the way in. It was the club rules, but nobody else got the treatment. That's why we didn't bring the covert equipment. On a second visit, they might trust us and wouldn't have to do the rigmarole, but on the first night, this was new territory to us, and we couldn't know where we would end up.

He led us down some steps into a dark and dingy, basement area. Neon lights were the new thing here! Add to that carpets which hadn't been changed in twenty years and you couldn't get much seedier.

'I wish we had the camera on,' I said to Dom, as some bikini-clad tart in a thong came rushing up to Harry as she had probably done a thousand times before, attracted to his perceived power, unless it was part of a routine, choreographed act to entrap us. Only dodgy people doing deals came this way, and Harry, by the ease with which this all panned out, had brought many a bent geezer here before. For a moment we mooted buzzing Paul to get him back, but ultimately it wasn't worth the risk.

'I've fucked her and I've done her.' Harry showed us his totty port-folio. 'Would you like me to arrange something?' As he spoke, he was summoning one of his bitches for a dance on Dom. You can see, can't you, just how tough, life on the BBC payroll was.

'Nah nah, I'm a bit tired tonight; maybe another night,' I replied when offered.

He promised us a party at his place – probably just as well. He clearly had a lot of friends in this gaff. You always knew in surveillance when all eyes were on you. Harry took us next door and this time we were ushered in – no pat-downs. This club wasn't busy but we'd climbed another rung on his ladder. No need to check us out twice. We were still being monitored though – a thick-set man in a red t-shirt was clocking us from the end of the bar. The scouts were out.

It was Harry's turn to flash the cash – large shots of green apple Schnapps flowing like there was no tomorrow. Then he raised the stakes. He motioned me to the bogs. 'Do you like a bit of the old [sniff] powder?'

'What do you mean?' I quizzed him. Course, I knew what he was on about.

'Charlie,' he replied.

I reckon he had watched this scene in some pirate Bob Hoskins rubbish. 'Yeah, I don't mind a bit of Charlie,' I responded.

He unwrapped the tin foil like an expert. It was already in powder form. Out came the credit card. I realised now that of all the things I had seen, all the risk assessments I had been made to fill in, all the stupid courses which I had bullshitted my way out of, there was nothing under the heading 'Snorting coke in the bogs with the Bulgarian mafia'. Fuck – what was I meant to do? Either I had to do it, or risk losing face. I was in the role. That meant it was in the job description. I would deal with London when I got back.

If I had to do it, I had to do it.

'I'm not using that fucking dirty rolled up note you've just used Harry; I'll roll my own,' I conspired. Fuck me, what would Nicholas Witchell have done in the same situation?! I couldn't get out of it. I was a big-time bent gangster from the East End who did dodgy things. Of course I was a cokehead.

I rolled up a fifty-euro note. I bent down over the marble surface, ready to whack it up my nose. 'Is this good shit Harry?' Like I gave a shit.

'Yeah, very good ... the best,' Harry replied.

Bang. The toilet door barged open. It was Dom.

In that split second that I was about to take one up the nostril on behalf of the Beeb, my mate barged in. We hadn't planned it. I didn't even give a thought to the greater consequences with my employer.

The door that led to the loo also took you outside. We hadn't talked through what we would do if one of us got separated and isolated. I blew it away off the top of the wrapper, and twitched my nose.

'That is good shit, Harry,' I lied.

'Very good, very expensive, Boss,' he confirmed. It looked like fine flour.

Dom hadn't even known we were in the toilet. 'I don't think you realise how perfect your timing was,' I said to him on the way out.

'I was just concerned,' Dom told me.

'That was brilliant,' I told him, buzzing. 'You saved me from having to do a line of coke.'

And I would have done it, too. For the story. I was living off the adrenalin. Had anybody on the BBC payroll ever gone this far for the story since Donal MacIntyre around the new millennium? I loved the idea that I could put in the receipts next month for all the dodgy contraband I had bought and consumed for the most famous broadcasting organisation in the world. I wouldn't of course – these kind of characters left very little paper trail.

Dom had played a blinder, unzipping his flies, and carrying on as though it was business as usual. Harry had pushed past him on the way out. Dom mouthed 'OK?' to me, and we both exited back towards the stage area. I don't know if Harry was topping himself up after an earlier hit but he was on hot coals now, unable to sit still, eyeing up his shag for the night while recounting his previous conquests.

'Are any of these girls available to ship back to England?' I asked.

'Yeah, yeah, Boss, everything is possible,' he dealt.

'Are they Romanian girls or Bulgarian?' I faked my interest.

'Both – we can achieve everything.'

I told Dom we needed to get into the prostitution game. Harry kept promising me anything I wanted. I was gutted we weren't filming. There was no point carrying on for the night. Our relationship was good. We were in.

He wanted us to go to the Peep Show Club on Maria Luisa Street right in the centre of Varna. This was classic Harry – rarely in bed before five, never up before three in the afternoon.

'I'm asking no money now from you, Boss,' he said. 'I already have been myself to two orphan houses. I spoke to my man in Turkey by Skype today and he said we're gonna do this.'

'Look Boss, it has been a long day,' Dom butted in. 'You need to call the wife.'

'Yeah, yeah, good call.' I was grateful for the get-out.

Harry was hugging me like the grovelling little shit he was, telling me it would be his honour to collect me and my wife from the airport on our return. I told him we needed to confer – she was nervous but hopeful – but I would bring her next time.

'It has been a pleasure,' I lied. 'And I think we can do business.'

We agreed to meet the next day.

By 03.00, we were back at the hotel. Harry probably can't piece together the rest of his night. More 'Pump My Pussy' and then the same again, without the song this time. In the morning we would see if he was true to his word that one of the 30,000 vulnerable orphans kept under minimal security in this country would be ours.

†

We decided we had to film the next meet. There was no time to hang around – we needed to do the deal. And we would sell it to Harry accordingly. I was a busy man with businesses to run, and I didn't have time to live the life of some playboy chasing him around Europe. The only problem was that Harry wasn't answering his phone. I knew he barely saw daylight but I feared the worst. At 19.00, he finally surfaced.

'Boss is really pleased,' Paul told him. 'He thinks you are a good guy and wants to do business. Boss is going back tomorrow to speak to his wife. You need to produce the goods here, Harry. This is a good opportunity for you to get in with the boss.'

We had strapped the Dictaphone to the handset.

'I've got some business to do, but I can meet you at the garage at 10 p.m. tonight,' he took the bait.

Fuck – I didn't want to meet in some garage, waiting for him to show or not, potentially exposed to God knows what. I told Paul and Dom to go. 'Boss doesn't piss around meeting people in garages,' they told him. On covert camera, he said he could show us the kids – boy or girl – anything, and then came the bombshell. It would be tomorrow. Shit – change of plan. My lovely wife Sangita wasn't even in the country.

I didn't care about shafting her. I rang London pretty damn excited, telling them everything except, of course, I never mentioned the coke. My debrief was simple – be patient; there was plenty more to come. Harry was going to show me some kids. It was on.

Harry knew I didn't have the money on me this trip and we had already escalated from a bonding session to doing the deal in twenty-four hours. In reality, he had hardly checked me out at all. I wanted to know how he could fix this so quickly. As I said, I clearly wasn't the first.

'I'm gonna take you up to the orphanage,' he announced. He told us to get some crisps and biscuits and stuff to take in. What the fuck was this all about?

Inside he introduced us to the owners, whom he clearly knew well. Jesus – they were complicit too. Deep down, I didn't like it. Were these people who we were going to be dealing with? Were we buying direct from an orphanage? Paul was rolling. Harry told us to walk around and take a look at these kids. We knew nothing about them.

I told Dom to ask him in Bulgarian what the score was. Dom translated back that Harry wanted to get a feel for the kind of children we wanted. It was a recce. In fact, it wasn't even that. It was bullshit. Waffle. The Emperor's New Clothes. These weren't our kids. This was just the brochure – a gallery. Borderline genetic engineering designer babies territory if you like, except these were already born – just show ponies in Harry's Game. This wasn't real. It was another test. Harry was trying to show he was credible. I took it that he wasn't. I told Dom to tell him we were off.

And on the next plane home.

By that night, I was back in London. My last words to Harry were that I didn't have time to fuck about. I would be back if he got his act together.

'The way things are going there's nothing happening, mate,' I had told him. 'I've got businesses to run; I've got a wife who wants this baby more than anything and she's giving me grief. I can't keep flying out there.'

He told me to come back in a week.

At the next day's meeting at Television Centre, I bigged him up, painting this all-powerful man who pulled the strings all along the Varna coastline. He was a gangster into strippers, he pimped, he was in with this orphanage – the works. I told Sangita that she would have to be right in there next to me if we went back, playing the subservient wife in my shadow. I didn't feel she was really up for it.

Paul, Dom and I had a private conversation. We thought it best that she didn't actually come at all. I just needed Harry to ring Paul to say we were on, and I would be the one to deliver. Just one problem. It had all gone quiet.

Over the next three weeks, Harry wouldn't answer, or we were fobbed off. All we could do while waiting was send Sangita with a cameraman to Varna to shoot some peripheral footage under the pretence of making a holiday show for the BBC. The chances of them running into Harry and his gang were slim – it was a thriving tourist area.

We, meanwhile, had to bide our time. Like all undercover stuff, you want it there and then but you have to stake them out. Then Paul called. We were back on.

On Sunday 15 July at around 21.30 Dom's mobile had flashed up. It was Harry.

They spoke for no more than three minutes. 'Dom, listen to me, I have news,' he began. 'There are two for the boss to see and choose.' He sounded urgent. 'I am 100 per cent sure,' he continued. The babies were in Bulgaria and would be ready at the end of the week. 'There are no complications. One is child of woman who does the special job.' He was indicating she was a prostitute. 'The other I'm going to tell you about when we see. They are healthy.'

He also told Dom that he could traffic the children himself to the UK for a little more money, again suggesting a honed practice and a safe route perfected over many trips.

Harry said Sangita was to say nothing, not to let her emotions and mouth run away with the story. 'You know how this business is,' he protected himself. 'I'm gonna call you again Tuesday, maybe Wednesday. 'And Boss must be ready to come Friday.'

This was the moment I was waiting for. Every time Paul had updated me since Varna, I thought it was a no-go. I had got to dreading answering the phone, fearing the op was going to rat shit. We were now speaking so regularly, always in character – even Paul had started calling me Boss! But this was the call I wanted. It was high-five time – albeit cautiously. This was brilliant, but I didn't want to get back out there for a no-show. I wasted no time in jumping off my desk. Those risk assessments could wait. My mind was all about the end game – what if he did show up with the kids? What was I allowed to say to them? When did we call it off and go to the authorities? I had three hats to juggle.

The Boss man met the security advisor and I had to wear some journalistic responsibility, too. I had to think on so many levels. It must be safe, and I had to be in character but we couldn't have any shit afterwards when the BBC got grilled for leading questions I might ask on camera in the presence of the kids. Editorially and legally, I didn't want anyone to insinuate that we had in way doctored anything when we exposed Harry. We hadn't and we wouldn't but we had to tread carefully – it was a standard objection in the guilty to say we had played with the edit.

We decided there was no role for Sangita. She had done the general shots – the voice-over at the end would all be she would get. There wasn't time to risk it by introducing anyone else or to build new trust beyond our existing circle. Thankfully, we wouldn't now be checking in as man and wife.

I took my time getting back out there, only arriving nearly a week later. We needed to plan for simple things like making sure that the overt team and the covert team didn't bump into each other. Paul and Dom would fly back in first to check everything was running smoothly. Sangita and her team stayed at a different hotel. We kept contact to a minimum, never mixing on the street, hotel bars our only shared office.

On the plane, I was straight back into character number one – Boss man. I would enter on my clean passport. (I had several, dependent on the role.) If Harry checked he wouldn't see any of the journalistic visas or unusual countries that my other documentation might show. Game on.

I had been back in the office for three weeks, answering emails, filling in forms and going home to Sue as Craig Summers. Amazingly, I had also spent ten days in Baghdad doing a security review. Paul had kept me abreast by text. In my other role, I had been driving around the Iraqi capital in fifty-degree heat on full alert.

Suddenly I was back in the part. This was the end game and I had to get it right. Conversations replayed themselves ... 'Pump my Pussy' was back in my mind, along with the coke ... his Audi and his Irish missus were there, too ... I needed to remember to tell him I had moved some cars around and that could be a meal ticket for him, too, especially after the eighteen months he had spent in a German jail for something to do with bent motors. When I told him I had done six months in the UK, it had sealed the deal – I was the genuine article from the proper school of gangsters and that was my badge of honour.

All these random details were flying around my mind and I had to get them in the right order. Then Harry needed to tell me we would see the kids the next day. I didn't want to make any mistakes. This was the end game and I had literally become the Boss man.

We picked it straight up at the airport – Paul and Dom also back in their parts. That's why it was crucial he had kept up the language with me in between the jobs. It had to be natural and without hesitation and we went full on for an Oscar with another big car – Dom taking my bags like the big shot, Paul calling me Boss.

I couldn't know if Harry had anyone snooping at the airport. I wouldn't have taken the chance if I had been him. That's why there was no back-slapping or over-the-top greeting again at Varna. Our TV faces were on. In the car, our driver spoke little English like last time. We knew not to talk business just in case. Back at the Kempinski, we briefed ourselves and eased off the role behind the closed doors of the room. There had been regular contact with Harry. Tonight at ten, he would bring some photos. Paul and Dom would meet him. It was looking good.

We decided straightaway that, with the overt team led by Sangita out and about, we wouldn't go outside but would get him to the hotel. Paul had told him that the boss was busy and very tired but that if Harry was serious, we had to do the deal now.

There were BBC cost implications for the job, but it was now or never. If he didn't play his hand, we wouldn't be back. At home, no questions would be asked if we delivered. If we over-ran or didn't produce, it just made getting clearance for the next story all that bit tougher. I loved splashing the BBC cash, but I also wanted value for money: if that flash cash seemed extravagant, I knew it was for the role. It wouldn't matter a jot so long as the show aired and justified itself with the big pay-off. Some doubters in London had already written us off because of the multiple trips. I wanted them to see the show and say, 'That was brilliant, Craig,' and then I wanted to go out and do it all over again with the next load of fiddling scum that would come my way. I loved the thought that a barely educated Craig Summers was providing the meat for some of the BBC's finest journalists. That's why I would knock back the large ones in Business Class on this trip home. Who would ever have thought that I could end up doing this?

I showered and selected my most on-the-job shirt from the assortment I had brought with me. Dressing was stage one of getting in the part. Dialogue wasn't a problem – I didn't need to prepare my lines, because I knew I would talk through Paul, who would relay it back as 'Boss says'. I sensed Dom was slightly edgy. Normally Paul would film and Dom would play the role, but he was stepping out of his comfort zone on a backup undercover camera.

Just before we went down for dinner, I sketched out on my notebooks exactly where I wanted everybody sat. Dom was to my left, out of range. He would be the runner to buy drinks and fags for Harry, far enough away to get a wide shot, and equally, if he got a slight panic on, far enough back not for it to be noticed. I told him not to worry about the camera – just let it run. He didn't want to let the side down either. His name was very much on the ticket and he wanted future work out of the Beeb just as much as Harry wanted a piece of Craig. We would also put my phone on the table, permanently off but still sending an audio feed back to London. We had it covered from three angles.

By nine, we had eaten and were at the table. I would see him tonight to bond; we would meet tomorrow to deal. That was the plan, and I wanted it done, as much for the buzz of the story as all those other concerns.

At ten, Harry walked in. Compare that to our first meeting – I knew he was serious, showing me the respect my legend merited. There couldn't have been a more obvious green light than being on time. We greeted each other with a gangster handshake where I pulled his finger like a trigger on a gun. The boys were sat exactly where I wanted them. I gave Dom the first fifty from my wad of 7,000 euros of BBC money.

I excused Sangita – the 'wife' was pretty nervous about all this and didn't want to be around. He told me he did business with men, not women. It had been the right call to bin her – she would only have put him on edge. Women, in his eyes, were only there to shag or to sell for shagging.

We chewed the fat, talking the usual shit, and then I went straight in. 'Have you got anything for us ... girls?'

He said yes. 'Twenty thousand up front, twenty thousand for the girl and then twenty more to get the child out and do the paperwork.' He explained his favourite routes out – it was always Cherbourg to

Rosslare. If need be, he would travel to the UK with the parents so it didn't look suspicious. We all clocked it – the bigger trafficking story was waiting for us, and Harry clearly had lots of fingers in many pies. False adoption papers would be a further cost, he informed us. They had no passports.

At that moment, I had no moral conscience. I didn't think, 'Fuck this is real, and it does happen.' Conclusions, as always, were for later. This was a job and all I wanted was the story. Producing the cash wasn't going to be a problem but he wasn't getting a penny off me yet, if indeed at all. I would need a receipt for that, for sure. I'm not sure what the accountants at the Beeb would make of it – one baby, £20,000. That's why it was all about taking him right to the wire. The money might have to be real at some stage but we couldn't ever hand it over.

Around eleven, after an hour's chat dipping in and out of cars, drugs and other business, I dragged it back on track.

Harry whipped out his Sony camera. 'These are the girls,' he said into every single recording device.

Yes, yes, yes. We had him. We needed only the meet with them now, and this guy was finished. The stills showed a girl of around eighteen months from a poor family. 'She's really beautiful. What do you think, Paul? Do you think the wife will like her?' I passed the camera, knowing he would film it.

'This girl is from a single parent – she's very beautiful, too,' he said, showing us the second image.

Paul and I did exactly the same again. I knew this was moving on. I didn't give the children a second thought – the responsibility was with the parents. It was them who were selling their kids to escape poverty. 'When can we see the kids?' I went in for the kill.

'Leave it with me,' Harry replied. 'I will arrange and I'll call you tomorrow.'

I reminded him that I was a very busy man and I would be off in the next day or two. We declined another night of pumping Harry's pussy and Dom and Paul saw him out, before we all retreated to my room to strip down the camera gear, and call the producer Annie, monitoring in another room. All the tapes were good to go – we had the lot and so did London. Thankfully, it wasn't one of those 'Shit, it hasn't recorded' moments.

Checking the car park to make sure Harry had genuinely left, we met the rest of the team on the beach to chat it through and to make the next plan. I rang Sue and told her it was all going down tomorrow. I would be home in a couple of days.

It was time to see the kids. At breakfast the next day Dom told me it would happen later on today. I hated the waiting period. Something was bugging me. Harry rarely surfaced and everything told me we wouldn't hear from him before four or five o'clock. That was obviously getting towards the end of a child's day.

By 13.00, I was restless, so I killed time with a swim. Around 16.30, Paul knew it was time to make a move. It was definitely Harry o' clock. We rigged up to record but Harry's phone just rang out. Shit, what did we do here? We needed to bury this today.

Half an hour later, Paul's mobile went off. It was him. 'Harry, Harry, what's happening? We've not heard from you. Boss not happy.' Paul was straight back into the role.

Then, the bombshell.

'Problem,' Harry declared.

'Problem? What problem?' Paul couldn't believe it. After last night, all we needed was a ten-second shot of the children with the cash on the table and we were home and dry. We had the story but literally didn't have the money shot.

'Problem – the children aren't available now,' he bullshitted. They were more than available less than twenty-four hours ago. I motioned to cut the call.

'Harry, Harry, I must tell the boss,' Paul hung up.

Fuck. Was last night a stitch-up? Like the orphanage, were they actually the kids? And if they weren't, then who were those children? We clearly had it, but then we didn't. Had Harry played us? No, not really. All we had done was have a few drinks with him and I knew deep down things like this never ran smoothly. It wasn't like going into Tesco and putting a baby through the scanner. He might have been genuine – it could have been something really simple.

Paul and I gathered our thoughts for a moment, talking it through rationally and conferencing with Annie. There was only one thing to do. Ring Harry back. And let's raise the bar. It was time to introduce the money.

'Boss not happy; he's wasted a trip over here. You promised the children would be available. He's tired, he's busy. What's the problem?' Paul did the talking as always.

'Major problem, major problem, I promise you,' Harry snapped back.

Too fucking right there was. We had you, Harry, and soon the authorities would, too. 'This isn't good enough. Is the boss going to see the children today or tomorrow?'

Harry told Paul it would be another two weeks.

I was fuming. 'Harry, Harry, it's the boss here,' I grabbed the phone. 'This isn't good enough, mate. You've called us over. I've got my wife waiting. You promised me.' I didn't want to hear about his big problems. 'Listen, I don't fuck about and I don't expect you to fuck about. I don't want problems; I want solutions. I'm not hanging around. I'm going home tomorrow.'

His apologies fell on deaf ears.

'Are you definitely sure you can't show me the children tomorrow?' I gave him one last chance.

'I'm really sorry, Boss.'

I hung up. Then chucked the phone on the bed, punched the wall, and screamed out the biggest 'Fucking hell' you would ever hear.

The next day we all flew back to London. There was only one thing on the table at the next day's meeting. It was time to pull the plug. Harry's Game was over with no result. At some point everybody had to move on, and that was now. I'd genuinely thought we had it in the bag. We still had no explanation. It could have been Harry; maybe the kids had been promised to someone else; perhaps someone higher up the chain blocked the deal; or were we too slow in showing the money? I couldn't be sure. I just knew this was how dodgy people worked.

Alison Ford, now at BBC Breakfast, and Gary Smith, head of Home News, hadn't been on the trips – they had a slightly clearer perspective. Leave it a week, they urged, and let's see where we were up to. Wise old heads who hadn't been caught up in the moment and who were, of course, working on many things simultaneously so coming at it with a broader perspective, they didn't share our frustration. They would wait – it was a massive story, and it only lacked the ending. I rang Paul straightaway.

'We've got a week, I think,' I told him. I urged him to call Harry once more.

For the next couple of days, Harry didn't pick up. That didn't concern me – that could just be lifestyle. If his problem was genuine and he still wanted to deal, he would call back. He wanted to see those batches of £20,000, he too had a paymaster to deliver to, and I was his ticket out of there with all the dodgy motors I would be farming out to him next time around.

Two days later, he came good. 'Tell the boss, I am really really sorry. It was out of my control. I can't tell you what happened. It's definitely on now. If he can come out next week, I will definitely have children to show him.' He suddenly put us back in the game. This time, I thought we would get him.

I would need to get into the part one more time, and this really was it now for everyone. If he only wanted to fuck us about, he had done that more than enough – I wasn't jetting in for any more fun and games. The fact that he was calling us repeatedly in a week of phone tennis told me that it was happening. Just short of two weeks after our last visit, it was time to get back on the plane and run through the entire Boss drill all over again.

We didn't meet him the first night. He wanted to see us at McDonald's at four the next day.

'Which McDonald's?' we asked.

'I'll tell you which McDonald's when you get in the taxi. I will call you and you pass the phone to the taxi driver.'

From nowhere Harry was starting to get serious and operate like a proper crook. A man who never seemed to have a security tail was now getting into the role himself, keeping locations under wraps and on a need-to-know basis. We knew that we would have to be ready to go at a moment's notice, strapped up all day with the gear when the inevitable change of time came for the meet. If he said four, clearly that was the one time you could rule out.

I had also changed my game plan. I would openly show Harry some equipment – my Nokia N95 videophone would film the children so Sangita could take her pick later. He couldn't really argue with that, and there would be no need to pat us down if I had put my cards on the table.

The next day, the inevitable happened. 'It's not four, it's now six,' said Harry. Then he hung up.

Fucking hell. Here we go again. I was pissed off big time. I would have done the same. You never set a pattern. At least there was no problem yet. Paul and Dom were a little more doubtful.

'Do you think we've fucked up somewhere? Have we made a mistake? Maybe we're being led into something completely different?'

I felt Harry was just testing us and told them so. I knew we had covered our tracks, and there was plenty of time. It was summer so it wouldn't get dark here until half nine. I really didn't think he would bring the kids in pitch black.

At seven the phone rang. 'Put the taxi driver on.' Harry was calling the shots. He had completely blanked us on the 18.00 call. He was playing it proper now. In a matter of twenty-four hours, he had gone from being an apologetic pimp who was putty in my cash-rich gang-ster hands to gaining my respect by knowing how to play the game after all, and perhaps these had always been the rules of engagement. It didn't matter if you played shit for eighty-nine minutes, then nicked it in the ninetieth, you still walked away with the points. Harry had just subbed himself for someone much more impressive. Maybe Dom and Paul were right.

Then again, I thought, what will be will be. It looked definitely on, and Harry was obviously working with someone else. He may have been pulling my strings but I also recognised that every time he had called me, someone had just rung him.

We got to the McDonald's early – it was no more than fifteen minutes away. I checked for police first of all, but nothing. Then I looked for the heavies. I saw a couple of dodgy looking guys who may have been the muscle, but there was nothing obvious. Just around the restaurant was the standard play area. Next to it, one man was on his motorbike yakking on his mobile, looking in our direction. He hung up when I clocked him, and sped off. This was definitely it – that was a sign and an error. Harry had his scouts out and we didn't know who was or who wasn't. Maybe we were meant to see that or perhaps not but, either way, I knew it was on his terms and we wouldn't know how many he had brought with him. To stay in the part was the name of the game: do nothing you wouldn't normally do at a McDonald's. So I sent Paul in to fetch some burgers.

Then I spotted Harry. 'There's the Audi,' I said to Paul.

Game on. He parked up. Next, I glimpsed what I thought was the business end of the deal. Right behind him as he wandered over to our car were a couple and a young girl. Was he really about to deliver?

Harry and I shook hands, apologising for last time amid our usual gangster greetings.

Fatia had a black-hair pony tail, and like half the kids out here had two little Gypsy earrings. They had clearly dressed her up to put her in the shop window. This wasn't some snotty little kid. She was a cute little three-year-old in a pink summer's outfit – dressed to trade.

I was told her mother was too poor to care for her; her father looked even more dubious – a fat slob with a massive gut, barely hidden by his stained t-shirt. Initially, she clung to her parents – though I don't believe they were actually related. To me, Fatia was just their cash cow. As un-paternal as I was, no parent, however desperate, could sell their off-spring. That was the bottom line.

I picked Fatia up, playing the doting dad. Of all the roles I had assumed over the years, this was my least comfortable. Mixing it with the football scum, wiping coke off a basin, or walking into a war zone – that was what Craig Summers did. I played out of my skin now with all that goo-goo nonsense. At my worst, I still beat their best when it came to parenting.

She responded a little – her brown eyes wide-eyed at what was probably more attention that she was used to. I held her, while her mother and father lit up a fag. They didn't strike me as poor.

Occasionally Harry would hold her, too, and I kept up the act, leaning across and holding her hand. The parents would only look me in the eye when I asked questions. She was as much a tool in my game as she was in theirs.

Within twenty minutes we were done. It was time to make our excuses and get out of there. We were all desperate to get back to check what we'd recorded. After all the false starts, it would be game over to try to set this up again – but if we had to, then we needed to know now. I definitely had the shots on the Nokia, and that would do if needs be, but the more you've got to pick from, the more you can ultimately nail them with. We also had a second meet planned for the next day, but you could never guarantee that these things might not get pulled at the last minute – especially if one of Harry's back-watchers had spotted anything untoward in the way we had been operating.

I took one last shot of Fatia to make a final fuss of her. As a sign of goodwill Harry urged Dom to give the parents twenty euros or so. That's how things were done out here. Let's face it, how much goodwill can you afford a couple who are about to flog their child to the highest bidder? Dom told me that the mother had asked Harry in dialect if she could see the child again once she was sold. Clearly, that was bollocks. You don't ask a question like that without breaking down in tears and she didn't.

'I need to know very very quickly if you want to go ahead,' Harry pushed. 'This has got to be done very soon. Papers need to be sorted and money needs to be exchanged.'

'I think the wife will like her but obviously I can't make that decision. It's a woman's decision with babies. You know that, Harry.' Craig Summers had finally found his maternal side. 'I think this could be the start of big things between me and you,' I tossed him another big fat lie.

In the taxi, my mind was racing. Still in character for fear of whoever might be around, but buzzing inside, I knew it had all been worth it. Gary and Annie had been right to stick with it. I couldn't believe we had pulled it off and when I told the driver to floor it back to the hotel, I only did so to stop myself from ripping the wires out of Paul in the back of the cab. More than any shots I had filmed undercover, these were the ones I wanted to see immediately. I knew what we had. I just needed to know we had filmed it.

It was time to be professional. High fives were for later. At the hotel, we couldn't get out quick enough, almost forgetting to pay the driver. We legged it across the lobby to the lift. Going up, all anyone could say was 'Come on, come on' and then back in my room Paul ripped his shirt off.

'We've recorded something. The tape has gone.'

I was concerned for a second. He meant it had finished – all sixty minutes were used. 'When did you start taping?' I asked.

'Just when we met the kids,' Paul answered.

He rewound the tape. That next second lasted an eternity. It always does when you have your finger on the play button, waiting for the images to spring into life, hoping they're at the right height level to ensure you've got the key players in rather than filming some lamp-post. We stared at the screen, waiting. Then they were all there. Harry, the parents, Fatia, McDonald's – the lot. We rushed the tape to Annie in a makeshift edit suite.

'Where are the children now?' she asked like a mother.

'I don't know – we went our way; they've gone with the parents,' I replied. I really didn't care. Just press play on the damn tape.

'Where's Harry now?' she continued.

'He's disappeared.' I didn't have the heart to tell her he was probably already unblocking powder from one nostril and pumping pussy.

We could have followed him to see if his dirty work took him back on himself, tidying up his day's work, but the truth was that if I rang him and said I had the deposit, he would have jumped any time. He would definitely be back for more. We had him. Harry was finished.

The next day, around lunchtime, Harry came to the hotel to pick us up. His guard was clearly down, and he had dropped the tail. This was rank amateur behaviour. You didn't see me turning up without Paul and Dom. After months of cat and mouse, he trusted us implicitly. The lure of the euro was too big for his coke-bulging eyes. What a difference a day made. He had gone from highly trained security operative back to the gangster he was.

We could have left first thing this morning. We had enough for the story, finally. We all agreed what a bonus it would be if suddenly after months of to and fro, he was the gateway to some sort of bigger network – the kind of conspiracy people said Madeleine McCann might have disappeared into. He had potentially promised us four children to look at. It was time to see how genuine his web was.

We pulled up outside the courthouse, not too far from where we had been staying. It was busy and sunny. A daytime outing in itself was a rarity for Harry; either the atmosphere was so touristy that the environment was brilliant to blend in to, or he no longer gave a toss. When we met our first 'customer' of the day, I thought he was taking the piss. He had clearly put everything on Fatia. Today was just about him looking like a player. In the same way that we wanted to unravel a web, he wanted to show it off so the boss would come calling again.

'That's no good, Harry,' I stared at him. 'I need to see the flesh.'

Child number one was no more than a photo. In walked the supposed grandfather of a twenty-month-old child, sensationally here behind the mother's back and wanting to sell. My first instinct when I saw him was that he was a low-life scrote. Again, there was no way of verifying that he was who he said he was. His story was just ridiculous, coming to trade with neither the knowledge of the mother, nor the child in his possession.

Harry was lining up any old peasant. Twenty minutes with one, then wheel in the next one.

The grandfather only wanted money – the picture he showed us depicted a poor mountain scene, a rundown building behind the child, the background implying a hand-to-mouth existence in a small community. Unlike Fatia's show pony parents, your old fella here hadn't really pulled out all the stops. Here's the reality check of what a bastard he was. After Harry and his superiors had taken their cut, would he even walk away with 600 euros? What on earth was his life like if that was so life-changing? It was a piss-take on every front. At McDonald's I had promised Harry a decision within five to seven days. I could knock this one back right now. Boss's wife not like. He would soon get the message.

Next came Nazar. It all just spelt poverty. Her dad and his brother had brought her. It was like something out of a different era. The dad wore a blue vest. He had scruffy black hair, lacked some teeth at the front and had that oh-so-trendy YMCA-type tache. The brother was wearing a white t-shirt that looked as though somebody had thrown black paint down it. These were your classic Romany Gypsies.

Then I saw Nazar. She was stunning, her brown hair in bunches and her ears pierced, dressed beautifully in a mauve t-shirt and shorts with a blue necklace around her neck. That old granddad before should have taken notes. Make a bloody effort if you want to offload your kids for cash. I didn't care, of course, because it wasn't my problem, my child, my financial situation, my welfare state, my crime network or my legal system. But it was my story.

Her beauty knocked me for a split second – she would have been the one if I really was an East End gangster wanting to buy. When I held her, she was more responsive than Fatia. When the father lifted her up to take a photo, she looked me straight in the eye and put her finger in her mouth. She looked prepped, even at the age of three or four. This wasn't me at all, buying her a drink and spoiling her. If I had put the money on the table there and then, they would have let me take her, too. They were desperate for cash and didn't care for paperwork. Their body language just said 'Pay up and take her'. They wanted the money before I changed my mind, or went on to see another child. Harry had done a good job bigging me up to the Gypsy community. Of course, he controlled them, so he wouldn't have let me pay them direct – not before he had siphoned off the lion's share himself.

At the back of my mind, the programme was in the bag, and we were forbidden from actually handing over the money, so all I was bothered about was getting back, editing, and notifying the authorities. 'I think Nazar is probably the one the wife will like,' I told Harry as Dom palmed them off with another twenty euros for a cab back. 'We need to go back to London now, show her the photos, have a chat and then, if she's happy, we'll get the flight out in a day or so time, and work out how to get Nazar back to England.'

Harry was now my best mate – high fives and hugs again, jumping through hoops as though back on his coke, a massive grin permanently etched on his face; this the longest of goodbyes, but only because the cheapskate was dragging it out, flagging up whatever future business we might be doing. His guard had completely collapsed, neglecting of course, the key point that a deal is never truly done until it is done. The only thing done for here was Harry.

At the hotel, we reviewed the tapes once again. A specialist Romany translator confirmed the authenticity. McDonald's last night had been good enough, but I was glad we had come back for seconds. Nazar was just as good, and would have been the one. Crucially, despite the wildcard of the granddad, hanging around for more had established a pattern – there was a definite trade and an established network after all.

Events in the future would show that sometimes you stick with an investigation only to hit a dead end within a whisker of a sting, and this at times had been that close, but there was no greater feeling than hanging in for the long haul, building relationships, befriending the underworld, and then handing them over to the powers that be. Or so I thought on that last night in Varna.

There was one more call to make. At nine that evening, I told Paul to ring Harry.

'It looks really, really good. The wife is really happy,' Paul bullshitted.

'She trusts me but wants to fly out, probably tomorrow, to see the kids,' I butted in.

He wanted money; the parents wanted money; we had money. His guard was well past down when he asked me how soon I could get it. He knew the kids were a phone call away.

'The wife will bring the 40k for the deposit and the middle part – is that enough, Harry?' I asked.

'Not a problem Boss. That's exactly what the business deal is,' he replied. Down the telephone line I could hear the Cheshire cat grinning.

'Boss wants me to handle it now,' Paul came back on. 'I will do business with you from now. He doesn't want any more part of it on the phone. The boss's wife will come over tomorrow.' Paul wrapped it up by saying he would touch base as soon as the wife arrived.

'Will you want to see the girls tomorrow night?' Harry was already counting his cash.

'Yes,' Paul confirmed. 'Let's get it done tomorrow.'

My dear old wife Sangita never got to see the child she craved! She wasn't flying out here to see Nazar, instead heading to Sofia to try to talk on camera to the authorities and tidying up some shots in the locality, making sure we had good footage of the garage where Harry had met Paul and Dom. I would leave the experts to the edit and get the next plane out of there.

The next morning we went straight to the airport and left Varna for the last time. I had only the one regret. I wanted to be there when the Bulgarian police knocked on Harry's door. As much as I wanted to see his face when he got turned over, discretion was the only option. I had my doubts of how the local justice system would play out; I didn't know if Harry had any friends within it, but he had got away with all sorts up to now and had only done time in Germany. You could never really know if there would be any fallout, or any of these characters might wander back into another storyline in the future. Dom moved in these circles and was heading back to Sofia, too, but this was his bread and butter. This was how he worked. I knew he could handle himself.

If there was such thing as a textbook op, this was it – from the patience and long-term strategy to the role-playing involved. It gave me massive kudos and for the first time I wasn't only the guy pointing the camera in a tight situation. I had shown my journalistic skills, which a few years ago I didn't even know I had. I now brought something to the table that the BBC veterans I worked alongside didn't possess. I was another rung up the ladder, and defining my own role in real life, too, as well as the fake ones I could create for the job. In the modern era post 9/11, military nous met journalistic hunch half way and it worked.

We had resisted the temptation to film undercover one last time at the moment of arrest and, when we got back to London, Paul rang Harry as soon as he knew he was awake. After everything that had gone on at his end, the least he could expect was 'Problem, problem' from us. He was remarkably cool when we told him there was a slight issue with the wife getting over and we would be back in touch soon, possibly landing the day after next. He had no choice really, given the future riches that he was convinced were on the way. Little did he know that we were simply building in a delay; equally, we were unaware that the Bulgarian authorities now had him under surveillance.

Twenty-four hours later, we were the top story on all BBC news channels. There was one footnote to the reports: the Bulgarian police had arrested Hasan Ahmed Hasan. Harry's Game was over.

That same evening that we reported Harry had been taken into custody, we learned to our dismay that he had been released. It had all been a big set-up, he claimed. He pinned it on me, the gangster. He told the police that he had taken me to a genuine orphanage but that I'd told him if he didn't get me any children, I would use my contacts to sort him.

At the last, he played a blinder. I had been so convincing in the part that he took the fiction to a natural end, citing fear. Only now did that surreal trip to the orphanage, which at the time, seemed just bullshit, show its true hand. That visit was a double-edged sword. He was gauging our interest and whetting the appetite, but Harry was also putting his alibi into place. He had told the Varna police a complete pack of lies. I knew he had them in his pocket.

And then it got worse. They threw the book at the BBC, accusing us of misportraying Varna as a drug-taking, child-trafficking prostitute-ridden resort. Our footage showed that behind the layers of sunshine and tourists, there was some truth in that. They overlooked the films where Harry had told us he had smuggled children into Norway and Germany, citing conspiracy from the Corporation. It was a classic case of a home decision by the ref. Our story had been perfect – I hadn't overplayed the role and had never threatened to bring the muscle in. We had done everything correctly by BBC guidelines and appropriately in terms of leading questions to minors. Then we had handed it all over to the law. Meanwhile he had come to us with everything and told us that he could provide the kids, supply false documents and even accompany the children. He flagged up his trafficking via Cherbourg to Rosslare. He put his own criminal past on the table.

Annie told me that their people were writing to us and it was serious. No such letter ever arrived. I knew I had walked right up to the legal line, which was exactly what the job required. There was talk of me being summoned to Bulgaria to give statements. Again, that was just a smokescreen to turn it back on us.

As you would expect, the *Daily Mail* didn't fail to go into BBC bashing overdrive – reporters Michael Leidig and Glen Owen claimed that we were now dragged into a fresh row over standards; that our investigation had been misleading; and they flowered the whole piece up with quotes from Commissioner Petrov in Varna. 'It was a sad day' that the BBC should 'fall so low' he began. 'The BBC led this man on the promise of vast riches ... he was provoked ...' And the best of all: 'It would have been a brilliant story worthy of the highest honour, but the reality is quite different.' Typical political bullshit.

What staggered me was that after all our months of footage and multiple trips, Harry was in and out of custody within hours, and they drew a line under it without further investigation. I think anyone who saw the piece would draw their own conclusions. They made no effort to track down the supposed parents, brothers or grandparents; and when we rang Harry, of course he didn't answer. His phone was dead and they never tracked him after his release. The authorities had given him a green light to go to ground – nobody ever saw Harry again. Norway, Germany or Ireland would have been a good place to start looking.

Even though our work was undermined by his release, it had definitely been worth it. Madeleine McCann had indeed been a motivation for this story. She was the highest-profile child disappearance in living memory. Craig Oliver at the Ten had access to Home Office documentation showing that at least 330 children had been sold to UK citizens between 2005 and 2006 – and these were just the cases that they knew about. In terms of the Corporation, this was exactly what the BBC did – everybody knew that, and I knew that the public would know it was good stuff. For myself, my name was all over the story almost for the first time.

GUNS

It was October 2007 and I was heading to Prague to buy guns with Allan Little. I was as excited as I had been about working with John Simpson. Our paths had crossed briefly in Pakistan and Afghanistan and I knew that I was working with a pro whose reputation in Newsgathering was exemplary. He was very busy, running a tight line on other stories and due back out shortly in Sierra Leone, so we wouldn't bring him in until we had to, but I knew that when we did, he was the kind of journalist who would give it his all. His work would invariably be seen at the top of the bulletin.

Dom and Paul were also back on the job – the pair of them had more than proven themselves in Bulgaria and their network of contacts in Eastern Europe was second to none. The former was a massive Allan Little fan who had developed a Balkan obsession after reading Allan's book. Also back on board from Harry's Game was the best cameraman in the business, Tony Fallshaw. I had the A-Team back together. The lads had come in to pitch just a couple of weeks before, and in no time, we were up and running. No bloody Business Class this time – we were to drive all the way.

Operation Trident had been everywhere in the UK – there had been a few shootouts in Birmingham and there was significant gun crime in Manchester. The police were making very big statements about getting all the guns off the streets. Just two months before, young Rhys Jones had been gunned down on his own estate in Liverpool.

'We've got access to buy some guns,' Dom and Paul had said. 'What do you think?'

It only needed a two-word reply. 'Fucking brilliant.'

Once again we were back down Romany Way – Dom had befriended a gypsy boy called David. Together with his dad, they ran a cab firm in Prague. His English was poor, but access was first class. In the world of Eastern European gangsters, he knew everyone. I wouldn't have been surprised if his and Harry's paths had crossed at some point. Who could ever know? I just took it on trust that Dom and Paul had worked their magic through third parties and had penetrated the right people. Their stock was also high after Harry's Game. I didn't ask too many questions; as long as they hadn't broken the law, I didn't need to know. In this game, their reputation lived from one story to the next. My job was to join it now, and devise the cover story. This was a lot simpler than the story with my estranged wife Sangita – though, of course, Craig Summers was still an East End gangster. Never stray too far away from the character that you needed to play.

I now owned a couple of pubs in London next to West Ham. Some Albanian immigrants had been giving me grief and were coming down heavy with their threats. I had even seen weapons on them. I couldn't go to the Met because all the booze and half the cash going through my gaff was bent, shipped in from Europe. Paul's relations were from Ilford and had done some work for me in the pub; Dom was his mate from Bulgaria. Dom knew David. I needed to get to Prague to buy a couple of pistols. It didn't get any simpler or more complicated than that, and I loved it.

Within two weeks of Paul and Dom bringing us the story, the producer Claire Gibson and I were hiring a car and driving to Litvínov – about ninety minutes north of Prague, and home to the CZ gun factory. (As lovely as Claire was, how dull was it listening

Belize Jungle patrol, 1985. Another country, another era – soldier boy.

Just back from the Falklands, 1982. Prince Philip inspects.

Three Dogs and three hours on the dusty road from Tora Bora to Jalalabad. Fatigue hiding behind the shades!

Zim, 2008. About to slip under the radar.

The Keshwa Chaca, believed to be the last remaining Inca rope bridge, spans the Apurímac River near Huinchiri, Peru, in the Province of Canas.

Kabul City, 2008, the suicide bomber's vest.

Ciudad Juárez. Distraught – their son and grandson slain in the drugs war.

Harry's Game. The first meeting – Varna, Bulgaria.

Just north of Mazar-e-Sharif, Afghanistan – a typical Afghan family.

The museum at Halabja, northern Iraq astride a T55.

Firdos Square, Baghdad. Seconds after avoiding that rocket.

Banda Aceh. No words needed.

Sadr City, Baghdad. John Simpson and our translator Leith leaving in haste.

Seconds before the World Cup Final 2010. I'm on the panel!

Surobi, Afghanistan. Death Valley. Nick Woolley on camera, and our own police escort watching us.

We made it! At the top of Tora Bora with my old mate Kev and my new mate Ran.

Five minutes ,
Friendly Fire, 200₃

2003 – tasting the
sound of freedom,
moments after
Friendly Fire.

Inside Juárez Prison
where the guards
wear balaclavas for
fear of reprisals in
the outside world.

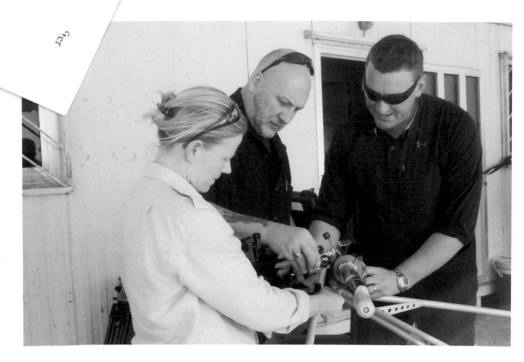

Tigris Rowing Club, 2010. Sir Matthew Pinsent and Sarah attaching cameras to the boat.

Haiti, 2010. Chuck, Matthew, Ian, James and, oh … William Jefferson Clinton.

to her Robbie shite all the way? I took control of the dashboard and whacked up some Springsteen: car rules at play here – driver picks the tunes.) We were prepared to sit it out for a couple of days when we got there if we had to wait on the guns. Our aim was to show how quick and how easy it was to buy them, and how often decommissioned weapons were coming onto the open market. You could spot a decommissioned gun because the barrel would be full of lead so you can't fire the bullet, and the firing pin would have been removed. Otherwise it looked the same as a normal gun. A metal smith could easily bore out the barrel and make a firing pin to shoot. This was the cuts 'n' shuts of the gun world.

Our other objective was to link them to young British gangs in the UK. We had to drive because we wanted to take the haul through a British port – that was the route they were entering the country by. We fell short of notionally supplying a genuine order to any such gang – we didn't have time to penetrate that world. This was a quick hit operation.

Claire and I arrived on the Thursday after a day and a half of pegging it across Europe, overnighting in Dresden. Allan and Tony jetted in on the same evening. It was going to be a pretty simple task, and we'd be out of there come Monday morning. My first job was to identify the gun shops. Frankly, this was a doddle. Can you imagine knowing where to find a legitimate gun shop in London? Here I could just wander in and buy a decommissioned gun – and, as we wanted to show, do it without any paperwork.

So I did. They were just like hunting and fishing shops – like a Millets – generally with only one or two people ever in there. 'I'm interested in buying this one,' I said, straight into the story. It was as simple as that. 'How easy is it to buy a pistol? Do I need paperwork?'

I already knew the answer. I would need to show some ID to get a real gun but nothing for a decommissioned one. The ID was just to show who I was and they didn't care to make copies. In return I wouldn't get any paperwork back. It was all a bit casual. Editorially,

I couldn't really buy a live gun over the counter. I would have had to take that to the police and that would have ruined the programme.

They wanted 250 euros. It was brand spanking new – immaculate condition. So close to the CZ factory, almost all the weapons on show were in this state. After twenty minutes feigning interest in their entire range, I whacked five 50-euro notes on the table and got my gun – cash talked. It was as easy as buying chocolate at the newsagent. Next I bought a replica with bits of the gun cut away – this would be the weapon we would take through Customs, the sort nobody would use but might hang on the wall or occasionally wheel out for one those nonky re-enactments that freaks attend on bank holiday weekends.

I left with both weapons. I didn't expect to get caught at Customs. I knew it was that easy. If they pulled me over, I would play the BBC card, while protesting my ignorance of the fact that I wasn't meant to bring it back in to the country. The truth was somewhat different – I had been told that the sum total of guns going backwards and forwards across the English Channel was in four figures. This would get you at least five years inside.

I needed to see Allan. We met in the underground car park of the hotel and started rolling while I showed him exactly what I had. We deliberately shot here to make it look even more seedy.

'Can this weapon be re-commissioned and used on the streets in the UK?' I said yes.

'Can you explain how it's done?'

I made it sound like any old monkey could do it, which they could.

'What else are you going to do when you're here?' he asked.

'We're going to meet some real gangland members and I'm going to buy some illegal weapons.'

It was a tame start, but we had established the parameters. As yet, we didn't really have a story. That evening we would make plans over dinner – that was the theory anyway, but while I sat there with my first genuine opportunity to get to know Allan properly, Dom was yakking in my ear, anoraking Allan over his Yugoslavia book.

Outside in the car, too embarrassed to come and eat with us, our contact from the Gypsy world was waiting for us. We had met briefly to introduce ourselves last night at the hotel. He looked like Gollum, but I quite liked him. He would refer to me as the boss – of course. I felt he was easily controllable and, unlike Harry, not really answerable to any bigger authority – well, just his dad – but he equally was sniffing out a bigger future with bigger bucks out of me, if he pulled this job off. I sensed he had a few dodgy sidelines – his BMW looked like a ringer. If I asked him about it, he would merely shrug it off as *katastrofik*. If he didn't want to talk about something, it was always *katastrofik*. Some of the players we would meet in the next twenty-four hours – *katastrofik*.

When he finally came into the restaurant to join us for a drink, we were in the middle of taking the piss. A day after meeting him, we too decided everything was *katastrofik*! Our plan was for Allan and Tony to get some general shots of Wenceslas Square in Prague and then film another exchange between Allan and myself – more theatre just for the camera. By night, we were going to drive to the outer suburbs of Prague to meet David's Romany boys, who in turn were mates of the gangs in Litvínov. David was extremely well connected in this world. In time I would see that he always succeeded in keeping himself just outside the circle of knowledge. He knew enough to take you there, but didn't know any more than that, so he could never be convicted of anything himself. The location was set – outside a kebab shop! That in itself made me think this wasn't for real. Gangsters didn't do business in front of kebab shops. Paul and Dom assured me that David was reliable so I took it on trust, even though he didn't give that air. He was just a typical Eastern European character – a bit like Bill Sykes, always puffing on his fags. When I pulled him up on his fake clothes, all he said was *katastrofik*. That probably confirmed it. He wasn't stupid though – he clearly had danced around a lot of deals and other people seemed to respect him.

By seven, we were in position. It was a dark, freezing night and I had pulled the hoodie on my fleece up to make me look a more imposing 6ft 6. Two Gypsy guys in their mid twenties were waiting for us. I didn't consider the meet a danger.

'He's here to buy some pistols,' David spoke to them in dialect. 'If you can't help, is it OK to speak to the guys in Litvínov?'

This was the new pecking order. You couldn't go to Litvínov without coming here first. They couldn't help us but did promise to call 'Martin and the boys' there to see if they would assist. And what exactly were we after? I told them straight. I wanted a couple of 9mm pistols. They would call David later that night. I turned and walked away.

Just feet from the car, I couldn't resist any longer. 'That was *katastrofik*,' I said to Dom. I didn't want to blow the job but I couldn't resist. I was pissed off. I wanted to buy there and then and get filming, but then if they were proper gangsters they wouldn't have sold on the streets. We all got in the car laughing and filled in Paul, who had been waiting. I quizzed him on how far Litvínov was – we would have to go right up near the German border.

Back at the hotel, I briefed Claire. Once again, it was the usual waiting game but David had assured me it would happen – we had only two days to nail the story.

First thing the next morning, Paul knocked on my door. 'David's just called. It's on for tonight.'

I got the sense that the Litvínov gang were used to dealing with bigger fish than me, and the lot last night weren't really serious players. David, too, was just the driver with connections. Nothing more, nothing less – that was how he wanted it.

I spent the day preparing my head – there was nothing to do but kill time. We were on for 19.45. Litvínov was an hour and a half away. Usual rules applied on not filming at the first meet but the SIM in my mobile was sending a broadcast quality audio feed back to London. That phone would remain switched off at all times – the sound would be one of those slightly crackly undercover recordings where you put subtitles up. It was good enough to air, but that little detail added to the theatre. I had never ever suffered by not filming on the first date. As Harry showed, you would be more than enriched with footage later. I didn't want to leave anything to chance – potentially, these guys could have been anybody from gangsterland.

We set off soon after four. I told everyone we needed to be firm when we got there, show them that we were the real deal and stick to the cover story at all times. I talked the boys through my Albanian nightmare one final time. The car journey was all about getting back into the part. The more miles it took to get there, the more in character the lads became. I left the hotel as Craig Summers, ready to record. I got out of the black BMW a proper East End landlord.

Litvínov had seen better days – a real northern Eastern European one-horse town – cute but with nothing really there. It wasn't industrial, but not far off it. An oil refinery had been the traditional source of work for many. It smacked of high unemployment, and the kind of place where everybody knew everybody else. Oddly, it was the birthplace of the supermodel Eva Herzigová.

Our instructions were to meet at a bar called The Radniční Sklípek. It must have looked pretty unusual, the four of us getting out of the BMW and leaving it outside in the street. We just didn't look as if we were from round these parts. It was that kind of place. David stayed outside on watch while Paul, Dom and I wandered in as casually as we could.

To the left was the dining area; on the right was the bar. A massive set of stairs led up to a huge Victorian-type building. We made for the left to tactically choose a table. I positioned Dom to the right and Paul on the other side. I would always take the middle ground. The boys lit up to create the mood, and ordered drinks for the table. We couldn't just sit there and wait – every prop added to our authenticity. Adjacent to us, a couple in their mid thirties were having a romantic meal.

Dom would occasionally step out to check with David if anyone was coming – they were always on the way, he would assure us. Beyond that, I didn't want Dom to do much of the talking. If any of the three of us was slightly less confident, it might be Dom who would say the wrong thing. I was loving my latest role though. I knew this was either going to be a complete load of bollocks like last night or I was about to meet some very tasty people.

After fifteen minutes, Paul's phone rang. It was David. They – whoever they were – were on the way, fitting us in early before a night of drugs, prostitutes and gambling. Just like Harry. David didn't know exactly who to wait for. He was just on lookout, a bit further up the road.

Suddenly, a car pulled up. The gangster vehicle of choice was now a black Porsche Kian – tinted windows, obviously, adding to the part.

'This is it,' I told the boys. I was pumping. I couldn't wait to get started and mix it with some new thugs.

First through the door was smooth-looking Daniel, of German/ Austrian descent and English speaking. He wore an Armani suit with a black polo neck – classic gangster attire. His two bits of muscle were both wearing black Puffer jackets. He was dressed to tell me he was in charge; the other two to tell me they were the hired heavies. I decided to ignore them arrogantly, waving Paul to introduce me. It was about setting your stall out as a serious player.

Paul and Dom got up to shake hands. I refused eye contact and waited for Paul to do the detail. Finally, I pulled myself out of the chair slowly and eyeballed Daniel for the first time. I knew from the cut of the suit and the way he handled himself that this was a proper gangster. The stakes had been raised. I felt no fear, just a greater awareness.

I made no effort to greet him in his native tongue. I was there to do business. I didn't want to come across as Delboy. The other two, Milan and Martin, spoke no English. (Of course, everybody over there speaks a little English in a way that we don't speak a lot of

156

anything. They would pick up the odd thing here and there.) Milan didn't need to. I got the size of him through his tone when he removed the romantic couple from the restaurant. 'Fuck off and eat your meal next door' was the same in any language right around the world.

I watched the couple get up to go. Their evening was over. We never saw them again. The senior waitress escorted them out, plates in hand. In a way, it was quite comical, but it also told me that these guys were feared in the local community and this was probably the normal chain of events on a Saturday night. When the boys were back in town, everybody would know to leave without even turning to glance their way. Their respect was built on fear.

The waitress locked the door. Finally, I shook hands. Then, stage two of the gangster code of conduct – phones on the table. I couldn't know for sure if the Nokia was recording, but it had never let me down yet. I loved that buzz that they could pat me down if they wanted and we could establish the transparent trust on the first meet, but that I had broken it straightaway. I knew they would live and breathe each moment with me back at Television Centre.

The door opened. The waitress was back with a tray of drinks.

'What are you after, and why?' Daniel didn't mess. Neither of us bothered with small talk. The next thing he said knocked me for six. 'Come outside. I want to talk to you.'

I hadn't envisaged this. If I had thought of it myself, I would have done the same. It was a smart move splitting us up. We could test each other for real. What the hell was he doing, though? My mind was racing but I stayed cool on the outside. I gave Paul that look which said that if I wasn't back in five minutes, make an excuse to go to the bogs to find me. Daniel walked me out of the room, closing the door behind. I was on my own.

He led me down a low-lit corridor towards the toilet – the stairs were on my right. I hadn't clocked this passage as I visually recced the room when we came in. I didn't know there was a bog. I was playing catch-up with a hard man – never a good place to be. He had the upper hand. His concern, I'm sure, was more that we weren't under-cover police rather than that we were about to spring one on him.

'What do you need?' he asked me again.

And I trotted out the Albanian line as we had rehearsed.

'We've got contacts in England. We can sort things out.' He was one step ahead of me. That wasn't what I wanted. The point of the mission was to buy here and transport home. I didn't want this to become real back in the UK – that wasn't my brief. Clearly, though, with more time and budget and a different agenda, he might just have been on the brink of opening up his entire bent world to me. I had to let it go.

'I don't know you from Adam,' I batted it back. He was standing right up close, in my face. 'I'm not going to ask you to do anything on my behalf. I look after my own manor.' I threw it back, gangster to gangster.

I knew he was testing me. Either he didn't think I was who I said I was, or he could check out my cover story. If the roles had been reversed, I would have assumed automatically that any cover story wasn't real – but I had years of training in making up fiction. Daniel would always want to deal, once he knew he was safe. I felt comfort-able, but not 100 per cent. This was the closest I had ever been to justifying my legend. My main concern was being separated from the other two. I suspect he did that every time, and that his two heavies would report back on the body language and anything else they could figure out, sat in silence back in the bar. We had more than met our match this time. Harry should have watched and learned.

Daniel and I started to exchange small talk, but even this was a test. 'How long are you in Prague?' he said. 'I have a good friend from London you should meet. He owns a nightclub in Prague. He will know your pubs.'

Luckily, I had been to watch the Hammers so many times that I had based these two drinking holes on reality. I could only come unstuck if this friend was a Hammer, too, and also used to drink at the same pubs. I had no choice but to ham it up. 'Yeah, we could go out tomorrow if you want,' I upped my game.

'Yeah, yeah, I can arrange that. Maybe go to a casino, get some girls.' His response was standard in this part of the world. I didn't feel quite so much on my back foot now. 'Come on, let's go back to the room.' He was showing me the trust – or so I thought. We never made it. 'No, no,' he pretended to change his mind. 'Come out to the car.'

Shit. He had me back where he wanted me. I thought we'd just established an equal footing talking about the night out but he was just reeling me in. I knew better than to be lulled into a false sense of security but he was stamping his authority all over me. He had been in this game long enough to know that predictability was a downfall – keep moving the goalposts and you stay one step ahead. I couldn't know what he had waiting for me outside in the car. I knew David wouldn't get involved. I later found out he wasn't even there.

Daniel opened the boot of the car. There was a blanket lying inside. For a split second, I wondered what lay underneath it. He really had come to do business. There was no time on either side for a formal courting process. He stuck his hand and pulled out a booklet. It could have been so much worse.

It was from the CZ factory. 'I can get you anything in this book,' he promised. His gang had 'acquired' dozens of weapons from a break-in there. I wondered how many times that place was prone to an inside job – it was after all, the main supplier to the Czech military.

Only now was he happy to go back in the bar. He must have felt that Paul and Dom might have covert gear on but that, as the main man, I wouldn't risk it or lower myself to be the monkey. The organ grinder did the deals, not the dogsbody work.

When we re-entered the bar, the biggest waft of smoke you could ever imagine engulfed me. Paul and Dom had been chainsmoking for England. Clearly, conversation had been minimal between both sides and the boys were tense as to where I had gone. The language barrier itself, despite Dom being just about able to communicate, was an obvious obstacle to banter; the frostiness of the unknown was the bigger problem. I glanced at both of them. Their faces told me they were fine. I gave them the look back to keep it going. Then, I filled them in on the book Daniel had given me. Daniel did the same to his heavies.

Dom was picking up the odd phrase like 'pubs in East London' and 'Albanians with guns'. Both he and Paul studied the catalogue like experts. Between us, we could probably navigate our way through all the weapons on offer.

We had been there around forty minutes. I felt we had earned the trust. All tests had been passed so far. Then Daniel threw in another wildcard. 'Your pubs in East London – what are they called?'

I could answer that, of course, because my story didn't stray too far from my reality. But it knocked me back again. A little bit of hard-man posturing, then a bit of camaraderie, a change of location and then a test ... this was how he operated. I realised that there would always be tests – no such thing as being in with these guys. 'The Boleyn and The Queen's Arms,' I bullshitted.

'What's their number?' he came straight back at me.

'What for?'

'I want to check it.' In total control, he handed me a piece of paper to write it down.

'I'm not giving you the number. Your phone should be switched off. We said at the beginning all phones off.' I was buying myself time.

Then I scribbled down a fictional London number. I didn't think he would check it there and then. I backed myself that he didn't care for the detail – it was a trick to see if I flinched at the question. Could your cover story still hold water when specific details need to be added?

I turned it back on him. 'I don't know if you're police,' I said. 'Or if we've come to the wrong person.'

'What is your number?' he asked.

I gave him the number of the Nokia that was recording. If he rang it, he would see I was genuine (even though I obviously wasn't.) He would get the voicemail.

He didn't even try.

Then he let his guard down. As he turned to Martin and Milan to translate, I could see the wry smile on his face. I felt myself going up in his estimation. He paused for a moment. 'Look, we can do business.' The tone changed. 'We would like to meet up in Prague tomorrow night and meet up with my friend and get to know each other properly.'

At last, he was taking me up the next rung.

'Yeah, yeah,' I lied. 'I have some business to attend to during the day but I'm always up for a good night. Are there girls involved?'

'There are always girls available in Prague,' he replied.

Dom and Paul laughed, and with it went the tension. They feigned interest in the guns, Dom saying we wanted something small.

'That's not a problem,' Daniel replied. 'We can sort that out.'

We were on, all set for tomorrow night. Martin rose from the table to shake my hand. I realised then that he probably did speak more English than he had let on – or at least understood it. They had played dumb to see if the boys would let their guard down. He wouldn't have got up from the table if he hadn't followed the conversation between Daniel and me.

'I'll sort the drinks,' I offered, producing my customary huge wad of euros to impress.

We shook hands again on the way to the cars as David pulled up. Daniel wanted to know who he was. In his mind, he needed to account for all of us. I told him he was just our driver while we were here. In the car I made sure David floored it out of town – a massive grin lighting up his face. Now wasn't the time to hang around or risk picking up a tail. Let's get straight back to the hotel.

'What are you so happy about?' Dom asked him.

He just smiled.

'You fucking haven't, have you?' Dom laughed.

'Ah, Gumar girl, Gumar girl,' David replied.

While we were inside mixing it with the mob, our driver had been off getting one from the local Gypsy hookers. He should have been watching out for us. We might have needed him at a moment's notice. It was shocking operational behaviour. But it broke the ice in the car after the tension of the previous hour.

The dirty little prick. '*Katastrofík*,' we all cried in unison. Thank God nothing had gone wrong. If his blow job had blown the job, I would have killed him on the spot. Instead, it made us come to our senses.

'I don't believe we fucking got away with that,' I said to everyone. 'We're out of our depth here. If we had enough time and money, we could carry this on. This isn't a news piece. This is a one-hour documentary on *Panorama*. We can't go to this nightclub tomorrow. We're now in with some serious players, and we don't have the support.' I never spoke like this during an op. I wasn't frightened – I just knew our brief and, as much as it went against my instinct, I could get us all into some serious shit if I took the matter into my own hands and pursued the thing. I had no choice but to call in to Claire.

Then came the bombshell I didn't want to hear. And it has happened to anyone and everyone in broadcasting at some point. 'It didn't work – there was no signal.'

Perhaps Daniel had known that all along, too. He was that good that this may have been the reason this bar was chosen. I couldn't believe it.

'We couldn't call you,' she said.

I had made the rule – no calls during the op. I was gutted. I couldn't regret not having any covert gear on – an hour and a half from Prague in a little village where secrets stayed secrets – we couldn't risk a pat down. Today showed how close to the bone things could get, and who knows what would have happened if our cover had been blown.

'We need a meeting when we get into Prague,' I told Claire.

I wanted to discuss it with Allan and I needed to ring a mate of mine in the force back in London. I was pretty confident that we had stumbled upon something bigger than what w'd come looking for. We were back in an hour. Gumar Schumacher absolutely caned it back to Prague.

I asked the boys how they felt – what had gone on when I was off with Daniel?

'We smoked a ton of fags,' Paul said.

'Yeah, that was a bit scary,' Dom said.

In turn, they asked me if I felt we were out of our depth. Harry's Game wasn't even in this league. All that had saved us was the cover story. It was good, but I hadn't put it in place in anything other than a casual way. Look how close we had got, based on the minimal amount of detail. These were serious gangsters – and we didn't have the resources. If only we had known how easy and fast it was to penetrate this underworld, I knew *Panorama* would have commissioned us.

Back in Prague, I met with Allan, Tony and Claire. Only one question mattered. Did we have enough for the Ten? Claire rang London. She told them everything.

I had to step out of it at this point – what followed wasn't my call. My job was undercover and security. London thought that if we showed the original gun coming back through Dover unchallenged, then we had a story.

I suppose we did. It wasn't enough for me though, and I couldn't let my frustration at budget control or lack of vision in the bigger picture bother me. The need to get Allan out to Sierra Leone on another story also meant this was the end of the line. These things happened.

My friendly copper Nick also advised me not to get further involved. 'That's serious crime,' he said. 'My advice is to withdraw.' And he knew how capable and experienced I was and how badly I wanted it. I expected all these answers, of course, before I rang him. He also pointed out that we didn't have the support of the

Czech police: after what had happened when we handed everything over to the Bulgarian authorities, who could know how much help we would get here?

Claire made the decision to pull the next morning. I knew it was over. That meant if we were done, we needed to get out of there quickly. There was a meeting in Prague to be avoided – inevitably our phone would ring soon. Plus, what would happen to David? Could he really be safe as our middleman? We were about to sell him down the river. I was chuffed though – this was as good and as close as it got. We just couldn't get any further. I still held up hope that Daniel would call. If he asked for a meet earlier in the evening, we could get him on film.

It was a lost cause. My phone never rang.

To be safe, we then took the decision to turn all the phones off. We cut our losses and made for Dresden, then headed back to the Channel ports. Allan's role had been small, by his own admission. At Dover, Tony Fallshaw was waiting to pick us up on the long lens from high above the port. He had flown home ahead to make the shot. The general shots of the white cliffs inevitably set the scene – an image everybody would recognise as Dover. Once out of the port, we pulled up high on the cliffs so Allan and I could park up on a bench to mock up some more theatre. We hadn't bothered to film coming through Customs – that border was so casual, we were pretty confident we would sail through without needing to produce our press cards. Allan did no more than explain the journey of the replica pistol and how we had breezed through British border control – just like many before and many more since.

The word from London was 'no more' – do not pursue. The story was dead. Daniel or whoever never rang that Saturday night. The only piece left in the jigsaw was to call David. Surely, the gang would ring him to see what happened.

'They've gone,' he had told them on the Sunday. 'Their boss was not happy with how you treated him in the toilet. As though you didn't trust him. He's going to take his business elsewhere.'

'Well tell him if you speak to them,' came back the reply, 'that if he wants to do business he is welcome back any time.'

We had stumbled upon serious gangsters after all. I later learned that in the town of Litvínov, where just some 27,000 people lived, there had been violent demonstrations by neo-Nazis towards the Gypsy community. It had become infamous for its violence. A three-year investigation also showed that people with controversial pasts had infiltrated local politics, and corruption went straight to the top. Long before we turned up in 2001, pop singer Martin Maxa was shot in front of his music club – he was one of the few who had dared to defy the ever-growing trend of staged fights on the bar scene, quickly followed by a visit from the organisers of the scraps, who would then provide bouncers for your club. Maxa refused the offer and was shot in the head. Much of this 'business' controlling this small town and linked to multiple murders and random violence followed a trail to companies owned by another man called Martin. This was the one of the three I met in Litvínov.

We'd had literally no idea what we had walked into. Dom and Paul's intelligence had been perfect – better than they could have ever known. David had delivered. I had levelled with the meanest of the mean. That others didn't have the time, resource, budget or drive to see the story through was simply '*katastrofik*'.

SEX TRAFFICKING

Almost immediately, Paul and Dom were back in touch with David. Guns were no longer on the agenda. It was November 2007, and David now knew that we worked for the BBC. We all knew from Varna and Litvínov that one crime led to another. We had to probe David for more.

Girls were being sold as prostitutes, earning their money and then being moved on as sex slaves. The sex trade was very much alive and kicking.

On this occasion, I was going to buy women and traffic them into the UK. Richard Bilton would be my reporter. I couldn't know that this time we would be in for the long haul. In complete contrast to Guns, this was a story we would stick with. My new cover story was simple.

I owned a couple of houses in Hounslow and I needed girls. Around Slough and Southall, there was a hidden illegal community called the Faujis. Often living twenty-plus to a house, they worked for peanuts, sending the money back home to India or spending it on alcohol and sex. My new property would be high-end brothels run by a madam – I needed a couple of really good-looking girls to come and work for me. My clientele didn't want trash.

The story had now moved to Slovakia, an appalling borough of Košice named Luník. It was the worst council estate imaginable. High rise after high rise, burned-out cars in the street. Designed for 2,500 inhabitants, it had three times that number – many with illnesses ranging from head lice to meningitis. There was just one school and most of the residents were so poor that they didn't pay rent. As far as the developed world was concerned, it was hell on earth.

Košice itself had a very small airport. Dom and Paul again met me with all the usual bullshit. We hired the biggest fuck-off Mercedes we could get our hands on to show credibility. You drive a car like that around and you show you mean business. Clearly, no two-bob whore would do for us.

If we got lucky on the first trip, we would come back for a second, when Richard would join us and film overtly. We made our plans in the four-and-a-half star Hotel Dukát. (Our options were severely limited, given the poverty of the region.) There was already a meet on for that first evening. David was bringing 'Peter' and his nephew to the hotel. Despite the cock-up recording in Litvínov, we stuck to the rules – no filming first time around. We knew that if we could pull this one off we would be heroes; this was definitely worth sticking with and we weren't under the same kind of constraints as we had been in the Czech Republic.

David's phone rang. 'Yeah, they're coming. He speaks some English,' he confirmed.

This immediately made me suspicious. If they spoke a bit of English, had they been talking to anyone before us? People from this region didn't really speak English, especially the Gypsies. I couldn't be sure who I was meeting.

Then a couple of scrotes in shell suits walked in. They told me they can get girls, and they are already working the train station. That was not what I came for.

'Can I keep the passports or do you control them?' I asked. That is a pretty standard pimp question.

'You do what you like with them,' one of them replied.

We had come to report on girls who unknowingly had been forced to enter the sex trade – not those who had been banged so hard they could no longer hear the InterCity coming. This wasn't the story we were after and I told them straight. 'I don't want girls who have been fucked three or four times a day and are hanging around a train station.' I was speaking the only language they knew.

Daniel in Litvínov had set a new benchmark for the premier league of gangsters – I couldn't take these guys seriously. In terms of how much I respected them, they were closer to the grandfather who tried to sell me his grandkid behind the mother's back in Bulgaria. There was me, sitting inside an almost five star hotel with the sound of Christmas in the air outside, talking to a couple of low lifes who looked like they should have been kicking a football around Moss Side.

Thirty-five-year-old brass that hung around railway stations – this was not high-end stuff. David had introduced us to trash, but when was it any other way. First rung always disappointed. Once rejected, inevitably we would get told we would be introduced to someone else who may help us. And they soon delivered.

'We'll introduce you to someone ... but he's in England at the moment.'

That was no good at all. 'My flats are going to be ready in the New Year,' I tried to press them. More to the point, what the hell was he doing in England? Immediately that told me this may be a player, or perhaps they were about to expose the route. That would take us to the heart of the sting without even trying. If he was the man, he was clearly on a deal right now.

We were promised top of the range – no munters – borderline models. We had a lead.

Conscious of previous battles in the office, trying to get various departments to chip in to fund a story, I decided to withdraw. Did I want to stand around a railway station looking at old birds riddled with God knows what? There was no point staying until we had more. After two days, I pulled the team. Yet something in these two did give me a small hope. They were prepared to show us the way – or maybe that was always their role. Probably it was because I was flashing the cash. I loved it, too, peeling off the notes for Dom so I looked the big cheese once more. He would then hand them a few euros and settle the bill. In the role, I was too important to cross their palms with silver myself. My dual methods of accounting were at work here – I would never waste BBC money by outstaying my welcome when a job was done or on hold, but if the gig was on and I needed to get in the part, I would spend it like there was no tomorrow. Sometimes flashing my wad backfired.

David didn't stay for dinner. 'We know where you're going,' we all joked. 'Gumar girl, hey?' (*Katastrofik*, I'm sure you will agree, if he caught something down at the station.)

We were almost alone. Only the odd American visiting to do business in the local steel industry was in the restaurant. Clearly we stood out, and the maitre d' saw us coming. 'Because you have spent well at dinner, I would like to offer you a really nice glass of brandy,' he flirted.

I didn't drink brandy. Ever. We got the whole history of the bottle, then he poured three glasses at the table. David re-entered bang on cue. That made four.

David was giving me the *katastrofik* eye. Maybe he had seen this one before. I took a sip. It was good but not for me. We let Dom down the lot then called for the bill. And there it was, right at the bottom.

Fuck. Five hundred quid – and we had to pay for the whole bottle.

'What's going on?' I summoned him back.

'The brandy, Sir.'

'No, no, no,' I told him straight. 'You offered us the brandy.'

'You've got to pay the bill,' he insisted.

Bloody *katastrofik* indeed. I had gone from one extreme to the other, from being the Boss to having my BBC hat on. How could I justify that? 'We didn't ask for it and you didn't tell me the price. Get the manager.'

'No, no, no, I know the maitre d' very well ... he's very trusted here,' the manager said.

Then they went off for a cosy chat before returning to deliver the punchline.

'I'm very sorry. You have to pay, Sir.'

I agreed but only to fob him off. Then I called the boys together. My plan was to check out at 05.00 – our flight wasn't until eleven. I had spent so many nights in hotels, checking in and out at all times of the day, that I knew that if we got out early, the bill would still be sitting there in the morning. A barely computerised Slovakia wouldn't be working that quickly. I knew the receipts would be sat there on the side. At five, I marched downstairs.

A young girl, who had been there all night, was working the reception. In reality, she was bored stiff playing on her phone. She asked me in average English if we'd had anything from the minibar so I added a few vagaries for authenticity.

'Could you check the bill, please?' They hadn't put the dinner on. 'That's it?' I said.

'Yes, that's it – did you have dinner last night?'

I denied all knowledge! She swiped my card and we left via the back, never to return. They were crooks – it was probably their standard trick each Saturday night for every naive fat American in town. I loved blowing them out of the water.

We returned home. Step one was over.

We had been told to wait for Peter's call – a different Peter. We would react to whatever came next. At Television Centre, we agreed that only one thing mattered – buying clean girls who didn't know that they were going on the game. A call from Paul suggested that Peter would be back in Košice in ten days time. He had gone to Ireland. Ireland – was that part of his network? Then, out of the blue, David called Paul to tell us about Kent. There was already a booming trafficking operation there. Kent again. Always Kent. The guns from Prague had shown how easy it was to get into Britain there.

Did we try to force the issue with Peter in Košice, or did we take it on a plate in Kent? And was there a link between the two? I needed to complete a deal in Košice, with the girls being handed over and me being given the passports. Equally, there was every chance we could work the story backwards if we got lucky over near the ports. My decision was to run both stories – grasp anything we got a sniff of. We could have unearthed a goldmine here. Enter Štefan the Boss, Štefan the Translator, and Rudolf the Muscle – no really! Paul had done the dirty work on the phone with Štefan the Translator – he was around eighteen years old, the only one who spoke good enough English. They would meet us at 15.30 on 4 December at the Holiday Inn in Rochester, Kent.

It was time to get back in the role, so I rang the Prestige Hire Company at Heathrow and booked the best damn car I could. Craig Summers didn't do things by half. I picked up the top of the range VW Touareg – it was in immaculate condition with just forty miles on the clock, which made sure there was no sign of it being a hire car – this would be my vehicle in their eyes. I tossed a couple of magazines on the back seat so it looked lived in, and whacked it on my credit card so it couldn't be traced to the BBC. Then, I booked two rooms at the Holiday Inn – there was nowhere better locally according to the map. We would collect the two Štefans and Rudolf at the retail park down the road.

Our plan was to use the bar area in the hotel and to keep it short and sweet. We didn't know much about these guys – three days ago we hadn't even known they existed. This was only about establishing contact and credibility. As ever, I rearranged the tables to control the meet and dressed for the part in my leather jacket, Rolex, jeans and boots – of course I had plenty of cash on board. When we met them for the first time, Dom heard them call me the 'British Mafioso' in Slovak. I loved that.

As I floored the two miles from the retail park back to the hotel, the tyres were smoking. I drove like a gangster, too, bragging about my new car. There was no way Paul and Dom would be getting their hands on the keys. Had I ever been happier in a role? Definitely not. Out of the car, we introduced ourselves properly. The pick-up at the retail park had been over within a minute.

Inside, I told them I needed to trust them before we could do business. 'Have you done this before?' I asked. They had. 'Where are the girls from?

Slovakia, again, was the hub. 'Slovakian girls are very beautiful,' Štefan told me. The girls were between eighteen and twenty-one.

'Were there any problems bringing the girls in to the country?'

Last year they had brought eleven in. All those girls were now working in Cambridge and Peterborough; Štefan had family there. Already he had more proof of form than Peter. This was looking very tasty. We gave them fifty quid for the calls and taxi fare and agreed to meet again soon. Suddenly we were back in the game. Then things just got a whole lot better – Peter had been back on. We now had two live stories running out of the one cover story. We had to get straight back out to Košice. Peter was home.

✝

We booked the Hotel Bristol and went straight back out but not before I had checked their brandy prices online! There was no way we could go back to the Dukát, plus the Bristol might impress. Richard Bilton and the cameraman Julius Peacock hired an apartment and put all the gear in there. Everything was ready to go.

At the bar of the Bristol, sipping on my latte, I could see this was where dodgy people met. All of a sudden, a top of the range black BMW pulled up. Against the backdrop of the glass-fronted exterior, two guys appeared dressed in black, with hair shaved at the side, cropped on top. They were the spit of Martin and Milan from Litvínov. You could tell they weren't normal – their eyes scanning the bar area.

'Who are the people?' David translated their conversation with the barman.

'They're English,' the waiter said.

Then a huge guy walked in, smartly suited and carrying a briefcase. The three got in a huddle at the smoky bar. I knew we were in the right place. I told Paul straightaway that we needed to call our contacts, my worst fear being that they disappear. David made the call.

They wanted to meet tonight in the Hotel Gloria Palac. Bingo. We legged it straight to the hotel. My mind was racing – we would get the overt crew to shoot their arrival and do a mini recce to see if they could film either through the window or get in there themselves. Julius was a genius who could work discreet magic from his laptop. The location couldn't have been more perfect. Positioned in town on a corner, the hotel had huge glass windows. When night fell, we got there early, nabbed our window seat and arranged two extra chairs, knowing that they never came alone. Julius filmed from across the road. We couldn't have been more chuffed with their chosen venue. David would come in to help with the lingo – the Gumar girls would have to go elsewhere. We ordered drinks to the table and waited.

After fifteen minutes, two shady characters turned up. One of them was Peter. The other one might have been, too. Everyone was called Peter.

Peter was a completely different character to the other two we had seen – a bit bigger, a bit bulkier, jeans and a jumper on. His mate was in the standard shell suit, with a bumbag around his waist. Only Peter spoke anything resembling English. I told David to quiz him.

'Can you provide?' he asked.

(My instructions were simple. Tell him that I've been here before, and I don't want to waste any more money. I need a top up every six months and I don't want girls working for me that look tired and withdrawn and have been done too many times.)

Peter looked at me and gave me that universal handshake that overrides any language. 'I know what you are talking about,' he said. 'I can get you girls.'

'Are these girls working as prostitutes now?' I asked, not wanting to fall into the same trap as the bloody railway station.

'No, no, no, they come from Luník; they are poor girls ...'

I interrupted him. 'I don't want poor girls. I want good girls with good teeth, beautiful hair. I want pretty girls. I'm bringing in people who want to spend a lot of money.'

'Ah, yeah yeah yeah, no no no ... girls good-looking in Luník just very poor,' he assured me. 'I tell them they are gonna work for you, and you are gonna look after them. You can break them in easy. I help you.'

This was great stuff, if true, but obviously I needed to see the girls, and I suspected they probably weren't at the high end of the market. He explained to me about their passports – he would take care of that. Getting them in and out of the country was no problem – he clearly had a tried and tested route. I could even sell them back to him, and he would move them on to Ireland. That was all I wanted to know.

Richard Bilton had shot the lot from the other side of the street but we had none of this on film. I needed to arrange a dinner for the next night so we could go through it all again on camera. They hadn't patted us down – euro signs were all they saw. In the meantime, we needed to get some general shots of Luník – even our interpreter from Prague said the place was frightening. David would drive Julius the next morning and keep moving and rolling on a tiny camera. It wasn't the kind of place where you wanted to stop.

We needed to make a plan. I went down to the bar area to arrange the seating. It was only a small place and I wanted to commandeer the big table. That would mean getting there a couple of hours early. I told the bar manager I needed it for an important meeting.

'We don't reserve tables,' he said. I slipped him twenty euros. 'No problem, Sir.' And he slipped a glass on the table with a reserved sign propped up against it. Local rules always applied.

As the meeting drew closer, Richard and Julius got a table in the restaurant opposite – it really was that easy. They would film Peter arriving. We got kitted out in my room, checked my buttonhole camera in my shirt, and drilled everything a couple of times. All we had to do was to get him to run through everything he had said last night and mention the girls by name, and we had him.

The bar was busy by the time Peter and his sidekick came in. Before they reached where we were sitting, a guy two tables to our right got up and said something to Peter. Fuck – he had been there an hour. Who the hell was he and what did he say? Was that a business associate, a coincidence or some kind of back-watcher for Peter? I was on my guard now. Ten minutes later, a couple came in to the bar area to meet this guy and then left with him. On the way out he made a point of saying goodbye to Peter – did it mean everything or nothing? I couldn't know for sure. I certainly felt less paranoid now they had left, but it didn't mean there wasn't anyone else watching out for him in the bar.

It was time to get down to business. Peter asked me where the girls were going to live. I told him near Hounslow – there would be lots of people coming in to Heathrow who wanted a bit of fun for the night. That was my clientele, along with people who wanted 'private parties', and I needed them just after Christmas.

'Not a problem,' he said. 'But we need to talk money.'

I had a rough idea of the going rate but it wasn't the 10,000 euros each he was looking for.

'What?' I laughed in his face. 'You're joking. I'm not paying 10,000 each for a girl I have to break in. That's too much money.'

'Okay maybe between five and seven.' He automatically dropped his price.

'I want good girls. Good hair, good teeth and not been fucked many times,' I reiterated.

'Yes, no problem. I've got two good girls,' he promised.

'From Luník?' I asked, disbelieving again.

'Yes, from Luník.'

I had to be sure they were my girls and mine only, and nobody else got commission.

'Why should they be working for someone else?' he replied. 'What would be the point of it when she works with him and then she works with him?'

'I will put them on the coach. Somebody will travel with them to make sure they are delivered to you. You can meet them at Victoria. And I need the money up front.'

I had 10,000 euros on me. 'I don't do business like that,' I replied. I couldn't just hand over BBC cash like that and risk not seeing him again. 'Half up front, and half when I take the girls,' I bargained. 'I need to see the girls. Where are the girls?'

Then we hit a brick wall. 'The girls aren't here at the moment.'

My alarms bells started ringing. Was he bullshitting me, expecting me to just hand over the cash? Did he really have the girls? 'Where are the girls?' I repeated.

'At home,' he lied.

I knew it was bollocks. At best, I thought we would be lucky to get two old dogs. 'I need to talk to my boys, Peter.'

I walked away from the table to discuss it. I told Paul and Dom I thought he was a small-time crook, just after our money. Why come to this second meeting without the goods, and worse, not really knowing where they were? We were so nearly there, in that we had it all on tape, but we couldn't get over the final hurdle. Paul persuaded me to hang on, have a few drinks and see what else he had to say, so I fed him the usual waffle about football, sex, cars – again I promised he could have a foot in the door of my empire, bigging myself up to get the girls back on track, promising him imports into Slovakia.

'Okay, I call you tomorrow,' he assured me. Then his phone rang. 'I need to take this call. I need to take this call,' he said, excusing himself. He was garbling away in some sort of Romany Slovak dialect at twice the speed of anything comprehensible. I looked at David to see if he could pick any of the words out. He looked slightly shocked – he couldn't make it out either.

When he hung up I asked him if everything was OK.

'Yeah, yeah, problem, problem. I might have to go back to England pretty soon.'

That was perfect – we could meet him there, then come back into Košice to get the girls. We shook hands and waited for his call the next day. Meanwhile Julius went back through the tapes with a local translator – not even they could make out what Peter had been saying on that call. Had we been rumbled?

The next day, breakfast came and went, followed by lunch and no phone call. I was marching up and down wearing out the hotel carpet. I tried to ring him – no answer. David did the same and left him a message. Nothing. I went to see Richard Bilton. If we hadn't heard anything by tonight, we would have to call it in to London. Richard was equally as frustrated.

'Look, we've got some brilliant footage. We're nearly there,' he said.

But what could you do? We had nine-tenths of the show but with no pay-off, there was no show. I couldn't do anything except wait for that knock on my room door.

Then it came. 'We've spoken to him,' Paul announced. I was punching the air. 'But he's on his way back to England now.' Now I was punching the wall. 'That call he took last night – that's why he has had to go back.'

It had all looked so good. 'Why didn't he tell us that?' I asked Paul.

'He was too embarrassed.'

What was so awkward that he had to go back to England?

'What about the girls?' I quizzed Paul.

'He's definitely got two. He has to be back for Christmas.'

That didn't cut it for me. 'That's no good to us,' I told Paul. 'We've got nothing.' By now, Dom was in the room. 'Do you think he's bulls-hitting us?' I addressed them both. 'Do you think he genuinely has a problem and has to go back?'

I felt he was full of shit. It left me with no alternative. We had to go home, too. We never saw Peter again – not that one anyway. The story in Košice was dead. There was little appetite to continue. Home

News didn't think we had a story. Clearly, we did, but without an ending. We didn't follow the lead to Ireland on the grounds that the story was about trafficking through Europe to get to the UK rather than taking girls already on the game off the shelf. Either through lack of journalistic nous, frustration at the blind alley we had gone up, or for economic reasons, nobody was prepared to put their reputation on the line to try to nail down an ending. Richard didn't want to discount it. Pre-Christmas apathy didn't help either.

Privately, we agreed to keep an eye on it – we could always come back to it if David came good or something new sprung to light. Paul and Dom were as desperate as me. They would only get paid in part. The year was stuttering to a finish, and I was pretty pissed off. I told Paul that we had to finish the story. After the big bosses called the whole thing off, my parting shot had been to start ringing David and get onto Peter. My only concern was not to ring him every two minutes asking where the girls were. We were meant to be big time Charlies after all.

Paul did get a call – but it was from the gang in Kent. Košice may have been fading but Štefan the boss wanted to meet us again. The obvious thing to do was to try to link the two stories. There couldn't be too many different operations coming out of a city of nearly a quarter of a million people and ending up in Kent. Nothing ventured, nothing gained. We would concentrate on Kent until we knew better.

It was now 13 December and we were heading to Chiquitos in Stroud. We still needed actual footage. We got there early, and recced on the day. Dinner was set for 18.00 – we had already been in place for two hours. This time we upped the surveillance. A mate of mine in security had a painter and decorator's van. This was to be my trump card. Just parked randomly at some faceless retail park, who would take notice of the white van man, *Sun* newspaper hanging out his arse, his jeans more paint than denim? You would never know that it was fitted out with cameras inside. Julius was further up the road, armed with a hand-held camera, just in case.

Paul and I were also kitted up lightly. I loved my new gizmo. We were good to go.

They, too, had upped the ante.

'Štef wants me to do business with his cousin now?' I questioned Štefan the translator. I felt they had introduced a bigger player – I was getting further up the ladder, nearer to the source. But I needed to know who I was doing business with.

'He has two girls.' Štefan the translator wasted no time.

We shook hands on the deal as soon as he told me the figure he wanted to lease the girls. I was staggered: £400 for each girl, and £300 for Štefan. Dirt. Cheap. Dirt cheap.

'He's selling to you,' he explained. 'You sell on to others. One is twenty-three, the other twenty-five ... six.' He told me the girls were making £300 a day, working from the upper part of a pub, and had already been here for three months. Of course, that wasn't perfect because we couldn't show them being trafficked in against their knowledge and will, but that made it more important to me to show the link between Košice and Kent. Potentially, stumbling across the two stories at the same time was much better than what Paul and Dom had originally come to us with. If only we could get there. Everything we had on tape was gold dust. We simply couldn't end up on the cutting room floor.

I knew the deal was on, even though Štefan the Boss said very little. In fact, when I said to Paul that this was how you do proper business, pointing at Štefan the Translator who was just a kid, Štefan the Boss clearly understood enough to look pretty pissed off. He wasn't in control, and the deal was running away in a language he barely spoke. I knew I had to seize the moment.

'I want to see the girls on 5 January or 6 January,' I told them. All I wanted were the girls. Then the show was in the bag. If Kent Constabulary had come bursting through the door, I couldn't give a toss. In fact, I would have loved to have got busted just like in Stuttgart.

179

We had the agreement. There would be another meeting in the New Year. My houses would be ready. If something came up over the festive season, Sue knew I would push my Christmas dinner aside and be on it like a shot, tearing down to the Kent coast. That was unlikely. The next meet was set for 2 January. Deal done, now I had to sit down and eat a Mexican meal with these low lifes.

On New Year's Eve, we got the location. It was time to talk about the man from Margate. Štefan's cousin was running the show from there.

The fact that we got the call on the very last day of the year, when nobody was doing business, told me we were well in the game and they wanted to deal – badly. I had slipped back into being Craig Summers, eating and drinking all day long, watching The Hammers, and hosting Mum and Dad, who were over from Spain. I had switched off momentarily and parked the story. I wasn't expecting them to call.

Dom was in Bulgaria, so Paul and I tore down to Chatham. We were to meet outside an estate agents – only because they did most of their dodgy business from an internet café about ten shops up the road. As ever, we got there early to check out the location. I left the Mercedes round the corner – if only the license fee payer knew my attention to detail, to living the part so that there were no flaws in my story! Something like that, anyway.

We were both filming, but we knew we needed good light. Early evening in January meant that we had to over-prepare the scene. No noise from the street would help, and if I stood right next to the estate agent's window, there would surely be a light inside doing the work for us. Just down the street was a bus shelter with a lamppost. That would provide a perfect mood shot. Paul texted Štefan the Translator to say we were here.

'Are the girls still available?' I asked.

'Yes,' he replied.

'You don't sound so sure.' I was doubtful.

He confirmed they were.

'Am I going to be doing business with Štefan or his cousin in Margate?' I needed to know. 'I will respect Štefan but I want to do business with the bigger boss.'

I would say any old shit to reel them in. The game of cat and mouse would continue the next Sunday at Gatwick, with Mario, the man from Margate. Štefan the Translator told me that the girls weren't working at the moment, and that nobody was paying them. They were staying in Mario's house.

'This is different to what you told me. You told me they were working in a pub.' I was furious. The trail of bullshit was beginning.

'He's got other girls working in the pub now.' Štefan explained. I asked if they were for sale, too. 'He's just brought them up,' Štefan fobbed me off.

'Are they virgins – clean?' I must have sounded like a right perv on the tape.

'They're not virgins but they are like ...'

'Fresh,' I interrupted Štefan. 'And how have they been broken in? Have they been fucked properly?'

They had.

It was essential I spoke like this playing the role. I had to make sure I wasn't buying Hilda Ogden but equally I didn't want some frigid totty who had only had a knee trembler behind the bike sheds. They needed to know how to treat my clients properly. How did Štefan know that they were broken in? Well, obviously he had tried the product first-hand.

Within twenty minutes or so, we were heading back out of Kent. Events here had overtaken Košice, principally because the trail had gone cold there. Here, we had a potential sting. All I needed to see were the girls – get the job done. If we had them on film, we had hit the jackpot. Editorially, how it worked was no longer my concern. I would let the grown-ups deal with that in London.

The meetings were coming thick and fast. This was good news. We were rapidly climbing the ladder of trust the Eastern European way.

At some point, this had to pay off. If they could do this business at this speed, what was the bigger picture? How many times had they done this and used these same venues to meet? The estate agents must have been a regular RV.

On 6 January, I checked into the Sofitel at the North Terminal in Gatwick. Busy man that I was, wheeling and dealing, I would fit them in 'on the way out to Spain'. I booked a suite with connecting doors to another room, and we rigged up everywhere. My mate Alan from a specialist surveillance company came in and layered the place in hidden surveillance gear. Paul had a backup camera. I was clean. Annie Allison, the producer, was in the adjacent room with Julius and Richard Bilton.

Downstairs, the tropical garden area of the hotel was packed. Julius went down to pretend to be working on the laptop. As we greeted the Slovaks in the bar with a couple of initial drinks, he got his emails up on the screen, feigning interest in BBC bureaucracy. His laptop camera went to work. Nobody would ever know.

In the bar, I held court while Paul went to fetch Štefan the Translator, Štefan the Boss and Mario from Margate! When they arrived, I asked him what they had discussed in the car. The first answer established my character – there was to be no smoking in my vehicle. The second confirmed the hierarchy – the deal was with Mario.

I checked I was speaking slowly enough for them, urged them to finish drinks and ushered them up to the room to do business. I told them once we were done, we could have dinner, then conclude business next week after 'my trip'. If they'd had half a brain and weren't just looking at the pound signs, they could have checked every flight going out and wouldn't have found any sign of Craig Summers. That's what I would have done. I summoned the waiter and told him to whack it all on room 635. I motioned to Paul to carry the phones – he knew the drill.

'If the wife phones ...' I began.

'Yeah, yeah, you're in a meeting and you'll call her back.' We had both become other people far too often!

'Let's get fucking down to business,' I said, straight in there with Mario. 'I need to know – are you the main man I'm dealing with now? Is that correct?'

Mario needed this translating.

'I've never had Eastern European girls before. I've always used English girls before.' I pretended to ask for advice. 'I need to know the tricks of the trade if there are any. How do you control them? How do I look after them? Are there any problems with them? Do you understand that?'

Mario told me that you only needed to tell them once. 'They do not know much English. It is enough to show them by hand where to go and what to do,' Štefan the translator told me. He added that if I had a problem, I could bring the girls to Mario and he would sort.

'Will there be any problems with the girls?' I reiterated.

'No problem. I can trust them and they can trust me,' he reassured me. He suggested paying the girls between £250 to £350 per month but charging the punters between £300 and £500 a time, depending on what they wanted. It was clearly a well-worn strategy.

Back down in the bar, the pressure was off. I had met Mr Margate but I had two girls in the bag – one beautiful, one not so beautiful. I didn't really give a toss. There had been no whiff of any problem. I thought I was within a whisker of getting them. We had one meeting left. Within a fortnight, we were going to collect them from Bar 26 in Margate. Just one thing stood in our way – and we had no choice about it.

If they rocked up in Margate with the girls, then we had to hand them over to the Police Welfare Unit. It was time to tell Kent Constabulary we were about to buy sex workers. I was slightly wary of sharing our intelligence, for fear they might scupper or take over the op, but in the bigger picture, the professional standards of the BBC were all that counted. Thankfully, Kent Constabulary said that they would pay the money but we would run the show. I was more than happy with that. However, I did have a very big concern. They should have seen the schoolboy error that they were making – how and why was I introducing another person to the deal right at the final stage? That was why Sangita had got jettisoned with Harry. It was too late in the game. You simply didn't introduce a new player so close to the deal. I wouldn't know their undercover cop any more than the Slovaks would, and that meant there was none of that natural acting chemistry that Paul, Dom and I could carry off to a tee. If he misread me at the key moment, then we would look pretty stupid and be cursing ourselves forever.

On the Saturday before Margate, we went to meet the police to see if they had any better master plan than us. Dave Clark from the City of London police had been my initial contact on the story just before Christmas – he sent an unmarked car to fetch me from home just after half seven in the morning. I loved that – cruising round the M25, pretending to put the blues and twos on. I was itching for a go. I even asked if I could pull some muppet over just for a laugh. I could never travel on the M25 again after this – speed down the hard shoulder with your lights on – what the hell had everyone been complaining about all these years? We were genuinely running a little late. I took great pleasure in barging everything out the way on our way to meet the detective sergeant (DS) and the undercover cop (UC).

The car was one thing but imagine how much I loved running the meeting with the police. One problem. The undercover cop didn't show – he was running multiple identities too, and was on another job. The way I saw it, we could only really work him in as the money man. I would have brought him down especially from London to deliver the loot. But you can't work backwards from the sting with your cover story – this late introduction of the UC meant that I had denied myself the chance earlier in the piece to tell Štefan and Mario that I was too important to travel with the money. It was plausible to have someone carry my cash, but it was far from watertight. It would have got us in the shit big time if I had started messing around in Luník like this, but on home soil, given their readiness to meet plus the frequency of the meetings, it was a chance I was prepared to take.

It left me slightly uneasy; I was a control freak when it came to work. And rightly so. Someone had to have a plan and lead. I didn't deal in uncertainties. Also, the circle of knowledge on a sting like this is tiny: you never add people, you only lose them. Štefan got that – he had binned Rudolf the Muscle for the Gatwick meeting once Mario stepped up to the plate.

I loved it though – I was told the UC guy was a good man, a true pro and I was running the show. The alternative was that I handed over everything to the police and had to watch it play out from the back of the control room. On the ground, they would go on my shout. Thankfully, Annie the producer had been firm with them – this was our sting, and they would bathe in its propaganda glory if it all came off. End of.

The meeting lasted a couple of hours. Crucially, we agreed when we would call the mission in. The cops would have a van at the end of the road. On the exchange of the money, they would storm Bar 26 in Margate and arrest everyone. It was a classic military ops meeting. The DS would run the team of twelve on the ground. Richard Bilton and Annie were down the road listening. I loved it. I would take any opportunity I could to bark orders at the cops – this was a once in a lifetime opportunity – the stuff wannabe action men like me always dreamed of.

Next stop: The Hilton, Maidstone, a few days later. 14 January. Time to go.

Kent Constabulary had taken over two business suites. We were all in plain clothes and with plenty of time to kill. It was only 11.00. I walked everybody through the story one more time. This was my first joint mission with a police force – there was a lot riding on this for the various forces and individuals concerned. Kent Constabulary had an awareness of the sex trafficking scene, but were doing little more than keeping an eye on the story. When I showed them pictures of the Štefans and Mario, it was the first time they had laid eyes on them. They had no reservations. I was sure we knew more than them and it was in their interests to help us make them look very good indeed. While we gave them everything we had from the Kent end, they shared very little back. If they had, between us, we may have nailed that link back to Košice – they would only say that Margate, Chatham and Rochester were the UK hubs, heavily populated with Slovaks. In short, we were potentially doing them a massive favour.

Likewise, this was exactly what the BBC stood for.

I rigged up my covert gear. I had no two-way comms – they could hear me and talk to me but I couldn't respond. I felt the unmarked van was over the top but that was just the way nowadays. They would have three guys – we assumed – to take out. Then they had to make the girls safe. I was also very specific about one thing – when they burst in, they were to nick me, too. I wanted the whole thing to look real to the last possible moment and my credibility had to be good to go again. Remember Harry? Let go within hours. Has he surfaced again? Probably, in one of his other countries. The same could happen here. They could even beat me up if they wanted. These were three players who I'm sure were linked to Košice and we still had that on the back burner. For the sake of any knock-on effects of this op or any future Paul and Dom projects in Eastern Europe, they had to cuff me. Plus, from the point of view of my personal entertainment, it was a must!

Paul had got the confirmation by text. We were still on for 19.00. Nobody in the Hilton would have any clue a major operation was going down.

Unbelievably, it was only now that I met the undercover cop. That was rubbish. But he was a pro, and clearly could run several ops at the same time. On first impressions, I liked him professionally. His handshake gave me confidence. Dave Clark in London told me he was very experienced and I trusted Dave. It did concern me that it sounded like Kent Constabulary only had one undercover guy. When I showed him the maps and photos and passed him the intelligence, I also got the message back that he could see we had done the work

– probably a lot more than Kent Constabulary. Most importantly, though, he looked the part.

We spoke for half an hour. He had no problems with his role or the plan, telling me he had played the money man before. I assured him we would blur him out of any shots if he got caught up in anything. My instructions were that he wouldn't speak beyond the introductions and handing over the cash. Then we had our own meeting without the cops. Editorially, I had to be sure again. If the tapes ended up in court, I had to make sure again that nobody would say I had put words in anyone's mouth or that we had manipulated the edit.

That lasted another thirty minutes, then Paul, Dom and I went for lunch – pre-op, I was starving. Dave Clark was at the bar – he told me to play the part. 'They will arrest you and might be a bit rough with you.' He said what I wanted to hear. 'They know you are filming so go along with it.'

I loved it. I was dreaming of these 6ft 2 bobbies storming through the door and nicking me, and me mouthing back at them in the role. My blood was pumping and I couldn't wait to get started. We had three more hours to kill. What do you do so close to an op? I retired to my room for a rest and to rig myself up. I blasted out some Springsteen to get me fired up. Another day, another job. The first time you go to war you think about it a bit – likewise an op like this. The second, third, fourth time you do it, you just find the zone and run the drills like a pro. It's what I did and I wouldn't change it for the world.

Maidstone to Margate was forty-three miles. It was time to go and pick up Štefan the Translator. The undercover cop was driving. In the car, he got chatting, asking me about the Štefans, finding his role for the evening. In reality, the less he knew the better because, as the money man, then he would know less than nothing.

We were due to meet Štefan at 17.00 – at the side of a road. Bang on time, he was there just before the junction in the most unglamorous of RVs.

I wound down the window and showed him my money man. 'We're happy to do business,' I announced. There was twenty grand in the boot – with trackers on the case to follow the trail. 'Are the girls coming?' I said to Štefan the Translator.

All he was interested in was his money. I had also concocted some bullshit that I would keep him on as an interpreter. I loved doing that – promising people an afterlife once they had led other souls into hell. I got off on their big eyes dreaming of riches – you can't underestimate the motivation in seeing their faces when it all went tits up. Selling other humans for cash was disgusting – I couldn't wait to nail them. The extent of their crime was doubled in my eyes by their disappointment when their greed failed to come good.

We pulled in at the services between junctions seven and eight on the M20. Paul needed a piss. We were also way too early. When we headed back to the car, Štefan the Translator was not his bubbly self. My sixth sense kicked in. I told him that if he did well for me tonight then we could see what happened but he was suspiciously quiet. My guard was on.

Then his phone rang. He answered in Slovak and hung up.

'Everything all right?' Paul asked. 'Everything OK for tonight?'

'Yeah, yeah, everything still good,' he replied.

Paul and Dom tried to inject a bit of life into him. 'Who was that?' Paul asked.

'It was Štefan.' He had told him who was with us. 'Paul, Dom, the Boss and the money man.'

On those words, I lost my confidence. I had been 100 per cent certain. Štefan, asking who was there, made me nervous. In his eyes, who was this money man? There was nothing I could do. I had to pursue this, we were too far in, but something wasn't right.

We knew Bar 26 on a Monday would be quiet. All we could do was agree a cut-off time if it wasn't going down. Crucially, circumstance had played into my hands – my fictional houses were ready.

188

The Slovaks were aware that day was coming – I had always said first week in January. Both parties knew we were in the end zone. We were all set up to go.

When we arrived in Margate, we pulled up two cars down from the unmarked police car. That was a tactical park. The money stayed in the boot – the supposedly romantic couple keeping watch would always have their eyes on the rear of the car, leaving the cash there for Dom and the UC to go and get it on my word. That's when they would storm the joint.

Bar 26 on the promenade couldn't have been more depressing on a dark, cold Monday in January on the British coastline – it didn't get much worse than Margate in the winter. The bar was deserted, Margate a ghost town. Inside, there was a solitary barmaid and a couple of people drinking. The football was on the big screen but it couldn't have been deader.

Paul and Dom took Štefan to the bar; the UC sussed out the toilets and the exit at the back. I waited by the wall. I don't know if the bar was better for us for being quiet or if it had been rammed. There was something eerie about it, but equally it was perfect if you wanted to go unnoticed. There was nothing to do while we waited, so I did what any bloke would do in this situation – chatted up the barmaid. She was a bored blonde student type who didn't really care for customers – she wanted an easy life painting her nails. I bored her senseless, telling her I was a builder on a job. She must have been wondering what the hell we were doing in there – to me that meant we were playing the game perfectly. Štefan never came to the bar to hear any of this.

By 19.45, the other couple had left and I was getting increasingly edgy – they were close to an hour late. 'What's happening, Štefan?' I asked him.

'They're coming, they're coming,' he replied.

'We need to know. I'm not hanging around here. I'm here to do business.' I was spitting inside.

Štefan said he would call. I made sure Paul went out with him to watch his body language.

'They're definitely coming; they're just running a bit late,' Štefan told Paul. 'He's just doing a bit of business.'

I looked at the UC. We were both thinking the same. Events were following a familiar pattern. Half eight became nine and Štefan was starting to get agitated. We were probing him every five minutes.

'He told me, they are definitely coming,' Štefan insisted.

I'd had enough. 'Phone him now. I'm not wasting any more fucking time here. You've got me down here to do business. This isn't how I do business.' I read him the riot act.

He looked like he knew the game was up – all along he had been sent to front this no-show, and now he was running the risk of ending up dead in the back of my car. At least he would finally get to see the money. Štefan did make that call. The line was dead. Straight to voicemail. I was furious.

With Paul outside having a fag with him, I told the UC it was off. He had been on enough of these jobs to know when you had been stood up.

'I'm not a hundred per cent sure why, and there's no point arguing about it now, but shall we abort?' That was me being diplomatic. What I meant to say was that if the money man hadn't been introduced, we might have had them. We decided to give it a little longer. I ordered Štefan to keep trying. At 21.45, I told him it was his last try.

'You are dialling the right number, aren't you?' I glared at him. No answer. 'I ain't fucking doing business any more.' Then I got up to leave. 'Where are you going, mate?' I asked Štefan, as he went to follow me. 'You ain't fucking coming with me – you haven't delivered.'

I left Štefan there, and never saw him again. It was dead.

We debriefed back at the retail park, handing back the money. Kent Constabulary stood down their strike teams and we said goodbye to the undercover cop before chatting it through for an hour.

'I think we've been spooked,' I told Annie. How come it was all hunky dory then nothing? I'd heard Štefan say on the phone 'the money man is with us' and that was key. Štefan had clearly felt something wasn't right and must have relayed that back. God knows what became of the girls, if indeed they were ready to go. For me, Kent Constabulary had ballsed it up. We had no choice realistically other than to get into bed with them. Doing so cost us.

A couple of weeks later, the DS and his team came to see us at Television Centre. We handed over copies of everything we had – they too had begun spending big cash on this and knew we were on to something. We agreed that if they got lucky, we would be back in to film the sting. We handed it over to them on a plate. They didn't seem overly interested – or perhaps they weren't showing their hand. That call never came, even though by December Kent Constabulary had jailed two other individuals for human trafficking offences. Two years later, even bigger sentences were handed out to gang leaders running the sex trade out of the Czech Republic into the Channel ports. They were convicted, having been caught arranging sham marriages in Dublin. Ireland was always the key, it seemed – and we hadn't even gone out there, despite all the clues. Among all this, in November 2008 Britain's largest unit investigating human trafficking was shut because of cutbacks.

Paul did make one more call to Štefan the Translator and laid down the law – I was furious with him and he had blown any opportunity of big bucks in the future. He had stayed the night at a cousin's in Margate; Štefan the Boss was no longer returning his calls and he didn't know what had happened that night. Or so he said.

ZIM

To protect some of my former colleagues on future missions and so they may continue to operate in the name of free speech, some of the names and details in Zim have been changed.

The BBC had been banned from Zimbabwe since 2001; it seemed the obvious place to go next. John Simpson wanted to be broadcasting live from Harare on the day of the 2008 elections. This was the perfect pick-me-up after the botched job in Kent and a knock back from the BBC. I'd planned a fantastic exposé in Amritsar, and was all set to pose as an agent for a top sportsman who wanted his own clothing range. I would get in undercover with my fake website and bent business card and expose the sham coming out of these sweat shops. I couldn't believe News had turned me down.

By mid 2008, this was becoming the way. It was harder and harder to justify funds. More and more paperwork would bury me at my desk. This particular foot soldier was useless if he wasn't allowed in the field. So, when I got called to a planning meeting on 11 June, somewhat disillusioned, this was just what I needed.

Our only real presence out in Zimbabwe was a reporter called Ian Pannell, based in Cairo, who'd done some undercover work there. Ian would slip in from time to time and vaguely sign off on his reports without being location-specific. The Zimbabwean government had spent a lot of money buying top notch gear from China

– they had some of the finest jamming equipment going. That was what we were up against.

Intelligence told us that security was at its tightest. Border crossings were heavily patrolled – getting into Harare and Bulawayo, in particular, was a real nightmare. They were ramping up surveillance in rural areas, too. We knew that it would be slow, hard work, just to nail a couple of quality pieces. Robert Mugabe's boys, Zanu-PF, were in complete control. We had also been told to watch out for another group – The War Veterans. They were setting up roadblocks and checkpoints with Mugabe's Central Intelligence network. One hundred per cent vehicle checks and body searches were now the norm. Inside the country, we had two BBC guys, but Firle Davies and Brian Hungwe were probably under observation. We didn't tell either of them that we would be bringing John in – the less they knew the better, even if they did work for us. If Simpson got caught, it would be a massive propaganda story for Mugabe. There might also be repercussions for Brian and Firle.

John was too big a name for him to get a real beating but we knew that Mugabe would parade him, portraying him as a spy. All of us would be thrown into prison in Harare and the British Counsel there would have to pick up the pieces. That would also have been a massive story for John. Me, personally, I would have seen it as a failure of my professional ability. This time I didn't want to get arrested and thrown into one of the most notorious, filthiest prisons in the world. Riddled with AIDS as they were, bending over in the shower was not an option.

Nor did I want London bogging me down in debriefs and paperwork – every op had a knock-on effect for the next one, and it always meant more questions and answers and less time on the road chasing the story and building up my air miles! My biggest concern was that once we were there, there was no way John wouldn't want to go live in Harare. When we worked together, he would always listen to me but he expected me to have a plan B. We were obviously in the business of putting pictures and people on the box at a moment's notice. I knew we would have to have that conversation, and I knew too there was no point arguing with him. If we were there, he would expect it. To this day, I have never stopped John going on the telly.

Craig Oliver at the Ten told me it was in my hands. If I felt we could get away with it, then so be it. The BBC buck was being passed. Everybody knew John would want to broadcast but nobody really wanted to commit to it. Only after the event with the power of hindsight would they all pile in, sifting through the wreckage of any international incident. Somebody would pick up the broadcast – he would get monitored on BBC World and the next thing we would be on the run, always changing our addresses and moving around. John wouldn't tolerate packaging stuff up and sending it back, only to wait a week before it aired.

On 18 June, I landed in Johannesburg. Ian Pannell had discreetly stored a transmitter, laptop, camera, cables, external hard drives and some radio gear at a safe house in a secure compound in Borrowdale, in the suburbs of Harare. Our cover story to get in was that we were a British company called Sport and Leisure Tours, looking for lodges and safari game parks for sports fans to retreat to in between matches. The Lions were due to tour in 2009 – I would show them Africa as they recovered from getting walloped on the pitch. I knew my rugby and cricket. It was perfect, my favourite cover story to date.

As soon as we arrived in Joburg, I met with Dirk, an advisor from LGI Security who had been a policeman in Bulawayo. Dirk had helped Ian, and was going to be our security man for this trip. We had to find the quickest way in overland. There was no point flying directly there – John wouldn't get through the airport. Our plan was to hide him in the back of the 4x4s with a big hat on. He was just an old man travelling with us – there was no point in dressing it up; we just had to conceal him.

Before we left, I set up a number in London and recorded an answer phone message on a faceless untraceable number inside Television Centre to say we were currently out in the field and would return your call soon. If anyone in Central Intelligence went so far as to check out the number's authenticity, then frankly, we were already past the point of being in the shit. I also put a load of images onto my camera to show the work I had been doing was genuine and well underway. I loved it. I loved it. I loved it.

Secretly, I half hoped there would be a genuine enquiry or two when I got back! If we ran into grief at a checkpoint and got questioned, I felt that the potential of them getting too interested in our story was small. We also had two Zimbabweans and South Africans driving a Zimbabwean registered vehicle. We couldn't do any more if we were going under the radar. When we made it to Harare, John would stay put in the safe house. We would shoot the rallies and election posters under the guide of our South African cameraman, Nigel. John was not to go out. That, at least, was the plan. First we had to get there.

Dirk flew straight into Harare – being a local, this wouldn't attract any attention. Waiting with me was TT, also from Dirk's company, and Steve Fielder, a tobacco farmer whose land had been taken off him. Nigel and I flew up to Lusaka, the capital of Zambia. John and my old mate Oggy from Friendly Fire were due in the next day. On arrival, John couldn't have been clearer. We had about ten days on this job. The elections were coming. Don't even ask John about going live in Harare, I was saying to myself. It was definitely going to happen.

From Lusaka to the border at the Kariba Dam, we knew it was three hours max. We had to put our foot down, of course – we were being met on the other side. Standing on the basin of the Zambesi River, this was one of the largest dams in the world, approximately 130 metres high and 580 metres long. It took twenty years to build, took the lives of eighty-six men, and cost nearly $500,000,000 – in lay terms, about half of Simpo's wage. It was massive.

By comparison, the border post was nothing more than a glorified shed. That's why we chose to cross here. Our information told us that it was still barely computerised, and, at six or seven hours to Harare from the other side, easily the quickest way in. John, Nigel and I went first; Oggy and the rest of the gang followed. Our vehicles suited our story. The traffic was pretty busy – quite a few people were coming back and forth across the border. Getting out of Zambia wasn't a problem. It was never going to be. It was on the Zimbabwe side where the fun and games would start.

'Have you got any money on you?' TT said. We were back in the land of cash payments. TT went over to butter up Customs, laughing and joking with them. It was that kind of place – sleepy border mentality of the staff, busy border crossing. Result: nothing happens very quickly.

Then I spotted it. I glanced at TT, thinking, 'Fuck – they are not on the point of joining the twenty-first century are they?' There was a computer on the end of the desk. Admittedly, it did look like one of the early Amstrads but maybe they had got their shit together after all. Tediously, they were still writing the names of everyone passing in a big book. I was waiting for the Amstrad to whirr into action.

This was the moment of truth. I handed the passports to the immigration officer. One by one he wrote down every fucking middle name you didn't know you had. Then he opened up John's. He was travelling on his Irish passport. It was more discreet. We were all in the game of multiple passports, and plenty of visa stamps or journalist accreditation was always a bit of a giveaway. Paddy Simpson was less visible.

It was one of those moments where you daren't speak but also feel the need to fill the air with waffle so as to not show your nerves. Seconds turn in to moments. We've all been there.

'Simpson ...' he began to recite out loud what he was writing.

This was it. The whole world knew John Simpson. It was just a question of whether Immigration were paying attention or not.

'S-I-M-P-S-O-N,' he spelt out. Then his mobile rang. The timing couldn't have been better. 'I gotta take this call,' he apologised.

The chief got up and began shouting into the phone. Now, that was more like it. The officer who lifted the barrier up and down at the crossing took over. I couldn't believe our luck. Lifting John's passport open, he didn't have a clue.

'Blah blah Simpson,' he wrote, misreading John's middle name for his Christian name. I was trying not to laugh.

TT and I looked at each other. He gave me that look that I had seen so many times before, so I slipped the guard five US dollars. In a magic handshake, the money was gone. We were now in Zimbabwe.

Outside, the two 4x4s were waiting for us. We also had a forward vehicle to sniff out the roadblocks and any trouble ahead. Our plan was to stop overnight at a lodge: I didn't think it was the right thing to do to drive into Harare for the first time late at night.

We stopped for lunch about half an hour beyond the border. That's where John started buzzing. 'Look Craig,' he began, 'what do you think the chances are of getting to Harare tonight? I'd like to get in today. That would give us three days or so to gather stuff before the election.'

I knew this was coming. 'I don't know, John. I'll talk to the guys.' Obviously I couldn't really make that decision alone. TT, Steve and Dirk would know much better. The problem was the daylight. These places can be very different when the light goes.

'Isn't John tired?' they asked, knowing he had only just flown in from London that morning.

I told them that when John sniffs a story, we had to go. He wanted to push on. But we would have to go now. There was no time to waste. We were up and out five minutes later, abandoning lunch which had just been served.

We changed who would sit where. Steve drove the front vehicle – the local should lead. Behind were Dirk and Nigel shooting general shots in the countryside. The rest took up the rear. We all had comms between the vehicles. If there looked like being trouble ahead, Steve would radio back and we would take an alternative route. That could only mean one thing – through the bush. John

197

was tired but he was also in the zone, sitting there quietly in the back scribbling furiously into his notebooks. I had seen this in him many times – a lovely gentleman turning into a furious hack when he got an instinct.

Steve spotted the first roadblock an hour down the road. 'I've told them what you're doing ... pretty relaxed ... they probably won't even stop you.'

TT told me to get John down, hide all evidence of journalism, and make him to pretend to sleep. I had my five dollars just in case. I was expecting this to be the first of seven checkpoints. We slowed down. One cursory look into the car, and we were through. Happy days. I could tick that off. One down, six to go.

I didn't want to get too complacent but if all the checkpoints were like that in the rural areas, then we were laughing. The next couple followed just the same patterns. They looked like lazy officers who couldn't be bothered and weren't really paying much attention, if any. Was it really this easy? Why hadn't we tried this before? I put it to TT that if it was like this all the way, it was going to be a doddle. Would it be like this in Harare? Probably not. The War Veterans in the capital were actively looking for white journalists – they were pretty rattled at the moment. With the elections coming, there couldn't be a more tense time to arrive. This made my mind up.

'We need to think about an evacuation plan,' I said. My thinking was that if we had an injury or had to flee under the radar, I knew that most of the farms had airstrips. What would be the chances of getting hold of a small light aircraft and one of the farmers flying in from Bulawayo, heading south and taking us into South African airspace? TT and Dirk, being both ex-military and police, had serious contacts at the border. They didn't see this as a problem. Craig Summers was impressed with both of them. If the shit hit the fan, I knew I could rely on them.

On the horizon, the lights of Harare came into view. I knew now we would make it before night fell. That was no longer a concern.

I was just wary that the checkpoints into Harare would be a different kettle of fish.

'They're stopping everyone,' Steve radioed back. 'There's no way round.' And there were still three checkpoints after that. 'Play the game,' he advised. 'And see what happens.'

Steve cleared the greeting party. Once through, he pulled over up ahead out of sight to spell it out to us. 'They're looking for food. They aren't interested in anything else. Sort out some Pringles or something and you'll be fine. That's all it will be.'

Nigel and Dirk cleared the checkpoint. Next it was us. TT wound the window down; John was dozing, his Tilley Hat tilted over his sleeping eyes. TT greeted him in Afrikaans. The policeman looked in the car, then looked at us. I picked up the bottles of water in the footwell and two pots of Pringles and offered them to him.

'Everything OK?' TT asked.

He waved us on our way with his finger, easier than any of us imagined. If only Mugabe knew. They were obviously hungry and not being looked after. I felt totally confident for the first time – it was clear that the message from the top wasn't being passed down. Bribes would work. Anything you needed to get through. Just keep looking down, avoiding eye contact, offer them something, appear subservient, and avoid confrontation, and it seemed you could drive the length of the breadth of the country without anybody dragging you out of the car and uttering the words none of us wanted to hear. 'Mr. Simpson – welcome to Zimbabwe. We've been expecting you.'

I loved that we were in. I would switch off for the forty kilometres or so between the patrols but as soon as the radio clicked and Steve came back on saying 'checkpoint' then my heart raced a little and my brain upped a gear. I got back in the zone, but never needed to be on full alert.

Once in to the suburbs of Harare, we still had about an hour to go to get to that night's safe house. Pulling up at the lights was when you really had to watch yourself. At the first major junction, you would have thought we were in a war zone. Traffic was tearing in from every direction. Dodgy people frequented every corner.

'What are these?' I said to TT.

He pointed out the War Vets for the first time. 'They take over major junctions and sit and observe, and report in anything slightly strange,' he explained. In Ireland, they used to call them dickers.

I knew as well that our luck was cursed. The lights had been on green for ages and the front two vehicles had gone through. It was one of those moments on approach where they were always going to change. Anyone tailing has experienced that at some point. 'You're not going to stop, are you?' I asked TT.

Doing so would leave us directly adjacent to the War Vets on John's and my own side; speeding through would make us look like trouble, too. They changed to amber. TT just floored it. Years of procedure had taught me – always lock your doors. These guys looked serious. I had a word with myself. I needed to be right at the top of my game.

In total, excluding the War Vets, we had only encountered four checkpoints. Incredible, really. Mugabe had certainly done a good job in image management – the world perceived that it was a risk coming in. So far, we had breezed it. We made for Borrowdale.

It was a mostly white, affluent area in the north of the capital, like Sunningdale in Berkshire. Dirk pulled over when we got there. We sent Steve in to speak to the owner of the house to let him know we had arrived ahead of time. We didn't want to be hanging around. Could we move in now?

Considering our expectations for the journey when we stopped back at the lodge, we had made impressive time. One thing you can never know is how long to budget for if you get any checkpoint hassle. They could, in theory, keep you all day. Ten minutes later Steve was back, and we were in.

I knew what was coming.

It was a huge gated complex – nobody could see in. The walls were six to eight feet high. It was a six or seven bedroomed old thatched house, with beautiful land all around. We were bang out of the way. My only concern was that there was only one road in: if there was any tracking on the signal or we got tailed, then we were in the shit. We even had servants, preparing stew and dumplings for us almost immediately we entered. Wine and beer were in large supply. It was like being on holiday. But in Zimbabwe.

And I knew it was coming.

I thought I should probably pre-empt it because it was obviously moments from entering the conversation. He was scribbling away while we feasted. The election was a stone's throw away and the clock was ticking. We were so close to being there on the day that Mugabe would reach out to democracy in that sincere way that only he could do that it was a major risk. We didn't even have a story; all we had done was travel – but that in itself was some sort of achievement given the ban on the BBC.

And then John and Oggy ganged up. 'We want to do something for the Ten tonight.' Well, at least that got it out of the way. It was no longer coming; it was happening.

If we went live, that clock was ticking twice as fast. As soon as somebody picked it up and asked, 'Did John Simpson really say he was live in Zimbabwe?', then we had to move, and at some point they were going to catch up with us. I respected John's hunger, but it felt like an unnecessary risk.

'Let me get back to you,' I told them.

Professionally, as liaison between the local guys and John, I had to sound them out. I took them out into the garden to assess the risk and, believe me, this was proper risk assessment, not some BBC bollocks about sitting up straight at your desktop in case the Corporation got sued.

'He wants to go live tonight, doesn't he?' Dirk laughed. 'We guessed this was coming.'

They hardly knew the old trooper but they could see that look in his eyes. It was this killer instinct to be the best and deliver the story that nobody else could even contemplate that would always divide opinion on John – you either loved him or hated him. Luckily, tonight, he was among his own.

Like I said, there would be confrontation. We all knew it was coming. It didn't matter that John, Oggy and I knew that essentially tonight would be waffle. The kudos and the sense of victory, coupled with the 'watch this space' tease of what would come in the next few days, meant that if John Simpson could get on the Ten and deliver his 'live in Zimbabwe' report then he had won. The whole world would be watching. That wasn't about ego – John was from another era where reporters were qualified and were drawn to the story, not the limelight. He didn't care for a second career on *Strictly*. As with bin Laden, Gaddafi, Mugabe, he was attracted to evil. It really was a lifetime of showing up the bad guys to as many people as possible. It was impossible to say no – whether you were his confidant like myself or one of these old Colonials whose house it was and who had seen him broadcast from the most impossible places in the world.

'That's not the end of the world,' Dirk confirmed. 'But John needs to be aware that we need some time to activate the second safe house.'

Considering we weren't even meant to be here tonight, frankly, we were making life very difficult for ourselves. The new plan was to move first thing in the morning.

I went back in to give John the lowdown. He also knew me too well. I would tell him if it was a risk, but I would do everything I could to enable him to break a story. So, this time, he knew it was coming. 'Okay, this is where we are John. We can do a quick hit. It's got to be round the side of the house. Minimal lights. Then we move tomorrow.' I was making it up on the fly. 'In the meantime, I need to be working on an escape plan, if we have to move tonight.'

John had his way – as *he* knew he would. In the meantime, Steve went to fetch the broadcast equipment in his truck. This, for me, was the risk.

Steve assured me that actually it was quite easy to drive around the neighbourhood because he was well known. 'Even the blacks know me,' he said.

While Steve set up, Dirk, TT and I discussed our plan for when we went live. Could Mugabe's people triangulate the signal and sniff us out? What if they came down our dead-end road? John was only going out on the Ten – that helped. Airing on BBC World could have scuppered us.

We walked round the back of the house. There was one garage and a wall leaning over to the house at the back. TT and Dirk attached a ladder over to the house – the neighbours were on side and said we could park a car on their drive. We would run for it, climb over and take the car from there if we had to. It wasn't the world's greatest plan, but at least we had an option. Remember, too, these were huge houses on massive estates. I calculated there was enough time to flee.

It was good enough. I briefed John again. This time, I had to put friendship aside. 'Look John, whatever you do, you cannot say we are in Harare.' I was as blunt as Craig Summers could be.

'Well, what can I say?' He was asking me. After all his years in the game. To his credit, John knew it was a team effort. Moments later, I heard him sign off. 'John Simpson, BBC News, somewhere in Zimbabwe.'

He was ecstatic – still buzzing after all these decades. He couldn't have many ambitions left, but to say those words reduced the list by one. I knew it meant a lot. And it had been a long day. Out came the whisky. That was him saluting the team. Mugabe would be watching, and John Simpson was on his tail.

The next morning, Dirk and TT grabbed me. The owner of the house was happy, but we couldn't be doing 'lives' from here at night. It would just attract too much attention. Deep down, we all knew that. Now that John had declared our hand, we would always be on the move, looking over your shoulder. The boys had a Plan B – their contacts were incredible. I respected that. They knew a Welsh guy who had lived out here most of his life. His wife and kids were away so it wouldn't be a problem. If we needed to do 'lives' there was an office space we could work from. I relayed all this to Nigel and Oggy. As a pro though, I had to go to check the live position. There was no point making them safe if I made them redundant. That was the paradox of the job.

It was even better. I couldn't move in quick enough. Nick, the owner, showed us the tennis courts and swimming pools. The guest rooms were palatial. With a huge electric fence around it, it was the dog's bollocks. It was clear we could broadcast safely and easily. Nobody could see in and one of Steve's mates had a pad out here. Perfect! As much as I liked it, I was aware we could run out of safe houses if we carried on doing 'lives'. I hoped this would be good for forty-eight hours or so and we would take it from there. I didn't want to move every night and we were all desperate to hang on until the election. That would be some feat, to survive until polling day.

We were in a C-shaped building. The live position was in the inner bit of the C, surrounded by its own building, and we didn't need to rig it for lighting because we could take the natural aspect from the house. Nor could it be seen from the road. John loved it, too: to be live once in Zim was good, but was far from enough. He had set the bar high. I knew what else was coming. There was no way that John Simpson was going to sit in a palatial safe house in the middle of Harare and not be on television.

'We don't want John to come up before the elections. We don't want to jeopardise anything.' I was sick of hearing this from London. 'It's your call,' they would say.

Did they realistically think John wasn't going to broadcast? John was with people he trusted and I wasn't about to abandon him. We regularly spoke about it, often joked about it, and we both had faith in our local guys on the ground. There was no way any editor of the Ten worth his salt wasn't going to take a live from him in Harare. None of them would ever say, 'I don't want John Simpson on tonight.'

Yes – during the day we would lie low. John knew his day began at night. We would have a breakfast meeting every morning. Nigel and I would go out and do some general shots. We could send back radio, and John would scribble, but ultimately it was about keeping him hidden. Occasionally, John would push it and ask to go out – he wanted to go to Faraday's, his favourite shop in Zimbabwe. I told him we would take each day as it comes. After all, who has a favourite shop in Harare? He also wanted to go and have tea with the Meikles family. They were very famous in Harare and John knew them from way back.

I consulted with TT and Dirk. It seemed an unnecessary risk but TT also knew the family. We agreed to plan. There was no way we could get giddy on an old school tie. There's an old saying that you seek local knowledge wherever you go; TT and Dirk could pull rank in my eyes, however much John wanted to revisit the Empire! On the other hand, John would soon get frustrated not gathering news material himself. It would keep him sweet to give him a little treat out.

By lunchtime that day, we were installed lock, stock and barrel in the new compound – once we had avoided the added security of a ferocious Rottweiler keeping guard. John relaxed in his new imperial suite, while I took a sleeping bag and tossed it on the floor anywhere that would have me. Dirk and TT stayed in the house across the road. I told everyone to always be packed and ready to make a quick exit. In the middle of the day, it was always about the night and the Ten.

John had to write – BA's *High Life* magazine were waiting on copy and obviously that was crucial! Oggy and Nigel were talking about getting some shots downtown. This was now the norm – John and Oggy would suggest something crazy and I would consult with TT and Dirk.

'What do you think?' I would ask them.

'Crazy,' they would invariably reply. 'But we can pull it off.' I loved that. There was no point doing anything by half.

They wanted to film drive-by shots at Zanu-PF headquarters in Harare. 'You get one shot at this Nige,' TT said. 'They have their Central Intelligence guys on the side of the pavement outside and the corner of the road, and where we are going to drive down will put us real close to where these guys are.' It sounded like close to the knuckle stuff. 'Film from the back seat from the side window. Craig, you sit in the passenger seat, and we will shoot over your shoulder. You've got one chance, Nige.'

Two vehicles went out. TT counted us down to the building. 'It's on the left. Two hundred metres, one hundred metres ... that's it now.' I have never seen so many dodgy people hanging around, shifty behaviour the norm.

Dirk rang the mobile to ask if everything was OK. I told him we needed posters. We drove past and pulled over further up the road. Nick had tipped us off that near the racecourse there was loads of 'Vote Mugabe' propaganda. We did exactly the same again, in and out in seconds – always keep the car moving. That was all we could risk before heading back to the compound.

Imprisoned, John was by the pool writing with just Oggy for company. Straightaway they were desperate to see the foot-age. Nigel had had one shot at it and his rushes were brilliant, especially the images of Zanu-PF headquarters. He was just a natural with the camera – you either had it or you didn't. You could tell on instinct if the images were any good or not, and both John and Nige knew. They'd worked together many times in war zones over the years. Even though TT and Dirk had been used to working with an Australian cameraman, Nige proved you could show your worth when you only got one bite at the cherry. John and Oggy abandoned what they were doing – they wanted to make a package immediately.

John was chomping at the bit now. 'Shall we do a piece to camera?'

He was desperate to get out there. but this time I talked him out of it. 'We'd rather wait – let's see what occurs,' I urged.

We were that close to the elections – a package would do without John needing to lay down anything more than his voice. Of course, if they were on to us, it didn't now matter that he had signed off 'somewhere in Zimbabwe' last night. There was no mistaking the headquarters of Zanu-PF. Clearly, someone was in Harare, and if they had half a brain, that was John and a small team.

Still nothing from Mugabe's people – we were able to book in for another night.

You could see John wanted to get out there. He would grumble about it every now and then, and there was only so long he could carry on holding court, entertaining our hosts and Dirk, Steve and TT with stories from the life of John Simpson! As evening wore on through dinner, I had seen this many times. As exciting as those tales still were, I never got tired of hearing them. Everyone always wanted a piece of him and he knew how to serve it up, but he was never exclusive. It wasn't just the John show. He would always say, 'Ah Craig, do you remember the Friendly Fire?' – they were our stories together. We had seen a lot in each other's company. We had killed a lot of time as we were now, as well as chasing down the story against all the odds. Nick loved it – in his eyes John Simpson could stay forever, and the cycle would repeat itself. By the time we had cleared off, Nick would be sitting round a table telling stories of how he and John had sat round this very table telling stories. Over the years, the stories would get better, and Nick, inevitably, wouldn't stop telling them.

The next day, John was back on my case, asking to see the Meikles family. He wanted to get out. One thing I knew for sure – we couldn't turn up all heavy-handed. We couldn't go in convoy, and that would mean I couldn't go at all. That meant I wasn't really doing my job but I trusted TT and Dirk and their excellent local knowledge and contacts.

The Meikles epitomised the story of South African wealth. Their house had a driveway longer than my street. On the walls, paintings were worth more than my own home. They owned one of the most famous hotels in Harare. We couldn't go in there – businessmen allowed into Harare would stay there but it was the kind of place where lots of dodgy people frequented the reception, watching you. That was a definite no-go.

They were gone for an hour. John would get his high tea after all. As contemporary as his act remained, this was just a little John throwback to a time when reporting was a different ball game and the Commonwealth still vaguely stood for something. He had thousands of contacts in hundreds of places. A lifetime's work was never complete. He probably knew somebody important in every country in the world. And they knew him. It was a risk getting him out there but it kept him sane.

It didn't stop there. We sorted the trip to Faraday's too. He shopped like he might never be back – and that was a real possibility, of course. It was an old hunting store that had been around for years and he splashed £500 on boots, bags and wallets. God knows how he thought we would get the stuff back. John knew the owner there, too. At 1 p.m., he closed the premises as he would always do for lunch. There was hardly anyone on the streets. John had a shop all to himself. We literally pulled up outside, Dirk and I on either side. John had saved his biggest hat for disguise! As much as this wasn't part of any risk assessment, I felt I couldn't say no.

'That would be splendid if you can arrange it,' he would say in a way that was politely persuasive. I took the decision to give it a green light on the basis that if my duty was to look after John, I didn't want him to go nuts either. Plus, I was attracted to the danger. I would have filmed it, too, just for the two fingers it would stick up to Mugabe to show John Simpson shopping freely in Zimbabwe, but I didn't want to put anyone at Faraday's under any retrospective retaliatory risk. I had done well to keep him under wraps up to now. This would probably settle him for the next couple of days until the election.

Unbeknown to John, TT, Dirk and Steve were working with me through their contacts to get us into the Dutch Embassy. This was where the opposition to Robert Mugabe was supposedly living under the protection of the Netherlands. Dramatically, Morgan Tsvangirai had just pulled out of the election. The race was on to get to him.

'Do you think John would be interested in interviewing him?' Dirk had said casually over a cup of tea. I nearly spat my drink out. Neither Dirk nor TT was particularly media savvy. They were both ex-military guys whose job was to look after the client. I had told them we needed to look for stories, contacts, meetings, whatever they could come up with – it wasn't enough just to be here. But he just dropped it into conversation like asking me how many sugars I wanted.

Steve Fielder was actually very well known to and within Tsvangirai's party – the problem was that we had to keep the network of knowledge small to protect both Tsvangirai and, of course, John. The fewer people who knew about this, the better, and when you are dealing with the leader of the opposition, the chances were that a few people were going to get to know. Many of Tsvangirai's party, the Movement for Democratic Change (MDC), were ex-farmers. Some, like Steve, had had their land taken off them. That is how he had the access.

Andrew Chadwick, a former correspondent himself for the British press, had now taken on the unforgiving task of becoming Tsvangirai's spokesman. That looked like a job where you might get a knock-on the door in the middle of the night – if they were even being that polite. Initially, when we discussed getting into the Dutch Embassy, his response was 'pretty difficult'. From my point of view, I didn't even know where the embassy was nor how much surveillance it was under. Clearly, the secret police and Zanu-PF were watching it and him like a hawk. How would I get John there in the cold light of day? We had to tread very carefully. If we were on, I knew too that I wouldn't be going, much to my disgust. It would be Nigel and John only – we couldn't risk any more in the head count. To make things worse, the Dutch didn't want the BBC on the premises.

That night, just before John was about to do a live, Andrew Chadwick called. 'Could he talk about the meeting?' he asked Steve.

It was on.

Chadwick knew the game and knew it was worth it. If he could get a message out to the world on the eve of the election, the trusted John Simpson was the man to deliver it. It was a win–win situation. Simpson would look good and Chadwick's background enabled him to understand that; as the media aide, he knew the world would be reminded of the violent and dodgy democracy that Mugabe was orchestrating. At home, there were bigger stories – many had questioned why we were so obsessed with Iraq and not Mugabe. Oil was always the obvious conclusion. Now was a real chance to turn the spotlight back on this awful dictator. These moments came along rarely.

It was time to tell John. Then, in his giddiness, to remind him not to blow it now.

There would no more shopping trips etc. He was to remain non-specific in his location. We were that close, both to election day and to interviewing one of the few people brave enough to stand in front line politics against Mugabe, that we couldn't risk compromise now. We were way past the point of day one, where just to be here was the story. Now, the story was coming to us and meeting us half way. In my head, it was time to start making plans to leave. My brief to the guys cranked it up a notch. No messing now, and we are gone as soon as we had everything we needed on election day.

TT and I got up to leave. We met Andrew Chadwick in the car park of a Chinese restaurant a few blocks away. I had to assume that he was being tailed and we were now under a very serious threat of acquiring one ourselves, even though there were only two other cars there. Chadwick would have used this place before, I'm sure. I trusted him and TT that we were as safe as we could be.

I pulled up next to him and wound the window down. Like so much of my BBC life, it was like something out of the movies. We didn't have time to muck about. He got straight in the car, and cut straight to it. 'It's on,' he said. 'Morgan wants to talk.' I drove to keep moving and spot a tail. We left his car there. John Simpson was going to love this. Well, until he heard the next bit. 'Morgan wants to know what questions you are going to ask him.'

He was playing a game and we both knew it. As a former press man, he sussed that John wouldn't agree to that, however much he wanted the interview. It was all part of the game. That, to John, was like being embedded with the Yanks in Iraq. 'Look, we can't really discuss that,' I said on John's behalf.

Chadwick knew I could fob him off, but that word would get back to John. What did it matter anyway? The image of John and the inevitably defeated opposition leader would beam around the world – that was almost enough to warrant the story. And in return, the politician would say what he wanted to say, regardless of the questions. We all knew how it worked, and that both sides were doing each other a favour. To talk to the British, too, when everything Morgan Tsvangirai did or said was monitored, must have been some comfort to him. If you can't trust your own nation's media, you could still, at least, believe most of what was on the BBC. I warmed to him – maybe it was the British connection or perhaps he was just a rare human being in politics.

'You and John were blown up in 2003,' he said. He was good at the small talk but it also struck a chord. It told me he had checked us out. People would remember John reporting with his trouser leg blown off – who wouldn't? – but it took some effort to know I was there. That impressed me. I always tried to know the little details about people before I met them for the first time, too. It just marked him as a pro.

'I really need to know the questions,' he repeated.

'Can we call you?' I asked.

And we left it there to head back to the safe house. It was over in no time at all. I loved that. Arranging a secret RV with the spokesman for the opposition, picking him up at the local Chinese and then taking him for a spin with the secret police possibly in tow – did it get any better? And that's before we tried to smuggle John into the Dutch Embassy.

Everything now would be done by phone. We would speak in the morning. I was desperate to get in there and meet Tsvangirai, too, but not even I could swing that one. What use was I inside an embassy when any trouble would be waiting for us on the outside? It was my job to think about moving.

John would want that broadcast immediately – and rightly so. As soon as it aired, we had to be getting out of there. If we didn't leave the country immediately, we at least had to be ready. There was a lot to take in. Just over twenty-four hours to go to the election, and we were a phone call away from a man who could showcase to the world what a sham Zimbabwe was. By then, if we didn't get caught in the process, we would have survived until election day. John, through our contacts, had sniffed out the big exclusive and I had chaperoned him to the sting. High excitement and tension. This is how we worked every time. There was a lot to sleep on.

In the morning, we made a tactical compromise. It wasn't worth not sending over the questions to Chadwick. We all agreed it meant nothing except that we showed willing and gained their trust. It wasn't what we wanted to do, but once we were in there, John could take Morgan places John wanted to go, and Morgan would probably not need much stopping anyway. Early the next afternoon we left the compound to shoot election day footage.

On the local TV, it was as though we were in a different country – it was a total and utter farce. Either they didn't bother or it was all Mugabe. How did those journalists on that network work like that? Through fear, I presume. They weren't really journos at all – they were publicists.

We knew we couldn't realistically get near a polling station. They were heavily guarded by Mugabe's lot. That would be a red rag to a bull. But we got as close as we could, knowing again we only had one chance to grab a shot and then get the hell out of there. John scribbled away hidden in the back. When we unleashed him briefly to do a tiny piece to camera to show he was really there, the old pro was ready to go and delivered it in one take before hopping back in the car. We never knew if anyone saw. It was a depressing collapse of democracy which made the interview with Morgan Tsvangirai now essential. For both sides.

Back at the compound, we spoke to Andrew Chadwick. Tsvangirai was now living back at his house, not far from the Dutch Embassy. In many ways this was better because we didn't need to involve the Dutch. In others it was worse – everything going in and out of there would be under even more scrutiny. Chadwick confirmed that we were definitely on.

Morgan Tsvangirai was born in 1952 in what was then Southern Rhodesia. He was one of nine children, his father a carpenter and a bricklayer. He himself spent ten years working in a mine, where he began his journey into politics, heavily involved with the trade unions. Ironically, it was believed in his early years that he was a big Mugabe supporter. In opposition, he had survived three assassination attempts and had been arrested and beaten several times – the most recent of these just a fortnight or so before we got here. The previous month, there had also been another credible assassination attempt on him, which delayed his return to Zimbabwe from Ireland. We would meet the lone voice against Robert Mugabe in the next day or so.

This was it. Dirk, Oggy and myself travelled in the Volvo. TT was at the wheel. Nick, John and Nigel took the 4x4. Sometimes something had to give, and it was here that I lost control. With TT driving because he knew the way, the back way, and the only damn way out if the shit the fan, my sole job was to have eyes in the back of my head. Before and after the switch.

Yes, the switch.

We had agreed the only way in was to be so bloody obvious about it that nobody would even think to look. Our plan was simple. Go in Andrew Chadwick's car. It was genius. They knew his car like the back of their hand and while they always watched it, I know from years of surveillance you can take targets for granted that you see every single day. Like us introducing the money man from Kent Constabulary at the last minute, it was any break from the ordinary that aroused suspicion. There was simply nothing unusual about Andrew Chadwick driving into Morgan Tsvangirai's house several times a day. It's just that this time, John Simpson from the BBC was lying down in the back under the covers. We had switched John about ten minutes away from the house.

This was the key to getting him in. But it made great drama too. The practicality of the two cars needed to happen but nothing escaped the attention of our cameraman, Nigel. All the scurrying around from one car to the next with the camera at all angles captured the tension of the moment. A straight, perfect shot from a long lens would have been bollocks. The perfection in the filming had to be that it could come out in any shape or size, just so long as it captured John on the move and breathless, exiting our vehicle and diving into the back of the car of the spokesperson for the opposition.

And that is exactly how it happened.

We all drove off seconds later. Suddenly my levels of awareness shot to maximum. They had to. Up to this point, we had just been two vehicles. Now we were one vehicle hugging the rear of one of the cars of one of the key players in Zimbabwean politics. By definition, we had drawn attention to ourselves. I realised, too, that at this moment, if we got pulled over, our cover story was over. There is no way in the world any sensible British sports and leisure company would be scouting for lodges and game parks in the capital on the eve of another of those hugely sensitive political moments in Zimbabwean history. Not unless they were stupid.

Then I saw it in the rear mirror. We were in trouble. A Central Intelligence Organisation car was tailing us. I knew all the tricks myself and we were definitely being followed. I couldn't know if they had seen the switch. That was the point with a tail – you could never be sure where it started because you can't specify that you have company until a car has been there right behind you a few minutes or so. I hadn't spotted it before John got out, so I had to hope we were safe. Most likely, they had routine eyes on Chadwick but we had attracted attention by being in his slipstream. I didn't like dealing in hope.

There was nothing to do except make Dirk aware and hold our nerve. Keep driving, don't do anything rash, pray the moment passes. Avoid pulling up at the lights. We pulled up at the lights. I stared right ahead. So did Dirk. It was one of those moments that hung in the air – a slow movie scene about to crash into fast forward at any point. Your heart races not out of fear, but out of mental psyching of what might be about to follow. It was just another day and just another job for the CIO, but every one of their subjects would have felt like this the first time it happened to them. I was pleased though, in an inverted way. If they had eyes on us, they didn't have them on John. He would be safer than safe if we were the focal point of risk. Our plan had worked. Everyone had done their job. I was happy that we were the Trojan Horse.

We pulled away. This just showed how good Dirk was and why local knowledge is king. There was no way in the world anyone other than a local should be driving. They went right. Dirk reckoned they might have seen us stop and were on routine patrol. Pleased to see that we were white, they left us alone. We carried straight on, now on a mission. However quickly you get your bearings in a place like this, you didn't know the alternative back streets and side roads that Dirk discreetly found his way on to, manoeuvring us back into the town centre, and losing our tail with no obvious signs of panic. I loved his coolness under pressure. Top-drawer pros who had the same anal attention to detail as me and didn't get a sweat on when a red light spelt danger were my kind of people. That didn't stop any of us breathing a sigh of relief when we got back to the compound.

Relief soon disappeared. I still had to be on high alert. Whatever John brought back was going to air almost immediately but obviously his return meant that our satisfaction of getting away from our tail was soon replaced by the joy of what Nigel had in his camera. He had been gone forty-five minutes. The return pick-up couldn't have gone smoother.

'How did it go, John?' everybody asked.

Ecstatic inside, John played it his usual cool self. 'Oh you know ...' he replied.

It was one of those moments for a broadcaster when, as long as it has recorded properly, you were in a quiet place. You knew that you were about to unleash a rocket which the world would then play catch-up with for the next day or so, but right now, you had a couple of hours of peace to yourself before you detonated. The ricochet was coming. Journalistically, you were in a content no-man's land. Except for the hard work at high speed that was needed to turn the piece around, of course. For John, at his age and with all his experience, this was still a massive deal. Make no bones about it, he wanted Mugabe one to one, staring down the lens. That was unlikely to happen until, if the day ever came, Mugabe needed John. But Morgan Tsvangirai was not far below. I knew John, and I knew he was happy.

That he was safe and undetected so far made this almost a perfect mission. We just had to get it out tonight on a live, get some election day shots in the morning and feed, and then it would be time to abandon our desperate search for safari retreats in between major sporting conquests! John said it was a good interview. Tsvangirai had answered some decent questions. Some of them were even the ones we had sent Andrew Chadwick!

I knew what was coming next, obviously. And this time, I couldn't argue.

'I think we need to do a piece for tonight, and I think we need to do a live. Let's see what London want.' John didn't think it. He knew it. He was underselling himself. It had to air now.

One thing that shone through was that for Morgan Tsvangirai, it was not an option for Mugabe to die in office. He needed to stand aside in real time. It was the old death penalty argument all over again – do you hang a mass murderer, or is their greater suffering to let them rot the rest of their days away? Did Mugabe have it in him to walk away from his corrupt, violent dictatorship? That was the moral high ground that Tsvangirai was walking across, and he was right of course.

He said not standing was the 'least of his concerns' because he couldn't swallow that level of violence. He had won in 2002 and 2005 and Mugabe refused to accept the result. A victory did not equal a change of plan. It was powerful stuff and both John and Morgan Tsvangirai knew it. John pointed out that this interview would be studied by Mugabe's people but also by African leaders across the continent just before their big African leaders' summit, which was imminent. I could tell by watching that the questions for Andrew Chadwick had become a nonsense – he pushed Tsvangirai more than once on his lack of courage, his inability to see it through for just a few more days, for not, as John put it, 'staying the course'.

Tsvangirai's message was clear: no armed intervention from an external democracy would help. You had to fight a dictatorship using democratic means. The bullet couldn't replace the ballot. And that was the soundbite that would resonate around the world. Our work was done. I made an instant decision on moving. Not to. It was too obvious.

My new plan was to lay low the next day. Nobody was to go out. The worst thing we could do was put John's piece out and then run. They would be watching the roads. I wanted to gather our thoughts, wait a day and discuss with TT, Dirk and Steve the best way to leave. Did we go the same way we came in, for speed? Should we head to Bulawayo or make for the Botswana/Mozambique border? (My air strip option was only to be used in an extreme medical emergency.) Bulawayo was nearly six hours away, Botswana close to nine. Mozambique would have taken even longer and there were a lot of war veterans and Zanu-PF that way. I knew that, as in all good military ops, the best thing to do was to retrace our steps, praying that the border crossing hadn't upgraded from Amstrad to ZX Spectrum overnight and also that the checkpoints hadn't suddenly sprung into life to do their job properly.

The next morning, Nick rang all his contacts. How did the land lie back to the border? Had anybody seen John on BBC World? Was it safe to go? It was like the first day of summer holidays – the work was done, we were just waiting to leave. Except it would be ten to fourteen days before the official confirmation of the result would come in. I thought it was a safe time to text Sue at home to say that Mugabe had won!

John also filed an excellent piece for BBC Online, laced with irony and straight to the point. He implied that the Dutch Embassy had been turned and that the streets outside were now virtually empty – Tsvangirai may have been better off seeking African refuge. The MDC supporters were resentful and gloomy; the streets of Harare were deserted because Zanu-PF had nobody left to beat up. He added that the official media rarely mentioned Morgan unless in a derogatory capacity – their main hour-long news show at 2000 was an hour-long advert for Mugabe. They never mentioned that the Zimbabwean Dollar had fallen to thirty billion against the US equivalent. The cost of margarine came in at around Z$420 million. That was one hell of a note.

Their economy, John said, was in free fall. No Western government had expressed their anger about the eclipse of Morgan; many African governments remained discreet in frustration. China continued to help with a whiff of diplomatic immunity. John signed off that Robert Mugabe's ferocious determination to stay in power should not be questioned. Equally, nobody should underestimate the ability of his own political opponents to destroy their own case. It was a brilliant piece – John at his considered best. It was also one of those moments in time where Morgan Tsvangirai hadn't stepped up to the plate.

We were by no means out of the woods but still, at least it would be better to get caught on the way out than the way in. We had delivered. The job was done. Bring on the next one. After all that, we were pretty blasé about getting out. We decided to go back the way we came. Our cover story would hold unless they were specifically looking for John. The further out of Harare we got, the better. It was exactly the same as on the way in – ill-disciplined checkpoints barely going through the motions, self-interest (food) mostly uppermost in their thoughts.

Until we got to the border. It was always the little detail that would come back to haunt you. Oggy had bought a zebra skin. To take it out of the country, the paperwork was a mile long. I just said 'Fuck it' and we would smuggle it through. Oggy was nervous that he could be accused of poaching when we flew back from Zambia into South Africa. The checkpoint was busy.

'Same routine again,' TT said.

'We need all the paperwork for the vehicles.'

We were driving Zimbabwean vehicles in to Zambia. I handed the guard the passports. One by one he stamped them. Just as he was opening John's, I thought now was the moment to pipe up.

'Oh, by the way, we have got a zebra skin,' I declared.

'Where did you buy it?'

'Harare,' I replied.

'I'll need to have a look at it.'

It was in the car. I paused for a moment. 'Not a problem,' I said. 'Can you just do the other passport?'

Thankfully, it meant he didn't have time to study the life and times of Simpson or any other name he was going under. He handed all the documents back to TT.

There was still the business of the cars – now was when John could get recognised. TT gave me the usual wink. A group of them came outside to the car.

'Is there a problem?' I asked.

'You can't be taking this out of the country. The paperwork is incorrect,' the guard moaned.

'Look,' I replied, 'we're in a bit of a hurry; we've got a plane to catch. Can I have a look at the paperwork again?'

TT called me over. I took the documents and applied the law of the land. 'I'll think you'll find that this is all correct really.' I handed them back to him.

His eyes lit up at the 100 US dollars inside. 'Let me just go and get this signed off and stamped and then you can be on your way, Sirs.'

I accompanied him back in to the office, while TT repacked everything. We didn't want to be lingering any longer. Moments later we were gone. Oggy's was another schoolboy error, but it had offered a good distraction from John's passport. It also was true to the cover story – all those sports fans coming on our tours would probably return with the same souvenirs. At the Zambian side, nobody cared. They stamped us in and we made for the airport to fly back to Johannesburg.

We had left at 05.30. At 19.30 we touched down in South Africa. John's interview was reverberating around the globe. Back in London, Malcolm Downing said that how we'd handled getting him in, around and out had been brilliant. It had been a big team effort – Dirk and TT were truly superb. It hadn't been a cheap story for the BBC but this was what we were all in it for: to get the World Affairs editor live in Harare was unprecedented; to interview Morgan Tsvangirai in such circumstances was way beyond the icing on the cake. In all the hours sitting around that big house, chewing the fat and waiting to go live, we had also given birth to another idea, which meant that John and I would be on the road again soon, literally into the unknown.

But before that, I got a real shock when Craig Oliver, editor of the Ten, rang me.

KATASTROFIK

'We want to give Košice another go,' Craig said.

It was now the end of August 2008 – nearly a year after our last visit, and seven months on from the cock-up in Kent. This was the last chance saloon – again. My gut feeling was that this was unfinished business. My mind was also elsewhere: I was supposed to be preparing for John's little brainwave, and if I wasn't careful the re-emergence of sex trafficking could run headlong into that. Given the amount of time and effort already spent on this story, as much as I was pleased, I didn't want to scupper the chance to a lifelong ambition. John, Robin Knox-Johnston and Ranulph Fiennes would have to wait.

David had spoken to a contact in Košice who could definitely provide girls. Annie Allison had gone back to Craig Oliver. He had agreed – one last shot. I needed no second invitation. I was so ecstatic that I would take any snippet of intelligence to make it work. Everybody knew we had a great story – and there was a lot of sympathy that we just hadn't got the girls. The story was 100 per cent true but the fact remained – no money shot, no show. It was time to meet Luboš.

On 31 August, we arrived back in Košice. Luboš was part of the same gang we had met the previous Christmas. He would take us to Peter, higher up in the chain. One thing was clear: none of these people were called Peter. At 21.10 we rang him.

We were to meet at the front of the station. It didn't get more rock 'n' roll than that. All sex and drugs seemed to be sold out of here. Paul and David went ahead. Twenty minutes later Peter met us in Herna – a small gypsy casino opposite.

'I hear you are looking to buy some bitches,' Peter began.

'Yes, but they must be in the UK and already in the sex business.' Paul clarified our position and complimented Peter on his English.

'I have been living in England and Ireland for the last fifteen years. I have businesses in Dublin and Dover. I do two weeks in Dublin, and two weeks in Dover. In fact, I'm travelling back on the 2nd. It takes me three days to get back.' He pointed at his new white refrigerated Transit van. By businesses, he meant girls. You wouldn't find him in the *Yellow Pages*.

Paul then specified that the girls must be aged eighteen to twenty-five.

'I can get them from here. It's easier. I can deliver them and it's cheaper,' he promised.

'We have tried that before and Boss has been fucked around. They must be in the UK and working. Can you help?' Paul asked.

Because of time constraints, and the fact that this was our last throw of the dice, we had changed tack. Our story stood up. It just lacked girls. We didn't need to go through the whole process from the start again. Peter then left to head in to the bar area, returning with his boss. His name, to my surprise, was Peter.

In Slovak, Peter 2 explained that his girls were for sale in Sheffield, Peterborough, Birmingham and Chatham. Ah, the elusive Chatham. This was a broader network than we ever knew. Dublin and Dover was all I had suspected. He told us that he would only sell – leasing came with too many problems. We could flog them on after for between four and five thousand euros. They were all clean and with no disease, though he didn't say how he knew. We could see them on his website, which, in itself, was a new development. He explained that he had his woman in England who we should deal with. She controlled the girls. As we exchanged numbers, he made it clear he did not want to get fucked by the police. No, I'm sure, he didn't!

Original Peter then offered to sell us some Dublin girls. We would speak tomorrow.

I wasn't exactly jumping through hoops. It all felt a bit déjà vu but they had cut to the deal much quicker and they looked less like scrotes than some of the other gangs. Plus, their talk of leasing showed me they had been in the game for some time, and the brand spanking new refrigerated van told me they were trafficking drugs too – sniffer dogs would not get a whiff of anything out of a vehicle like that. He was a player, and a regular one. I had to be optimistic. But it all seemed too easy and, this time, there was no way I was going to involve Kent Constabulary. I wasn't going down that route again. The next day, it was business as usual – nothing happened.

'I cannot get hold of the woman who runs my girls in England. She is not answering the phone.' Peter 2 said.

Lunch was cancelled. They did meet us though – at 18.00, back at the station. When I say 'us', I mean Paul and David. I told Paul to tell them that the boss didn't hang around railway stations doing business. That white refrigerated van was clearly dealing at the same time – get all your business done in one go at Peter's registered office, Košice Central!

'I will be leaving for England tomorrow,' Peter 2 announced. 'I will call you when I get there. I have three girls for sale in England at the moment. One is blonde with big tits and the other two are dark haired – all in their twenties. We will meet in London.'

By 6 September we had returned to the UK. They, had after all, said they were heading there. It proved to be untrue.

Paul took the call from an overseas number. 'Hello Paul. I am Peter speaking from Slovakia. We no come London. Problem in Slovakia. We must to stay in Slovakia. I am sorry. We come next week. Next week, sure. What day you in London?' It was Peter 2. I didn't know what to make of it. What they'd said in Košice suggested that they were for real. My previous dealings with Slovaks also told me that this was the normal way. It might just be that he didn't have any girls at this point, when he'd thought he had. Everyone was just a cog in a chain, grinding very slowly. What gave me belief was that he had called at all. We never rang him. That was a very good sign.

Two days later, the other Peter rang. He was now in Dublin. Predictably, he apologised for the delay – he had a couple of things to finish off back in Košice. Now, he needed to sort out his business in Dublin. Today was Monday; he would call by the end of the week. Every delay took me a day closer to the next trip with John, and I had to see this one through. We were so near the sting, and I had worked so hard on this – so many trips to Košice and so many stop starts. Annie Allison tackled me on this.

'You're going to be away for a couple of weeks,' she said. 'We're not going to get it done.'

'No way,' I stood my ground. 'Just tell them I'm away. It's got to be me or not at all.'

I wanted the glory. And I had done the work. But I was due to leave on 14 September. The next day, Peter in Dublin rang Paul. No surprises here, more delays – the other Peter had problems in London.

'Some personal things, you know,' he said. 'He gonna call me at ten tonight, then I will find out what the problem is.'

'So there's no meeting in London tomorrow?' Paul asked.

'No, my friend, I'm sorry.' Peter answered.

Paul reminded Peter that the boss was going to 'Spain' for two weeks and we were concerned they would be back in Slovakia by the time he returned. He assured Paul that wouldn't be the case. 'Tell your boss when he come back from Spania we do the girls business in London. One hundred per cent.' They agreed to speak at the end of the week.

I was now running dual lives. Ran and Robin were in for their briefing at the Hostile Environment Training Course near Reading and that was something you couldn't take lightly, as many times as

I had overseen it. The clock was ticking. At any moment, I was due to leave with them on John's crazy idea. But I might have to go to Košice. Or Dublin. Or Kent? Spain was the only place I wasn't going. By 14 September, it was too late.

Frustration got the better of me, and I knew patience was running out at TC. There were only so many times I could try to re-persuade Craig Oliver and Annie: everyone knew we were so nearly there, and it concerned me that my absence over the next fortnight would kill the story. Without me there, it would be easy for it to slip down the agenda.

I wanted to be in two places at once but there was no way I was going to delay or abandon John's trip. I was about to fulfil a boyhood dream. The chance to work with Robin Knox-Johnston, Ranulph Fiennes and John Simpson meant that I would be taking three of the world's greatest explorers to a place nobody went any more. I wouldn't be the star of this show but I didn't want to miss out.

And the BBC was paying for it again. It was time to unleash the Three Dogs.

THREE DOGS

I picked up the report in Dubai Airport. I was caught between a rock and a hard place. As I read the transcript, I felt it slipping away. I realised that if nothing happened while I was abroad, then they would call time. I was the lifeblood of that story – in my absence, there wasn't anyone to represent it. Nobody had lost interest, but it was yesterday's news. Here comes Craig again, asking for money to chase birds across Eastern Europe.

In one way, I wished nothing would happen so I could pick it up on my return. On the other hand, if nothing did happen the story was gone. There had been just a small development.

Peter: Hello Paul, how are you?

Paul: Hello Peter. Good to hear from you. I thought you had forgotten us.

Peter: Listen I speak to Peter in London and we have three girls ready. Give me email address and I send you pictures.

Paul: Hang on, Peter. You know Boss is in Spania and I must speak with him ...

Peter: Yes, I know. You can send him pictures. If he like the girls we do business when he come back ...

Paul: OK, this is good. Let me call the boss now.

Peter: You call me back?

Paul: Yes, I call you back for sure. Give me some minutes and I call you straight back, OK?

Peter: OK. Bye, Paul.

Paul: OK. Bye bye, Peter. I call you back.

I texted Paul immediately.

He had rung Peter back straight afterwards to say that I thought that emailing the pictures was excellent. There were three girls, aged seventeen, twenty-three and twenty-six. They were all in the UK. I loved it. It was brilliant, and I have never been more pissed off in my life to be sat in the Executive Lounge in Dubai. Compounding the problem, of course, was that I would soon have to turn my phone off and that meant an update an agonising three hours from now. I would have to wait until I touched down in Kabul.

I sat back and thought about the show we were doing now. Dee, John's wife, had pitched it to the BBC. It started as a joke back in Zim – that's what you do when you are sitting around incognito, waiting to file. You dream up shit, and later you get someone else to pay for it.

Sir Robin Knox-Johnston was born in 1939 – a world away. He was the first man to perform a single-handed non-stop circumnavigation of the globe. In 2006, he became the oldest yachtsman to complete a round the world solo voyage. Quite simply, the man was a legend. Sir Ranulph Twisleton-Wykeham-Fiennes was five years younger than Robin. He had actually served in the British army for eight years. Guinness World Records listed him as the World's Greatest Explorer. He had done the lot. North and South Poles, Antarctica on foot, and some doddle of a mountain called Everest. And then there was John.

The show was to go out on BBC2. I didn't give a shit if nobody watched it. This gig was too good to turn down – not that I ever rejected any free trip or work with John. The name of the game was that each Dog would take the others into their 'comfort zone' and we would see what transpired. And so was born *Top Dogs: Adventures in War, Sea and Ice*. It was almost completely different to everything I had done before, except that the terrain was still very tricky. And it just proved that if you had the right cast list, you could get any old nonsense commissioned! It was a jolly, but with risks. Nobody from the West had reported back from the Tora Bora mountain range since the Americans thought they had bin Laden there in December 2001. That's where the Dogs were heading.

When I touched down in Kabul, there was nothing on the sex trafficking. Paul confirmed that the email with the pictures hadn't come. Nor did it come the day after or the day after that. Peter in London seemed to be in some bother. But I had to park it to one side. In my mind, even if word came in that that op was live, I wouldn't abandon the Three Dogs. Sex trafficking was officially on hold again and there was little I could do. I had to let the Dogs off their leads. It was time to chase down the Taliban.

John didn't really know the other guys and it was a nightmare co-ordinating everyone's schedule. The proposed dates had got moved several times – it was one of those jobs. I was only going on the first leg. We were really making it up as we went: it was a classic case of coming up with the show before knowing what it was. At one point, we were in meetings with the Ministry of Defence and talking about flying into Kandahar to see the troops. That was all a bit too Geri Halliwell for me – I didn't want to be part of their propaganda, despite the military in me. In fact, they were borderline useless, unable even to offer us definite seats in the Hercs to get us out there. It was also changeover time for the troops in Kabul, which meant this was the worst possible time to ask the Foreign Office to help us. We were on our own.

Kandahar and Helmand were out of the question. I certainly wasn't sitting around in Kabul for three weeks, and there was no real interest for this type of show if Robin and Ranulph just shadowed John fishing out the usual stories in the capital. As part of the story, John still had to do his job. I only had one route in my head – let's do the Khyber Pass and get to Tora Bora. From Kabul to Jalalabad was about three hours, and that could mean anything in these parts. From Jalalabad to the Khyber Pass, it was in theory anything up to a further three.

The Khyber Pass was steeped in history and Tora Bora had shaped contemporary current affairs. Mention the Khyber Pass and most people see Sid James running around in his red uniform in the Carry On films. The truth was that it was one of the most influential border crossings in the world, an integral part of the Ancient Silk Road, dividing Afghanistan and Pakistan and the huge mountain range across both. To this day, it still bustles with both legitimate and illegitimate trade, but its roots go as far back as the Bible. It was an absolute must – take the three of them to a heartbeat of the Old British Empire, now confined to the history books even though their generation lived alongside it, and get one of the world's most respected journalists to al Qaeda's den. Nobody had confirmed it, but British and American Special Forces came within a whisker of taking out Osama bin Laden in the vast network of caves in this mountain range before Christmas of 2001. Who wouldn't want to go there and breathe in history?

Let your imagination run wild for a moment and wonder what went on in there. Remember, too, that the Americans helped build the network when it supported Afghanistan fighting the Soviets in the early 1980s. And yet today it remained an unvisited mystery, hiding a million secrets. To get the Three Dogs there would be incredible. It was like getting John in and out of Zim – but this time with celebrity in tow. That was the beauty of this show. Could the World Affairs editor deliver once again from the back of beyond, and could we do so while making a reality-type show, which wasn't what any of us had trained to do, and still feed the Ten at the same time?

I arrived two days before the Dogs. More than ever, it was imperative I sorted out the best vehicles for the trip. This was not the terrain to be leased a duff vehicle by the usual local fixers around the Hotel Serena, who saw big pound signs as always whenever the BBC turned up.

There were no specific threats at this time but, hey, this was Afghanistan. You always had to be on your guard, and despite having excellent BBC contacts on the ground, nobody could really say with any certainty who we would run into on our trip, especially once out of Kabul. Were there any extra risks in taking three old boys this way? Yes, a few. At the Hostile Environments Course back in the UK, both Ran and Robin had asked really sensible questions. Ran in particular loved refreshing his military skills – the soldier never dies in you. They had both read up like pros and had done their homework, never once asking a naive question. They were like kids in a sweetshop. Ran also got to use a defibrillator. This was a minor issue that I had to include in the risk assessment. Unscathed through all his adventures, he had actually suffered a heart attack in 2003. That was really my only concern but it was minimal. He would never complain, and I think you could say that he had more than proven himself over time!

Hanif, our fixer, took Oggy and me to see the cars. I really didn't want to be driving around in tinted armoured American 4x4s. None of us wanted to stand out and announce our presence. That's where there would be an incident. My suspicions were confirmed: one of the cars wasn't up to it. There was no way I was driving to Tora Bora with bald tyres.

Hanif was very well connected – I had worked with him many times before and the BBC trusted him. He also worked as a presenter on Afghan TV and accompanied Afghan dignitaries on trips abroad. He was the man to know. I told him to get it sorted by the time the Dogs arrived. New tyres, a service, and I needed to see it again – they were my instructions. Hanif didn't let me down.

When John, Ran and Robin touched down, I just knew I was on the brink of something special – a real landmark trip, and very different to what I had left behind. Yes, it was a jolly and there was no need to make the show, but John had stretched himself with the ambition for it. Journalistically, he gave it merit. To watch the chemistry between the three of them, even in these early stages, was inspirational.

For Simpo, this was old hat, his thirtieth, fortieth trip – we had all lost count. He was a seasoned veteran here. But for Ran and Robin, you could see the mutual respect in their faces and it was a pleasure to chaperone two men who still had an appetite for culture, even after all that they had seen. Yes – they would have been to places like this before, but the planet never ceased to amaze them. I looked at them looking at Kabul. You could see that they simply had explorer eyes.

It was so refreshing, rare and unexpected, too, that the boys seemed to know the place on their first visit. Robin was constantly dropping quotes out of a book as we passed landmarks – they savoured every moment because their trips had begun in the library and on the net before they left London. That first evening we had a meeting in Robin's room to sketch out what lay ahead. Against hotel rules, we had a tipple of John's whisky in the room. These may have been three old dogs, but they were still naughty schoolboys at heart.

And so, in the morning, we began. John talked openly to camera about the mission. He said they weren't doing it because it was risky, but that the risk made it difficult to report on. I thought that was a good turn of phrase. And more importantly, it was an excellent on-screen justification for getting up to a hundred grand out of the Beeb for making the show!

Robin really was living the role – picking him up on everything he said. John had stated that he hoped Ran and Robin would challenge him and it was his job to sort truth from rumour. Robin kept piling in, questioning John's subjectivity. John felt it was important to interview people who were hopeful. Robin contested that this in itself was selective and that John was shaping the story without considering whether it was representative or not. Ran would always be more cautious before stepping in. But they were challenging the old dog himself, and it was brilliant to see. Between the three, there was nothing but mutual admiration; in the context of the show, they all knew how to throw their heart and soul into it.

On our first proper day, I had received a tip-off. There was a major security threat near the heavily defended government area and US Embassy at Massoud Circle in Kabul. I was on a phone link which would notify me if anything came in like a potential car bomb or suicide threat. This was still daily life in Kabul.

First, we would head to the markets. I briefed the guys that we would spend minimal time on the streets. They should put nothing in their back pockets and be aware that anyone could produce a gun or the like at a second's notice. I told them that when I'd had enough, we would go – probably after no more than twenty minutes. The market had been attacked several times previously. Three weeks earlier, a stray US bomb had killed thirty people attending a wedding nearby. That all sounded too familiar. We knew there could be hostility towards a Western camera crew. Plus, as you might imagine in a developing country, the market was the hub of the community. It was packed, noisy and hot – your classic Third World hustle and bustle with appalling music and a stench of local spices. Meat was hanging everywhere – dried fruit, ox's tongue, heads of cattle and all sorts of tack that told you it was an open air pound shop where live food was the main product on offer, all sold to a backdrop of ever-present flies. It was vile.

I was on high alert. It was eyes in the back of your head time. John would be aware and he understood how I worked but I couldn't know if the other two were sharp enough. I had told them – leave everything in the car and take your lead from me.

Nick Woolley, the cameraman, was right at the end of the market. I briefed them all: if anything happens, you go forwards not backwards. The two vehicles would be at the end near Nick. We marched into the market – me talking all the time, constantly looking around. I was on the walkie-talkie too to Oggy. I wouldn't say I was on edge but it was time to be on top of my game. If anything happened to these three famous guys, it was down to me.

We pulled up at a stall to get the locals' viewpoint on life in the new era. Of course, this attracted a crowd, but nothing any of us couldn't handle or hadn't seen before. Plus, we had Hanif accompanying us, which reassured me.

I didn't expect the ambush that followed. Suddenly we were under attack. Handfuls of sweetcorn pelted us. Sweetcorn, of all the weapons in the world, was raining down on us. I was under attack by corn on the cob. This was either a joke or a sideshow.

At first, I thought it was kids taking the piss, but it didn't relent. And it hurt too – tons of sweetcorn on a bald head is not funny. Hanif said it would be fine, but to keep moving. I didn't want to pull out, but I was wary. The locals were intrigued and a lot of Afghans knew John. They had no real idea who Robin and Ran were. They could have been anyone.

Some people just didn't want us there. The women, for example, wouldn't appear on TV – they did not want to talk. 'I can't talk because of my family or relatives,' one of them said to camera.

There were a clearly a lot of people living in fear of the unknown in a male-dominated society. We pushed on further down. Maybe Hanif was right and the dried fruit stall just simply didn't want us there. The sweetcorn had just said go. I could see our vehicles a hundred metres away at the bottom of the street. Lots of people were following. I expected the curiosity, but I didn't like it. My head was on a 360 rotation.

From nowhere, a fight broke out in front of us by a stray cart. Hanif decided to get involved and break it up. The cart was the decoy prop.

'Hanif, leave it,' I shouted to him.

I didn't want him in there – he was my other eyes and ears. The crowd closed in on us. It was a textbook sabotage. Out of one eye, I was watching the three guys in the fight; out of the other I spotted John Conroy, the director and my two other cameras. Oggy was to my left. Something didn't ring true – it looked like a well-oiled drill. There was no reason for this to start up in front of us. I wanted to keep moving but I knew they had done this hundreds of times before. The fight lasted forty seconds, if that. We moved on.

I surveyed the scene to work out why. Alarm bells were now ringing. My instincts told me not to like it. We had been here around thirty minutes. That was my maximum. It was time to abandon. To my right, I spotted two guys. One was on a phone, looking in our direction, but not really in our direction. The second man was trying to shield the first. Was this somebody calling this in to say a Western crew were in the market, or was he simply ringing his bird?

'Look John, it's time to go,' I said. I didn't like it one bit. We were gone in minutes. I was relieved to get back to the hotel. I was relieved ... until I saw Oggy.

'You'll never guess what,' he said. 'I've had my phone nicked. It's got all my contacts on it and everything.'

'Why did you have it on you?' I reminded him of my brief. 'Fucking hell, that's the most basic mistake.'

'I know, I know.'

You couldn't get the moment back. And Oggy would be replaying the point of impact time and time again. It gave me a chance to reiterate the ground rules to the Dogs. I knew for sure that it was a staged fight, and that's what annoyed me about Hanif. He shouldn't have got involved but, typical Afghan, he couldn't help himself. We were pushed into the middle of the crowd and got fleeced. As ops go, it hadn't even stretched them – these petty thieves knew the drill. All for a phone. Robin questioned how I could be so sure that it was a mock fight. I watched the footage back and it was as I'd seen it at the time – completely without spark and starting for no reason. It was important not to be naive about these things or it would happen again. Lesson learned, I hope. Greater risks lay ahead.

Next came the minister. The Afghan police had actually done brilliant work with their checkpoints, thwarting dozens of potential incidents. This is why I didn't want a fuck-off vehicle for once. Our vehicle was one that any Afghan would have used. Otherwise, we would have added ourselves to the list of targets.

We were on our way to meet Saeed Ansari, a spokesman for Afghan intelligence. You would think politicians would be too busy to allow a couple of hangers-on to be in on the interview. But then, this was John Simpson. Frankly, I had never seen anything like it. The World Affairs editor of the BBC sat with an interpreter and a member of the government – two of the world's greatest explorers watching but only to tear into John afterwards. John's plan was to lure him into saying that security in Kabul was going downhill fast. The minister trotted out the official line – it was actually improving!

John changed tack. 'Do you think there's an extra effort at the moment to capture Osama bin Laden?' he asked. Fobbed off with some rubbish about what might happen if the UN put pressure on Pakistan, he interrupted the answer. 'Sorry, I'm not asking what ought to happen. I'm asking what is happening.'

John cut the interview short. It hadn't delivered what he hoped for. And Robin and Ran, like student journos, tore into him.

'What did you make of our spy chief?' John began.

'John, I've got a question for you,' Robin had been ready to pounce.

'No, I've got a question for you.' John was fired up by the indifference in the office. 'What did you make of our spy chief?'

'It's a comment he made,' said Robin, 'that you didn't pick up on.'

I think John could read Robin.

'He was quite specific that Osama bin Laden could be picked up if the Pakistani intelligence co-operated.' Robin felt he had John here.

'You have to tell the difference between fact and opinion. Nothing he said was fact. We're in the business of news – not the rhetoric of government.' John was adamant. He had seen it all before, but it was the first time for the Dogs. That was the difference – Robin and Ran felt they had a sniff. John knew it was bullshit. It wasn't enough to re-broadcast the words of a government minister just because you had the access. Your job was to cut through the crap.

Over the next couple of days Robin and Ran asked decent questions, often in the confrontational atmosphere of the throngs that would automatically gather when a camera crew turned up – especially when they saw it was John Simpson. They would ask the locals if they had been happier under the Taliban – that question always polarised opinions. We also took them to Friday prayers at the Mosque.

On the morning on 21 September, however, we all went down to breakfast unsure as to whether the show must go on. The previous night, a truck filled with explosives had detonated in front of the Marriott Hotel in Islamabad, the capital of Pakistan. More than fifty people were dead and over 260 injured, some of them dignitaries. The bomb left a crater twenty metres wide and six metres deep – the noise could be heard fifteen kilometres away. It was one of the most prestigious buildings in the city and the explosion came just hours after President Asif Ali Zardari had made his first speech to the Pakistani parliament. John needed to cover the story.

The truck had pulled up at the front of the hotel. Among the casualties were one Danish intelligence agent and two American military personnel, a US State Department employee, and the Czech ambassador. Thirty American marines had been staying at the hotel, and they were believed to be the target. Either way, whoever bombed the Marriott knew they had an international audience.

This was now the problem for the Three Dogs – if a major story broke while we were out here, it would put our show in jeopardy. We had a correspondent in Islamabad, but if John Simpson was in town, then he was the man. He could be there in an hour by plane. Equally if Paul rang from London to say that either of the Peters had been in touch, the entire show would be a no-show and I would have to go.

John was frustrated. It took him nineteen takes on the roof of our hotel for him to get the report out on the bomb, finally finishing just before the light went. This was the only time I had ever seen him need this long. John was in the wrong place. He knew it was waffle because he couldn't get close to the story. He had also heard that the bomb had been planted in retaliation for US air strikes. For a day or two, his heart had been ripped out of the Three Dogs.

What seemed like a cute little show with some journalistic merit was now a sideshow. You couldn't ignore the destruction over the border in Pakistan. In short, if we hadn't been making the Dogs, John would have gone without question. So close to the scene of the crime, it was right that the World Affairs editor report it live from the Marriott on the Ten, regardless of whether any other correspondent was there. The public expected to see John Simpson and John wanted to go.

London said no. It would be day three of the story by the time John arrived. Our correspondent there would cover it. We were told to carry on with the Three Dogs. It had shaken everyone: to John, it was a day-long frustration where his mind and heart were on other things; to the Dogs, it was a reminder of the random nature of self-destruction in this part of the world where the price of life seemed less than at home. As for me, I studied the footage of the bomb. They made it look all too easy. I had stayed with John in that very hotel several times and knew it well. It was just another hotel and another city. The victims never stood a chance.

The next morning, I re-briefed everyone. It was time to head to the Khyber Pass. Truthfully, the chances of any of us getting killed on this route were now increased. Much of it was bandit country, and outside the city, the chance of ambush was significant. I told everyone to put their flak jackets on if that happened. We would drive straight through it if possible; if not, we would get out and find whatever cover we could, leaving everything in the truck.

'If you get taken out, Craig,' Ran asked, 'who is in charge?'

I told him that with his military background it had to be him.

'If we see vehicles ahead being taken out with RPGs (rocket-propelled grenades), what do we do?' Ran knew that planning was the key to survival.

'We'll either quickly reverse, or de-bus and move back.'

John wanted to stop and film in a place called Surobi, about sixty kilometres east of Kabul. It was officially Afghanistan's most dangerous place. I reminded him about the ten French paratroopers, killed in broad daylight just a fortnight before. If we were stopping, it would be for minutes only. We could only make that decision as and when we got there. I would take advice and see how we were doing for time. My preference was to stop outside and film into its valley. That was the problem, you see. Anyone knows that once you're in the dip, you're cannon fodder. There was, however, no choice but to drive through Surobi to get to Jalalabad and meet the Khyber Pass.

Proving how precarious this was, I took extra care. In fact, I did something I have never done on any other mission. I went to see senior Afghan politician Mirwais Yasini, and arranged to tag along in his military convoy. That gave us a menacing presence, but of course it also made us a far greater target.

He took me into unchartered territory. 'Would you like to take weapons along for your own protection?'

I knew one thing. This wasn't in the BBC Health and Safety guidelines. It told you something about where we were heading if a major politician advised you to arm up in his own backyard. That gave me maximum confidence that he was honest; it also gave me zero confidence about our mission. 'I will need to discuss this with London. I don't think they will allow it, but I really appreciate your offer. With you and your own security detail travelling with us ... I think we should be OK.'

I never consulted Television Centre. My old mate Kev Sweeney, from our company KCM, was now working for me in Kabul. There was a security changeover at the Bureau in Kabul, so he was free to come. I had known him for thirty years and valued his opinion. We went back to see Yasini.

I put my plan to both of them. 'We take two AK-47s with spare magazines in bags. We put one in each vehicle. They stay out of sight, unless we need them.'

I also told John. He thought it wise, but didn't want to know. This was what we would call in the military a deniable op. Ran was over the moon, living the dream now, with me always living the dream!

I told Yasini's guards that these AKs were their weapons. If anything happened and we needed to use them, I would take control. How I would explain that back in London, I would deal with later. Even if I saved the Dogs from certain death, I am sure that would have been the end of me at the BBC. We walked a fine line, but I still believe it was the correct way to proceed.

We slotted into the Yasini's convoy. One road in, one road out, and scarcely a chance to overtake. It was the usual story. Mountain roads snaking their way home; around each corner, more of the same and more of the unknown – the drop down below too vast to look at more than once. You can see how the French paratroopers and many more before were sitting ducks. We had no choice but to nestle in the pack. When they sped up, so did we. When they stopped, we did the same – flak jackets on.

As we approached Surobi, Yassini's guards pulled over. Everybody out. Several of the French had been beheaded five kilometres away. Yassini pointed out the exact spot. This was as close to Surobi as the convoy would allow John to be filmed.

'At the risk of sounding a bit nervous,' John understated, 'is it a good idea for us to stick around here?'

'I wouldn't say a long time,' Yassini replied.

'Anybody who sees us is just going to stop in Surobi and say there's this long line of big-wiggers coming. I think we should go right away,' John chuckled.

It was a hauntingly beautiful spot – a complete contrast to the dangers held all around. Yassini explained to Ran that some of the French were ambushed in their car; others were on foot. Walking through Surobi was just foolish – we needed to get back in the cars. Sharpish. In truth, we had only stopped for television, but then we were in the business of making TV. Driving round the corner into the town was eerie. You know when you are not wanted – the streets were lined with pro-Taliban lookouts discreetly monitoring the road but not wanting to draw any unnecessary attention. All eyes were on us, our vehicles creeping at a steady speed past the market stalls that hugged the pavements.

'In 2001 after the fall of the Taliban, I came down this road,' John recalled. 'My cameraman nudged me saying he really didn't like the look of this at all. He highlighted the menacing stares of a group on the corner. At that point the axle on our car went.' Robin and Ran were transfixed. All ears were on John. The silence spoke volumes. 'Twenty minutes later, we had switched into another car and passed a Spanish vehicle coming along the oppo-site direction. There were three Spanish journalists in there, one of whom I knew. They drove into Surobi. This gang of people decided to stop them because they knew they didn't have any protection. They, I'm afraid, led them up a side path and shot them. Very, very depressing.'

Nobody blinked. John narrated the story with real gravitas and warmth. It stood as a chilling reminder of the dangers on the very roads we were passing. The way he told the story clearly indicated it could have been him. Robin and Ran understood the depth of that. For once, their questions and analysis dried up. They were taking it all in, even as men who had seen it before. Their eyes told you every-thing, scanning the scouts who were surveying them, each a possible bystander to atrocities on this road before, perhaps just the fortnight before. Their faces radiated one message. They would have to come back this way on the return leg. The safety of Kabul, as ironic as that sounds, was a long way away now.

'My military days told me that you never go back the way you came,' Ran finally broke the silence.

The further we left Surobi behind, the more the conversation piped up again. You could feel the Dogs relaxing once more, although they were still very much on their guard. John had built up the dangers at the place where the French and Spanish were massacred, and you could sense a few kilometres down the road that it was OK to talk freely again – their silence a dignified memorial to the victims here, and an acknowledgment that the jolly had real journalistic merit, too. It was time to push on to the Khyber Pass.

Mountains, small towns, and the odd hamlet all the way to Jalalabad. Then it merges into an open plain, with greenery all around. The very first time I saw this I had thought it was beautiful, but I had met John here many times before. The second time I came this way, it was just a mountain range. I didn't have time to be a tourist.

With heavy fighting between NATO and the Taliban at the border, we persuaded another army unit to escort us the final forty kilometres through the Black Mountains. John pointed out the route to Tora Bora – gateway to bin Laden all those years ago. With that sense of expedition in the blood of all three, who wouldn't want to wander that way? He confessed it was one of the remaining things on his To Do list, even though al Qaeda were still lurking and the area was mined. Way beyond the lifetime of the Three Dogs, perhaps John's little son might retrace his steps in safer times and enter bin Laden's vast network of caves for the BBC. For now, Tora Bora remained pretty much inaccessible. Finally, we reached the Khyber Pass.

'Ah, I love it here.' John chatted naturally, oblivious to the camera. 'So many of my times in Afghanistan have begun or ended here,' he raved to the Dogs. 'So full of activity, criminal, commercial, military, anything ...'

Ranulph couldn't believe he was here, as though this moment could have passed him by in life. It was one of the great crossing points in the world from a bygone era we rarely talked about nowadays but to their generation it was a time of daring adventure. Between 1839 and 1919, Britain engaged in three wars with Afghanistan. Many of the fiercest battles were fought here.

'For a Brit, the Khyber Pass has a resonance of our past,' Robin made the point for his generation.

'It makes your heart beat faster,' John was exhilarated.

At the same time, all three were wary. John pointed out a truck carrying goodness knows what. So much went through unchecked.

'This truck coming through here ... could have something very unpleasant hidden under the top three or four layers ... and nobody's going to search it ... he's only got to press the button and the whole thing goes up.'

He was spot on. Every excitement was also a potential threat. The noise, the smell and the bustle were exhilarating but you couldn't take your eye off the ball for one moment. Several factions of the transient community would often play on that nervous energy in the air. But John was moved to be here, too, and to share it with the Dogs, patting Robin on the back in an uncharacteristically non-British way. Each of them thanked the other.

'I used to be a typical kind of broomstick up the arse Brit and probably still am, mostly, but the one thing I learned from being in countries like this is that physical contact means a lot,' John apologised but didn't need to.

I knew that this story had gone from being Dee's idea, to an irritation with the Marriott bomb, to now reaching a thoroughly worthwhile emotional conclusion. To be at the Pass, however many times you had come this way, still stirred something in grown men, and to be with Ran and Robin made it prefect. So many times, John had been here with just a crew and myself. I sensed for the first time that showing the other two this border so steeped in history finally gave him somebody to share it with.

And the Ten wanted a piece of him, too. Oggy said that Craig Oliver had been on. They wanted John to be the lead that night. Neither John nor Oggy were convinced that they should go top on the bulletin. He had minutes to get the story out.

'This has become a no-man's land where all sorts of violence can thrive,' he began. 'The Pakistanis clearly can't do anything to stop it. If the Americans don't come up with something pretty dramatic, then this war will be lost. By changing the command structure, they're hoping they can stop the rot, but it's by no means certain. John Simpson, BBC News at the Khyber Pass.'

And the clue was in the out. John didn't have a story, but this time location won the day. They wanted those words at the end on the Ten against that mountainous backdrop, knowing that viewers would be in awe that even today, you could file from the middle of nowhere, yet in one of the tensest places in the world. John would never shirk at being the lead, of course, but it left him hungry to find a real top story. It was time to push on. And crucially, he had left the Marriott behind.

We had to make for the Tora Bora caves. No other reporters had been there since 2001. This was the journalistic merit I've been talking about. Thirteen vehicles now accompanied us towards Tora Bora – mostly through dried up river beds. Out of character, we were almost embedded. Tora Bora was no-man's land on Afghanistan's side of the border. The commander escorting us insisted we had to have such a huge heavily armed entourage – it was that dangerous. This meant hours of travelling though bandit country and then camping in the mountains overnight.

'I don't like this,' John said. 'I don't like all these soldiers. I've almost never done this in my life. My idea was always to get in a vehicle like this and just go out unnoticed. I think you are ten times safer on your own. The Taliban must know that we're in town.'

I knew John's tone. He didn't want to be part of a circus. Soon we ran into rough terrain. The vehicles were dangerously exposed. We came a cropper in the dry river beds – stones under the vehicles meaning we couldn't get any momentum to push on. Next, we hit a puncture. John wanted to walk. If the Taliban were on their game, there was no easier target than us. We'd taken our chances outside Surobi where the French were killed but we'd known we weren't going to linger. Now, we didn't know how long we would have to wait because of circumstance. You can see why I bollocked Hanif about the vehicles on day one.

This made Ran and Robin even more uncomfortable at staying overnight. 'From a military view, I wouldn't come in here unless I was dressed like one of them,' Ran said, concerned as he gestured towards our guards. Every moment we lingered gave the Taliban a chance to organise an ambush up ahead – and those guys never needed asking twice.

'It's almost like we are deliberately giving the Taliban an opportunity,' Robin replied. And if they didn't get us now, it would certainly never be so easy for them again. We were sitting on a plate for them. This was not a case of two great explorers' arses going. They were just talking common sense. 'It's almost as though we are going to create news by getting a mine blown up under us.'

Robin was right. We abandoned the crew vehicles to make for the checkpoint. From here, we became military – army jeeps would have to do. There was still no lack of danger. Parallel to the road, whose edges couldn't be defined, mine after mine lined the route. There was only one relatively safe way to proceed – follow the tracks of the vehicle in front. Just like in Zim, always trust the local knowledge – but this was completely different. There we would have suffered a beating and imprisonment at worst. Here, we could all end up like Stuart Hughes through the slightest misjudgement by someone else. The commander had told us it was his life as well as ours, which was as close as you got up here to a guarantee.

Despite the tension in the air, nothing was going to stop Ranulph and I standing in the back of the jeep with the AK-47s ready to go. As much war as I had seen, there was something playful in both of us. Who wouldn't want to be a big kid for a few moments and pretend they were in the A-Team? This was genuinely scary territory, and if something happened you wouldn't even know about it, but I can't say I didn't love it.

Finally, we made it to the top. We were there.

John has harboured this ambition for many years – to reach Tora Bora. The commander of the checkpoint explained exactly what lay beneath in bin Laden country. Through a break in the mountains, a green area came in to view – that was where America's greatest menace of recent times lived when the Taliban were in power. Occasionally, he added, the Taliban came to the peak of the mountain. Just two days before our visit, they had fired rockets on his men but retreated when the attack was returned. They were still there and very much alive and kicking. Just the place to stay the night then.

For TV purposes and no other, Ran and Robin under my supervision fired three shots each from the AK-47 into the valley.

'That kind of thing ain't for me,' John relinquished the opportunity. 'As a journalist, I don't want anything to do with guns.'

It was an ironic choice of words, given his lifetime in war zones. I think what he meant was that he shouldn't be protected because he was a journalist reporting the story. Robin said it was nice to do it practically but that was very different from having to do it for real. Ran fussed over his technique like the old pro, comparing it to other weapons he had fired. The decision was taken. We would camp for the night after all.

Oggy was on the phone to Television Centre. London loved it and wanted John live to millions of viewers, minutes later.

'How lovely to see you there.' The News anchor was momentarily caught up in the moment too.

This wasn't the *Holiday* programme. It was incredible that the World Affairs editor was there, and live, but the report was all about the backdrop and the unspoken story. Today, there was no news in these parts, but the 9/11 generation knew what the silent words meant. John was breathing in bin Laden's air and even though he was long gone, nobody had got this close in years. John savoured the moment.

An emotional satisfaction hit everyone when the feed was cut and only the view and sense of history remained. The Dogs all knew what they had achieved and that you don't come back to these places twice. Three wise old men who had lived a million lives between them knew these were precious moments.

'I couldn't bear not to have seen it,' John said with his guard down. When you've done your day job to the level that he had just done, even the most seasoned pros would be forgiven for forgetting the documentary camera was rolling too. It wasn't that he was caught off guard, but he spoke as though the moment were special beyond journalistic purpose, though it had that, too. In his job and mine, you see so little of the world for pleasure. It's all about airports and the story. This was heaven for John in that he had the story and so much more. The sense of wonder in his eyes, looking down into bin Laden's lair, would never leave him, regardless of what was still to come in his long and distinguished career.

'To wake up tomorrow and see what it is like in the early morning is going to be magical.' John summed it up perfectly.

They toasted each other under the stars and under the influence, and reviewed the previous fortnight.

'To the Dogs,' Ran proposed.

'The Dogs, the drunken Dogs,' John laughed.

This time it was Robin who found the words. 'We've still got that childish curiosity in us to see these places. We may have grown old in experiences, but we haven't allowed that to quench our thirst.' He puffed on his cigar, having hit the nail on the head.

I felt the same. It was a private moment caught in public. To sit around the campfire and hear the stories was just phenomenal. It was like Iraq in 2003, camping out under the stars with the American Special Forces. To be in the presence of three legends and such danger was the stuff of dreams. This was a different gig. Clearly, as safety advisor it didn't get any bigger. Equally, I was soaking up this once in a lifetime experience, sleeping outside in the still of the night and waking up feeling a million dollars. To be paid to do this in such company – well, it didn't get any better.

Only a dog sniffing around in the early hours presented any danger. I slept with my AK-47 by my side. Around me so did thirty-five of the finest from the Afghan National Guard. What an awesome experience. In the most dangerous place in the world, I had never felt safer. Normally, of course, when you've never felt safer, you've never been in so much danger. Nobody bothered us tonight.

We had shot ninety-six hours footage for a one-hour show. I wouldn't be accompanying the Dogs on their next two adventures. But I did have one last little surprise up my sleeve. There was no way we were going back the way we came, so I had chartered a rickety, old 1950s Russian propeller ten-seater to get us out of there. At take-off, I'm sure returning through Surobi looked a better option.

Little did I know that less a month later, I would be once again in Afghanistan with the reporter Jane Corbin, back in the same room where John had interviewed the 'Spy Chief' from Afghan Intelligence. This time, eyeballing me across the room and refusing to look Jane in the eye because of his religious attitude to women, I was within a breath of a suicide bomber from the same stable that wreaked havoc on London on 7/7. One vest could kill forty people.

I knew, of course, that there was a fine line between planned, needless violence and sporadic gang warfare, and nothing was more apparent to me as I jetted next into Mexico. Destination: Ciudad Juárez.

COSTAS

It had now been a year since I had first gone to Košice in search of sex. Several times we had got to the eye of the needle and been unable to reap what we had sewed. I had heard nothing when I was with the Dogs. Nothing, until I was flying out of Kabul back into London.

Paul had been on. Peter 2 wanted to meet. In the next forty-eight hours. He was driving back to Košice. That might mean we could see evidence of something in transit – girls or something narcotic in his refrigerated white van. It was unlikely he was going to turn up with a van full of birds but you could never know. He was either on his way back from a job and wanting to brag about it, or he was taking something back. That was clear. His asking to meet at such short notice gave me hope we might finally seal the deal. I was still buzzing from the Three Dogs but we had to be there at all costs. There was nothing to lose and we had nothing left to go on. I was certain he was a man of habit and that he would take the same route time and time again.

If only Costa Coffee at Clacket Lane Services on the M25 knew that this was Peter's office. It was a Saturday afternoon and the services were packed with the weekend traffic. It was perfect – just two stops before the M20 heading down towards the Kent coast. We had informed one person at the BBC that the job was going down – we had cut corners because I was just getting back and I couldn't keep justifying the story. I also decided to film, despite our lack of prep.

If I could get one shot of him opening the van to reveal the girls, we had made it.

Making the call that we were in a public place, I just thought 'fuck it'. It would only be Peter and his gang that could be in trouble. The location was so extraordinarily ordinary that there couldn't be any physical threat. The risk assessment was all his. By 14.00 Paul and I were at the car park, rigging ourselves up in the car for a meet an hour later. Peter rang to say they were entering the services. We were in position inside Costa Coffee. The meeting lasted no more than thirty minutes.

'Peter, my friend,' I greeted him. 'How are you, my brother?'

They were a gang of two – Peter, and presumably another Peter. The latter never said a word, continually glancing around. Maybe he didn't speak much English. He was definitely on watch. Everything was flying through my mind – has he got anything for me, were there girls in the van, did he want money now? All the time, the banging of cutlery and slamming of plastic trays around us provided an irritating soundtrack. I could see the sting now going on *Panorama* – it would be a subtitles job. If he wanted cash now, I would go and get it – my BBC credit card could get me ten grand at a push but I wouldn't need that much. Or I could rob Paul to pay Peter! Straightaway he told me that nobody could get hold of the other Peter. He had gone to ground with gambling problems. That was why I had never received the pictures in Dubai. He swore he had been ringing him every day but still no answer and still no pictures.

'Is Peter finished?' Paul asked.

'Peter in London is finished,' this Peter replied. 'It is *katastrofik*,' he continued. 'He plays the slot machines all day long.'

That lead was dead. The word *katastrofik* was very much alive, again. He told me Frankfurt was good for business. He drove the girls there himself. Germany was very good, too. Next he was heading to Belgium.

'Genk,' he explained.

'Kent?' I questioned his pronunciation.

'No, Genk. I am picking a girl up at 2 a.m.' He had girls in every port.

'Has she worked in England?' Paul asked.

'Yeah, yeah, no, no, Ireland.' There was that whiff again that the trade route was Košice to Dublin or Kent. 'I don't take back my girls. No leases. They are yours.' Peter rubbed his hands, talking like he wanted to deal. I felt this was respect for the job we had done in Košice. Perhaps we had played the part too well.

He was making anything between 100 and 1500 euros a day.

'That sounds good business,' I said.

'I treat them right, they never leave me,' Peter assured, even though, of course, treating them right meant putting them on the game.

I was desperate to get him to the van, but had no reason to take him outside. It was more important to keep the dialogue open. He promised he would be back in two weeks' time.

'I'm off to New York,' I bullshitted to sound in demand. I dragged the thing out to bait him to return with my standard Eastern European tease.

'Are there any other business you might be interested in?' One crook and one criminal sideline always led to another. 'If it's nice for me, it's nice for you,' he smiled like a game show host through his Slovak-cum-fake Irish accent.

There were more than just girls to his game. I couldn't keep him much longer. He had a ferry to catch and he wasn't producing today nor did he ask for money.

'When you go back to Ireland, maybe we come to Ireland for a proper chat?' I suggested.

'I will bring girls to you who know the job. Seriously, dick in hand, five minutes finished.' Peter made us laugh.

'All right, my friend. Stay safe.' I bid him goodbye.

We would meet again in another two weeks. After a further fifteen minutes, Paul and I upped and left. Once again, we would wait for his call. This time, it never came. We had to declare our hand at

Television Centre. With 99 per cent of the show in the bag, we had been unable to pay it off. I couldn't throw any more time at it and the Beeb couldn't post any more resource or cash the story's way – and now, they meant it. It was over.

Nobody seemed sharp enough to follow the scent to Ireland. We knew we would find Peter there – his wife was there, for goodness sake. It was yet another lead, but the best one yet.

'You're not allowed to ring them again,' Home News told me.

I didn't take it as a vote of no confidence. I understood it from an editorial and financial viewpoint. We had been here before and come back from the dead, but now they said Dublin wasn't part of the story. I disagreed. The net was far greater than any of us could have originally known. We had exposed Kent and Dublin as hubs and learned that the trade route was also a goldmine for other activity. Furthermore, Kent Constabulary had made arrests after our work with them. If I hadn't been on the Three Dogs, I would have found some way to work in a new angle and pushed for Ireland. I should have also gone to *Panorama* and asked them to take it from the Ten. The story was a timeless piece that would suit them perfectly, and they could return to it if we let it nestle quietly in the background. Collectively the Peters couldn't do the deal in the time span that making a TV show allocated them. I wouldn't have missed Three Dogs for the world but if I had stayed at home, I could have cultivated this to its conclusion. We didn't hear from any of the Peters again.

Sex Trafficking never made it on air.

CIUDAD JUÁREZ

'What do you reckon?' I bantered with Ian Sherwood on email, early in January 2009. Ian was a Geordie looking after the Bureau in New York.

'Do you have any contacts down there?' he replied.

It was one of those sleeping stories that I had kept an eye on from time to time. 'I haven't, but I do have a contact in Mexico City called Dudley Althaus. I met him in Afghanistan after 9/11. He writes for the *Houston Chronicle*. I'll put the word out.'

It was one of the fastest-growing cities in the world, located immediately south of El Paso, Texas ... a border town on that infamous Mexican border. Hundreds had been murdered. The gangs were in control and out of control. Welcome to Ciudad Juárez, the most dangerous city in the world. It was a difficult pitch to sell internally. The Ten were interested, but not overly. It didn't have top billing potential. *Newsnight* said they were in if the Ten didn't want it. BBC America couldn't get enough of it – they hadn't reported this story, nor had anyone really. There was also some interest from radio. I knew it was good, waiting to be told and they would see that when we delivered.

Two untold aspects, which were almost unique, fascinated me. Firstly, the role of the sicaritos. These were the child assassins on the brink of society – often only thirteen or fourteen years old. Eighty per cent of the 2,000 dead in the previous year or so were under the age of twenty-five. The other angle that was almost unique was femicide. In the past ten to fifteen years, violence towards women had gone up significantly, more than anywhere else in the world. There had been approximately 600 killed in that time. Added to that, three thousand missing women were still unaccounted for.

In another era, Americans frequented Ciudad Juárez – now they largely stayed away. In one street of bars belonging to the drugs cartel, sixteen people had been wiped out in two months. One of the main problems was that the cops were also bent. Many, whether out of fear or looking for better pay packets, were controlled by the gangs. Only recently had the government thrown in the army – 10,000 soldiers had been tasked with cleaning up the city. It was plain to see as well; the military had taken the guns from the Traffic Police themselves. It was that bad.

Matthew Price was to be the reporter; Chuck Tayman was on the camera. Lightweight covert body armour was the order of the day. I also had a medical pack. As fixers go, we had pre-arranged the best in Ricardo Garcia Carriles. He had been chief of police between 2006 and earlier that year. The army knew we were coming, too – they would be our escort.

We touched down in El Paso on 15 March. This was cowboy country but it was also like any border town, busy with people crossing back and forth and packed with bars. I made a mental note to visit one in particular, The Kentucky Bar. Just like the Khyber Pass, the border had the bustle of commercialism – again probably as much legitimate as otherwise. It was the way of the world. Many international businesses were based here – labour was cheap and it was the gateway to both North and Central America.

Ciudad Juárez and El Paso were pretty much the same place; it was the line down the middle dividing the two cities and the two countries which caused many of the problems. For Mexicans, the desire to get out was paramount. The privileges on one side of the frontier far outshone those on the other. You were either on the Santa

Fe Bridge side or the Bridges of America side. Indeed, many of the dignitaries from Ciudad Juárez chose to live on the El Paso side. That, alone, told you everything. Strangely though, when we arrived it just looked a military town, with hundreds of army vehicles hanging around and the odd civilian. Downtown Ciudad Juárez was idyllic – a lovely square and beautiful church the centrepiece of the attractions. But, like all these towns, everyone came out to play at night. We didn't stick around.

The next morning, Matthew, Chuck and Ian went to the border to join the horseback patrol on the American side. What a gig: I would have loved to have been on that, taking control from the saddle, singling out who was a crook and who was genuine. But I had to go back over to Ciudad Juárez to set up ready for the interview with the Mayor the next day. A bit boring, but that was my job; it wasn't all guts and glory. To be honest, I wanted to be that side of the border and it was fascinating travelling in with Ricardo. He took me in to the office, pointing out several crime scenes. He showed me buildings burned out by the cartels, and a huge restaurant on the corner of one of the avenidas that had been completely torched. Half a dozen guys had been killed inside – they hadn't paid up. We passed other memorials to multiple shootings and a house where bodies were found with heads rifled with bullets. I loved it. Horseback could wait. This guy had seen it all.

I watched him work, talking to the mayor and making his calls, and then he took me to lunch. He brought his own security man in tow. Obviously, Ricardo must have had plenty of enemies in his time, and I would attract attention but, to his credit, he still had the balls to ride the city and dine nonchalantly in public. To the watching world, he would never display any weakness.

We pulled up outside this huge restaurant – it looked like one of those no-nonsense Gaucho restaurants with a cowboy menu. The place was packed. The security guy walked in first. Through the front door, we passed the grill on the left. It was a huge big open-planned room with wooden chairs and tables and a kitchen at one end. As we entered, everyone stared at the former police chief, and then at the bloke accompanying him – obviously, I wasn't very Mexican. For a second they couldn't take their eyes off us, before they realised it was Ricardo and carried on eating and chatting. To this day, every time I enter a restaurant, I always sit facing the door so I can see who is coming in and out. As I went towards the table, both Ricardo's security guy and I made for the chairs and he got there first. Inside, I was impressed and pleased – the guy was a top-drawer operator, not that there would be much anyone could do if the cartels stormed the joint. Nor did it stop me shuffling my chair round at an angle. Old habits die hard.

Over an authentic Mexican lunch, I couldn't help but notice that Ricardo was knocking back brandy after brandy. He wasn't even trying to conceal it. He looked like he did this every day. He would soon stop if it cost £500 a bottle! Was this just the custom, was it the stress of the job that had got to him, or was he an alky? Unsurprisingly, he was delighted when I let the BBC pick up the tab.

That afternoon Ricardo showed me to the mayor's office in preparation for the interview. You could see he was afforded maximum security. The underground car park beneath was like Fort Knox, each car heavily armoured. You could see why the key players didn't live in Ciudad Juárez and needed this kind of protection. At the same time, Matthew and the others were picking up some cracking border shots of where the Mexicans regularly penetrated the fence. The Americans couldn't patrol the whole thing all day long but it was important footage, showing how locals on the Mexican side just ran for it with no thought of what their second day in America would be like without documentation or any kind of legitimacy, arriving with just the clothes they were wearing and presumably heading for a given location where friends and family had fled before. And it was happening all the time. We weren't running a story on border control, but it was integral to our piece on the most dangerous city in the world. Indeed many of the shops in El Paso were selling guns that found their way on to the streets of Ciudad Juárez, and much of the tension clearly came from the line dividing the two cultures.

That night, Ian and I crossed back into Ciudad Juárez to survey the bar scene, synonymous with much of the killing. Taking our chance, we got lucky, wandering as close to the border as we could – this time in an unofficial capacity. The captain of the Mexican army challenged me on whether we had permission to film. I lied and said we had. Those three famous letters, BBC, opened so many doors. He was happy to chat, too, explaining that he had 150 men here. Since their arrival in this area, the number of murders and shootings had fallen. But it had moved to another area and this was a huge city – they were always fighting a losing battle. His parting words went against everything I believed in when sniffing out a story.

'Don't go too far off the beaten track,' he advised. On this occasion I took him at his word.

The next day we were back in to see the mayor, José Reyes Estrada Ferriz. The office was very dark, very wooden and very close to the border. In fact, you could see it from his window, just across the rail track. I felt this was deliberate and Matthew took him to town on the fact that he didn't have the balls to live in his own city. Occasionally, he would stay over, but he had to protect his family. The signs were all there – he spoke very good English with an American twang. It's almost as though he was a Yank, freelancing across the border on a daily basis.

In answer to the question on why the police couldn't contain the violence, he said he had taken up the offer from President Calderón to use the military – corruption was right at the heart of the police. That's why a blind eye had always been turned. We had half an hour with him, and his mobile never stopped ringing. He could only see us first thing in the morning. Everything about him and his entourage said stressful life, a man with a never-ending problem which wasn't getting any better. He was on a hiding to nothing, and it would always be that way. The threats, he said, came with the territory. Hence, his close protection team. I asked him if he varied his routes.

'That's a bit difficult,' he replied. 'There are only two routes.'

But he did vary his times for going home, and he had the benefit of sitting in a VIP lane. Otherwise he would be unlikely to serve the three-year term without someone having a pop at him as he sat in traffic every night. It was a thankless task.

From the mayor's office, we were taken to a military parade – many wore balaclavas to protect their identity so there would be no repercussions in their civilian lives. Then, we asked to film at the morgue as the latest round of bodies were brought in. In the end, they decided that we didn't have the right permits, so Ricardo suggested we go out to the cemetery. Funerals were two a penny. Indeed, as we pulled up, a cortège was leaving. It was like a Clint Eastwood movie, bouncing along this dirty old track in the dusty red hot desert – this slow convoy departing the graveyard. As we approached, there was almost a stand-off as Ricardo wound down the window to ask if we could film and if they would talk on camera. We were gutted to miss the main event, as heartless as that sounds. Their crying and wailing would have been the ideal shot. As the statistics verified, the victims were young.

Our only other option was to talk to the staff at the graveyard. They would know more than most. The manager told us to walk down past these tacky ready-made wreaths for sale in the direction of the unmarked graves. That was the true face of war. Bodies that had been blown to bits or for whom no descendants had ever come looking were dumped at the end, paid for by the council. For some, they had found ID and attached a cross to them. To the right, little metal plaques stood on sticks – all unmarked. Further back, some had been identified and had roses on them. We spoke to the main gravedigger – a real cowboy-type character aged around sixty-five. He was paid per grave, and he did as he was told.

Day in, day out, he dug. That was all he did. It was a horrible job but somebody had to do it. He looked withdrawn, slightly haunted.

What on earth did he go home and say at night? I looked him in the eye and knew that 'seen too much death' look which made you immune to it. He had probably seen as much as me, but for him it had a lasting legacy. Each body that he buried was a message from the cartels. Mess with us, and this is where you will end up. And there was no emotion about it – you wouldn't get two days resting in a refrigerated morgue like at home. Here, you just get dumped in a box and buried in the ground. It was a strange, quiet, eerie place – a real rarity to find a marked grave. This was so different to the aftermath of the tsunami, when the unmarked graves were understandable. There, hundreds of thousands were killed in an instant and there weren't the resources to clean up immediately. This was self-destruction, and you would surely know if a family member didn't come home that night. We were talking only small numbers every day but the statistics came in the accumulation. There hadn't been a natural disaster wiping out communities in Ciudad Juárez.

Were they unmarked because they had brought shame on the family? Or was it simply that some had had hands and heads cut off and were nearly unidentifiable? It was that brutal at times. The price of life was minimal. I hadn't even seen such atrocities in Bosnia. If you were on the wrong side of the cartels, then you were doomed. It didn't shock me but it left its mark. Had anyone seen more death and burials than me, and indeed, had anyone seen more different ways to die?

It was the first time this story had aired at home. News were happy. Generally, it was a part of the world that the traditional audience weren't over-bothered about. Equally, coverage of Central America was poor on domestic television. I knew it was a fantastic story, and we would be coming back. I would position myself in the office as the expert in Ciudad Juárez security. Next time, we had to go out and film at night, hoping to get lucky. Of course, in Ciudad Juárez, our luck would be somebody else's misfortune.

By 13 November, we were back out there. In between, I scanned the net for anything and everything to do with Ciudad Juárez. If it was reported that there were more than ten deaths, I made a special note in my Juárez book. (When there was another free trip coming, like the class swot, I always gathered as much evidence as I could to help the story on its way.) I read an article which put the number of deaths for 2008 at 6,000. In the world of news, sometimes you only needed an anniversary or a landmark number to get a story moving again. Remarkably, the total number of women dead stood at 2,754 including the first decapitated female. It was clearly unusual for the majority not to be overwhelmingly male. Since 2006, a total of 28,000 people had died. To put that into context, it was more than the number of American military casualties in Iraq and Afghanistan combined.

And yet, since our previous visit, the story had barely been covered. I started up on the email again with Ian and drip feeding the Ten, whetting their appetites so they couldn't ignore me. There was no specific reason to return now, such as an election for which this would be a key issue, but Ciudad Juárez was clearly in meltdown. Our motivation to go was that if we didn't, somebody else would have our story. It was time to get back out there. Suddenly, Juárez was back on the agenda.

Money was again an issue: it was hard to justify funding a great story that on paper prompted minimal interest in Britain. The window to make the story was so short and things were so tight in stumping the cash that I had to fly Economy to New York. Not even Craig Summers wanted a news story that bad! Life had been pretty normal this year. I'd done a job on fraudulent call centres in Delhi, been out to check out South Africa for next year's World Cup and was just back from the Afghan elections with John. Oh yeah, I'd bought some armoured cars in Salt Lake City too. Nothing too interesting, then! I did the decent thing. As a Gold Card member, it was time to cash in some air miles and get an upgrade! Why break the habit of a lifetime?

When we landed, we were straight back out there. With body armour in tow and the med-pack on board, we hit the streets immediately with the army. Ricardo wasn't with us – his mother-in-law was in hospital. We went directly to overt filming. Darkness fell at 6 p.m. – that meant the curtain came up on trouble. As soon as the lights went out, the killings would start. We met our escorts at the police station. My adrenalin was in overdrive. I couldn't get out into Ciudad Juárez quick enough, organising the cops myself and urging them to let me drive! Matthew and Chuck took the front vehicle so if they came across anything they would be first there; Ian and I brought up the rear. Two cops were standing in the back, blues and twos on the vehicle, and their weapons pointing out. I loved it.

'Do you want to go inside the vehicle?' they intimated for safety.

I couldn't help my reply. 'No way, José.' I found myself delivering the punchline of the century.

We pegged it out of the station, hurtling down the road with grit flying everywhere. I took stills for the website as we flew through the streets. We pulled up at a checkpoint – Chuck jumped out to see what was happening and take some general shots. All of a sudden, there was a big commotion. The police sergeant was shouting into the walkie-talkie.

'Back in the vehicles, back in the vehicles,' he screamed.

The lights were flashing and we were off again. It felt like Formula One. I was hanging on in the back, like being on a ride at theme park. It was fun but scary, real life. I tried to lean round the side to see what was going on.

'Cuerpo ... cuerpo!' was all I heard.

'It's a body, it's a body!' I shouted to Ian.

We screamed round the bend, down a side street and screeched to a halt. There was a car in front of us. The locals were surrounding the black saloon – the driver's door was open and the police had masks on their faces. I shouted to Chuck to get in there and film. I rushed forward with Ian, taking pictures of the scorch marks on the side of his cheek.

'They are not bullet holes, mate,' I said to Ian.

'They are saying that's where he's been shot in the face,' he replied.

To the side of the car, a woman was screaming. It was her husband. We were standing in a crime scene, in a pool of blood with cartridges all around us, but none of the local police were bothered. It was a mess. We were contaminating evidence and they didn't care. I'm sure this was the same night after night.

'He's only a mechanic ... why have they done this to him?' the wife was screaming.

I knew there was more to this. As I took pictures, it was obvious that they weren't the gun shots. Then a copper pulled the victim's jacket aside. There were four large bullet holes just above the heart. They had shot him there just to make sure. They had done it up close with 9mm bullets, and they had rebounded and hit him on the face.

While I was taking pictures and Matthew was trying to get the wife to talk on camera, one of the police came running over to order us into the car. Something serious had come over the radio. We hadn't had this much luck on our last visit. Matthew and Chuck grabbed their stuff and jumped in, as we floored it out of one crime scene to another, with no idea where we were heading. As we approached a roundabout downtown, we saw a white Suzuki Jeep ahead, lights flashing. They were beginning to cordon it off. There was a body on the floor, covered with a jacket.

'Two people have been killed,' one policeman said. 'The other is inside the car.'

You could see that there were four bullet holes in the side and one at the rear; all around, cartridges lay on the floor. The gold of the bullet glistened in the night sky. I was stopped from taking pictures despite having taken loads already. Local TV had also turned up, and only those who knew the police officers were allowed to film. As I walked round the vehicle, the police telling me to move back even though I was with them, I spotted a priest coming across the roundabout and thought I had to get this. I was on a job and this was going to be the last rites shot. I kept telling the cops I was travelling with them but still they tried to move me. The priest lifted the body off the jacket.

The victim was seven years old. That hit home.

As you would expect, the clergy made the sign of the cross. The priest escorted the grandfather towards the body. As he saw the face of the young boy, he held his face and began screaming. He had already identified his own son in the car – a 28-year-old called Raúl. I knew we had a great story, whatever the human cost.

I needed to know what had happened. All along the passenger side of the brand spanking new white Jeep, it was just covered in blood. As I stood there taking the pictures, I was filled in on the details.

'The young boy tried to get out after his dad was shot. Because the kid could identify the gunman, he shot the lad. And as he tried to get out and crawl away from the vehicle, he shot him again. About five metres in front of the vehicle, he collapsed. The gunman shot him again,' the eye-witness told me in Spanish.

Chuck filmed the lot.

'What has he done to deserve this?' the wife bellowed. Another girl screamed his name.

This was a street on which many had been killed before. Fifteen had been slain on this stretch alone. Just for drugs. All the relatives and friends started turning up. It was hysteria. When they spoke, they covered their faces and didn't reveal their names, anxious not to join the ever-growing list of 'killed by association'. The jeep said money and, round here, that meant drugs. It was obvious to me that the victim had been followed. The previous victim was mowed down by his house – that told you he had been targeted. We hung around as long as we could. We had our story. Unlike our previous visit, we had struck gold within hours of arriving.

Ian and I discussed our plan. It was now half nine at night. We had some cracking stuff; all we needed was a piece to camera from Matthew to add to the one he had done in the back of the truck on the way to the first murder, and we had more than enough for the night. We would need to get back over the border to package it. Unless another murder came in sharpish, we would call it a day. Ten minutes later, the blues and twos were on again.

'This is crazy,' I said to Ian. We were bombing it down to a corner of a road on the side of a hill – all the street lights were out. It looked like we were walking into a trap. There was a gunman on the roof.

'Put your vests on,' I shouted to Chuck and Matthew. We took refuge in the drainage ditches beside the road. All of a sudden, we were off, running with the cops and chasing them, chasing proper villains. All the police had their pistols drawn. I loved it. The policeman motioned to the roof. 'Over on the roof, over on the roof,' I shouted to Chuck.

Two of the police were scrambling across it. Chuck desperately tried to get up there but couldn't make it. Nor could he see his footing because of the pitch black. Instead he followed the police into the house. This was proper brave camerawork, following them in, clearing each room. There was nothing. No gunman, no bodies.

I was gutted. I was all up for a bit of Miami Vice. What it showed was how bad things now were, and that the army-controlled police had more than their work cut out, racing from one incident to another on a nightly basis. Sometimes they would arrive in time; at others they would be left cleaning up the mess. Equally, there would be nights when the cartels or their hired hit men would flee and live to fight another day. Inevitably, both parties would run into each other again soon.

Driving back through downtown Ciudad Juárez, we were on a high. I pegged it back to the border. We all bantered about what we had seen – life was cheap and if you play these games you get burned. The child was unfortunate and the only one I felt something for but the dad was knee deep in shit. It was a proper cartel assassination. He had thrust this his family's way and deserved his fate. We had got what we'd come for.

The next day we had been invited to meet Ramos in the city prison. He had been a schoolteacher for three or four years, earning no more than $500 a month. He also had a second career. Ramos used to drive across the border as a drug mule. For that, he would get $500 per day! What a waste of a life for an educated man, capable of influencing the next generation. He was in the slammer for a decade. He had gone undetected for two years and had no regrets – he was feeding his family on a handsome income. Now, he had a lot of time to think and a lot to be remorseful about. He had been caught with drugs in his spare tyre. In that moment, his heart sank and he knew the game was up.

The prison was massively overcrowded. Ramos was one of four people in his cell. It was like an army barracks in there – the various cartels had their own blocks on each of the three floors. Previously, in March, there had been a massacre in the prison when some twenty people were killed. I wasn't surprised. If the police had lost control of the streets to the gangs, the justice system had also caved in on the inside. The gangs did their own security in their own cell blocks – some of them huge big Mexicans, tattooed all over with a fearsome look in their eyes. Being inside meant nothing to them – their power still reigned – and we were just wandering in among them with no warden accompanying us! I approached one of them to see if they minded if we film. It was no problem at all, though they asked for their faces not to be shown.

I wasn't scared, but I didn't want to hang around. There were some very nasty people in there, and it looked like a place where guards knew best to turn a blind eye. They were all in balaclavas – again, for fear of repercussions on the outside. It had taken 250 police and army to quash the two-hour riot last time. There was no doubt where the balance of power lay here.

That said, I liked Ramos. Predictably, I think he had found God inside. He knew he had fucked up. He was a genuinely nice guy and was now paying the price. Though, as was the way, the drug cartels were still looking after his family. Ramos alluded to this when Matthew asked him how his family were surviving now, given those vast riches before, and that meant one thing. When he came out, the cycle would repeat itself. He was a crook with a record; often the only work they could find when they came out was more of the same, plus he was now indebted to the mob for maintaining his status quo while he took one for them. His life was technically over – he was on a retainer. He would either end up shot, or back inside. An intellectual among thugs, he would quickly conclude that the smart thing to do was to avoid splitting ranks and dobbing anyone in.

He told us he had loved being a schoolteacher, but with two kids and his own mum and dad living in the same house, he needed the money. He actively went looking for the work, and in this part of the world, it was easy to find. Everyone knew the score about the unofficial industry of Ciudad Juárez. You were never going to be part of the familia's inner circle but you could be a very well-rewarded nephew or cousin.

He was better educated than me, and in truth society needed him out there. Now he was doing a decade inside because he wanted to feed his family. I didn't feel for him, but I did for the system. Despite his obvious crime, there was nothing dishonest or criminal about him. There was a demand for the drugs business; he was the supplier who didn't ask any questions. He was caught up in it. Ramos knew what he was getting into, he was not an innocent victim, but I found myself having some sympathy where my sentiment over the baby in the tsunami or Stuart's foot had been nothing but a functional reaction. I respected what he did for his family. If I'm being objective, there were still 1.5 million people in Ciudad Juárez earning $200 a month who hadn't turned to crime, and this guy was organised by the prison service to talk to us. He wanted to put his story out there so he would look good and society would look favourably on him. It was the age-old problem for us, a bit like like being embedded. If you want access, you will take whoever gets put up for interview. We weren't going to get a cartel member on camera.

Ramos was the most interesting person we met, even though there were both players and pawns in there. It was generally a housing estate for the low life, and your manor was your manor. A turf war could kick off again at any point. A cursory glance could cost you your life. He told me as well that he'd never thought he would get caught, and I could well imagine that after the first run, and then a week of scurrying across the border, followed by a month that turned into a year, you would start to feel invincible. Of course, as soon as you had entered the game just once, you were trapped in the system. Whether you were caught or not, you were trapped. And Ramos still had time to do. Lots of it.

Next, we went on a sightseeing tour of Ciudad Juárez, checking out the areas of interest, sniffing out where the cartels hung around. We saw, first-hand, the work of the baby assassins at a bar on the corner – that fascinated me, that they had used the kids as patsies to do their dirty work. It was almost as fanatical as some parts of the Middle East or Afghanistan – start them young. We saw one bar where 'Jesus, The Devil' had been gunned down, just three days after getting out of jail. He had been shot seven times in the head. We were on a murder tour of the city. At one house, fourteen bodies were found inside. In disasters and wars, you could understand it but that figure was incredible. Assassination was a stronger word than murder, but this was exactly what was going on. Our guide didn't know the story but they were linked to the cartels – people had stopped asking about the details. It was all so matter-of-fact, so normal and routine, so everyday in Ciudad Juárez. We had got the picture, and we had got the pictures. Why this story hadn't been investigated before and why Ciudad Juárez wasn't a watchword around the world like Lockerbie, Dunblane or Beirut was beyond me. This was officially the most dangerous city in the world and nobody was talking about it. I felt totally vindicated that Ian and my hunch had paid off. In fact, we had so much footage now that anything else was just duplication.

That meant that, as with any Craig Summers trip, there had to be some me time. I wanted to go up Main Street during the day to see how it functioned in daylight.

'Have you heard of the Kentucky Bar?' our chaperone asked. Ah yes, the Kentucky Bar! 'It's where the margarita was invented.'

It was the strongest margarita I had ever tasted – like fuel. So powerful was it that I had to have two just to be sure. I couldn't stand the drink, but I loved a bit of history. To be sat in this dingy bar that Hollywood A-listers used to frequent was the icing on the cake for a great trip. I toasted myself at the same bar where Liz Taylor and Richard Burton used to come to drown their sorrows and from which Steve McQueen and Jack Dempsey would crawl out on all fours. Today, there was hardly anyone in there, only the memorabilia on the walls signposting a different era and a glorious past. Nowadays, of course, none of the big names could take their chance on a night out in Juárez.

The next night, we were due to leave. Before that, we had one more job to do. We got the call that the funerals of the victims we had seen on our first night out would be tomorrow or the day after. We were invited to the house to see the father lying there in an open coffin. On the approach at the corner plot, five guys in sunglasses were standing outside looking very shady on their mobiles. That said a cartel house to me. You don't just have five burly blokes outside your front door for no reason. I took the wheel, staring at them staring back at us. With all of us crammed into the back of a US-plated 4x4, we must have looked dodgy, too. People like us didn't come down this way.

We couldn't find the victim's house, and I didn't really want to drive back past the house on the corner. There were no street signs. We stopped to ask for directions. I could see the local gesturing a left and I knew what was coming – I was heading straight back that way, one block along. I didn't like it one bit, but there were no other options. As I turned, I tried not to look across. The hairs on the back of my neck stood up. I couldn't stop myself glancing at the corner house. Then I floored it past to the top of the hill. I could see the mob chatting on their phones again in the rear mirror. In reality, we were only about fifty metres away all the time, but we just struggled to find the street – you can see how close the victim lived to the cartel.

Finally, we turned and saw a line of cars. I recognised one of the guys from the other night. We were told to wait while our middleman went in to clear the way.

'Look at them over there,' I said to Ian. 'They're just standing there looking at us.'

'Let's do something rather than sitting here like idiots.'

Moments later, we were in, much to my relief. I walked past the mourners, offering a hand to shake as we were led into a yard out the back. The return of the handshake told me we would be fine. In the yard, all the men were sitting around. When the camera came in, they turned away, hiding behind their hoodies and shades. From there, a doorway took us into the front room where the coffin was laid out. The casket said drug money – and lots of it. This wasn't a poor family. Chuck was free to film the family, head in hands all around. Matthew interviewed the victim's sister.

Part of the coffin was open – there was a picture of the father and the son. The man had separated from the child's mother. For that reason, the two weren't being buried together. The father would be the day after; later, the son would have a service with two other young victims. We asked permission to attend and made our way to the church. It was rammed. Even though funerals like this were happening every day, you always got a good send-off. Why? Because so many people were wrapped up in the drugs trade. There was the family ... and there was the family. The son's wreath, attached to this huge fuck-off Chevvy, confirmed that. Again, I recognised the grandparents from the other night. It had been the grandfather who had identified him. It was also the same priest who had administered the last rites at the scene. Today, the boy's coffin had a football shirt draped over it.

The priest kindly let us take some general shots inside the church but asked us not to film during the mass. The family asked us not to go to the graveside. I didn't really want to go back a second time to that cold, lonely place that we had visited earlier in the year.

We showed the boy the maximum respect. I felt less for his father and could only conclude that the parents had split because the mother had found out about the drug running. The boy actually lived in El Paso and went to school there on an American passport. He had no reason to be back in Ciudad Juárez other than to see his narcotic-peddling dad. That had cost him.

It was a strange day. And from there we left: one minute at a funeral, the next back at the airport. I was pleased to get out – in hindsight, our first visit had served as a fact-finder. This time we had got what our hunch had indicated and hadn't really busted a gut. Murders, funerals, the mob, and prisons – inside three days, and all daily reminders of the self-destruction that was Ciudad Juárez. We walked straight into it. It was a great story but it was on a plate. And there was no stopping it. In Ciudad Juárez, it wasn't really news at all.

DAD

I t was February 2010, when Paul Easter became my boss. He had come straight from the Intelligence Corps, where he had been lieutenant colonel. Things were changing at the Beeb. Even though they were nominated for awards, trips like Ciudad Juárez would be more highly scrutinised than ever. Cost and manpower came to the heart of decision-making as never before; form-filling was rife, meetings relentless, and getting funding for stories was a process of self-justification that never ended. In the new leaner keener BBC, if you couldn't do it on multi-platforms, forget it.

From the start, I didn't get on with Easter. While we were fine socialising, I sensed I was being looked at with suspicion – a top-heavy cost who was away a lot, and who then came back with raucous tales of adventure and a massive expenses claim. I never failed though, Sex Trafficking the only time I missed out (narrowly) on delivering the goods.

Easter hadn't been long on the job that time he had rung me in Baghdad, where I was covering the Iraqi elections with John and dealing with everything that brought, but was also in the process of spending a quarter of a million quid of BBC cash buying armoured cars from the States. My trip was scheduled for my return. He rang to cancel it. I was short with him, explaining that you didn't just go and spend that kind of public money over the phone. The professional thing to do was to get out there and handle the deal yourself. Goodness, over the years I had inspected every vehicle as though my life depended on it, and as we had found with the dodgy motors that Hanif tried to flog me in Kabul, it was the right thing to do. Besides, I was on assignment. It was neither the time nor the place.

I felt the noose tightening. I wasn't on his team. It had started when he mocked me early on for being in a photo on the wall with John. True, I wasn't the face on TV. That didn't mean I didn't have my place in the great stories of the past decade, many of them with John.

My opinion was that he was the wrong man for the job. I didn't think he understood the media. I was a guy at the coalface and he was destined for a desk. I was brought in to be the deployable security guy who got his hands dirty. That wasn't his style. As good as the adventure had been, I knew my days were numbered or that my role would change. Though I had never been one for the money, I realised I had reached a ceiling in terms of pay and bonuses. The trips were my pocket money out of a fun BBC budget that I lived off but didn't have direct access to. If they were drying up, then so was my appetite. I had started to think about an exit plan.

Then, on 1 April, my mum rang. 'Your dad's died,' she said.

'What?' I was stunned.

'Your dad's died.'

I had spent much of the previous two months going back and forth to Spain where they now lived. Dad loved it out there, and Mum said she had done it for him. It wasn't the typical 1970s and 1980s dream of that generation that made them go. It was actually my idea, one they had never even considered. Dad had never been happier.

Sadly, he had been seriously ill that February and had just recovered. Then we lost him. All the deaths that I had seen and, finally, one came along that ripped my soul in two. I knew several things were on a collision course. Nothing felt right any more. I would still do the World Cup in South Africa that summer but everything happens for a reason and Dad's massive heart attack at the age of seventy-nine was a sign. My heart was no longer in it either.

He also had skin cancer, albeit under control, and he spent Christmas 2009 in hospital with pneumonia. He had begun to talk the odd bit of nonsense, slightly deliriously. I am bound to say, he had a good innings. After he had recovered from the illness in February, I had taken him out for some lunch. He was eating for the first time in ages, and there was some colour back in his cheeks. While I was at the bar ordering him a bitter shandy, he was telling Sue all about his childhood on the farm. Much of what he said was strange. It was classic preparing-for-death language, going deep into his past as his circle came round for the final time.

Back home, Mum asked me to take him up for a shower. He had been a strong old boy, but I could see how bony he had become. I propped him up with a book and went downstairs to get him a drink. Dad looked tired. He didn't seem the same person. When I came back up, he was asleep. The book, which the old Dad would have read in an afternoon, was barely opened. After the previous visit to the hospital, the surgeons told us that they had found white shavings around his lungs on the X-ray. He was too old to operate on and they didn't really know what it was. Dad had been determined to carry on as long as possible. Now, even though you never think your own dad will die, he looked defeated. From downstairs, I suddenly heard him scream out. I asked Mum what it was. She told me that it was now a regular occurrence to hear Dad wailing and screaming through the night. Nobody knew why. Was this the near-death experience – literally a nightmare of a lifetime's experiences flashing by? Was it pain from the lungs? Was he more in the subconscious than the conscious? I couldn't know.

He was rolling around in the bed, so I woke him. He had no idea of what had gone on. We were due home the next day and I asked Mum if she wanted Sue and me to stay. Dad was due to start taking heavy medication and, deep down, the writing was on the wall. Mum said to go and to keep in touch by phone.

When we returned, Sue's dad was also unwell. We looked at each other, thinking the same. This was definitely the last year for both of them.

When I rang a couple of days later, I could tell the drugs were kicking in. Dad just sounded completely different, but in a good way. He was chatting for England, as though the tablets had given him a new lease of life. At the beginning of March, we went out again for a long weekend. Everything he talked about was clear and concise. The weather was picking up, and he was the most coherent he had been in months. I suddenly began to think everything was going to be fine. I genuinely went home unconcerned.

Sue's dad was eighty-seven. He was a man who had nine lives – a miner and a smoker, too. He had caught MRSA in hospital and had his toe removed. He also had only one kidney. No longer able to live in his bungalow, he had moved in with Sue's sister. That, in the short term, eased the burden.

We had a lot on – we both had full-time jobs and one minute we were in Spain, the next going up and down to Mansfield for Sue. I would ring Spain to talk to Dad. He would ask me if I was getting ready for the World Cup, talking like it was twenty years ago. The nightmares had gone, he was eating a bit and definitely perking up. Mum said it was solely the drugs. I was heading into Easter feeling a lot more relaxed about the situation.

Just before the bank holiday weekend, I had agreed to meet Chas Staines on the Thursday. Chas was an old buddy from my security days and we would hook up every few weeks or so. We agreed to meet at the old fire station at Waterloo. The night before, on the Wednesday, Dad had called. The medics were putting him on an oxygen bottle.

'What do you mean?' I had said.

'You know, one of those things you walk round the house with, strapped to you to help you breathe,' he replied. I asked him why they were doing that – he said the doctors had recommended it.

'That's not a bad thing. That's not the end of the world,' I told him. I knew that the portable oxygen machines were brilliant.

'That's it now; I'm trapped. Speak to your mother.'

They had delivered the big bottle to the house and given him a small portable one for when he was out so he didn't feel housebound. The medics were coming back a day later to set everything up properly. They didn't need to.

Dad died the next day.

He was from that generation where they didn't talk about things, but even though we weren't close, I couldn't pinpoint anything that would have caused him distress in flashback before the drugs gave him the short-term relief. Born on a farm in Scotland in 1930, he had worked all his life and hadn't been an evacuee during the war. Like many dads from that era, he shared very little with me. He once told me of his biggest disappointment – getting turned down for a coaching job at Swindon Town Football Club when he came out of the military in 1972. He had also been an extra in the movie *The Wooden Horse* and played the role of a stretcher-bearer in the classic *Dunkirk*. His own dad had left his wife and served for fifty years in the merchant navy. He had sailed convoys across the Atlantic during the war, dying in 1969 in the Greenwich Seaman's Home. I knew virtually nothing of his DNA. In fact, I can't say I knew Dad well at all.

It was only in death, of course, that I realised this. Even though a friend of mine had told me when Dad was ill to say everything I wanted to or be left with a lifetime of regrets, I never got round to it. It's stupid, I know. Of course, from having not really known him at all, I suddenly wanted to know him like there was no tomorrow. But now tomorrow would never come.

If I saw a picture, it would upset me. A lifetime of dodging and dealing with death professionally now crashed into my personal world, and all those bodies and families that, machine-like, I had dealt with as part of the job ... well, I crossed over onto their side of the road for the first time. I don't know if I had lots to tell him, but

I wanted the right to do so. He loved all my stories and adventures, watching everything I did. He knew about the baby at the tsunami and Harry's Game – stories I would have given minimalistic details of to Mum and Sue. I didn't think I needed to unload this stuff, but he knew more than most. Dad would never say he was proud of what I had become since he dragged me out of that court to the army but he did let me know in the way that his generation did.

'I saw you on that *Panorama* ... I read about Friendly Fire ...' That was his way. And I was grateful for the life he had chosen for me after I turned my back on school. He had played a blinder, and I wouldn't turn the clock back. Occasionally over the years he would bring it up jokingly but he never ever judged. 'Did that really go on?' was as tough as his moral line went.

When I would say that of course it had, he would urge me to tell him more and to get to the good bit, always interrupting at the crucial times, asking a million questions. I was an audio version of the books he loved to read, playing the narrator. His desire to know the story perhaps said we had more in common than I realised – both military men, but with me given the chance to take those skills into the modern era of media, something only the Oxbridge elite would have chanced upon in his day.

As he would listen to me recounting the stories, he was living them with me in person. I think in the end we showed love in this way, without knowing it. His enthusiasm for my stories met my desire to tell them – it was an unspoken thank you from me for showing me the way at such a young age, and a massive show of pride from him that he had steered his boy from going off the rails. When I took that call after four or five pints with Chas, I knew that there would be no more stories. This was his last chapter.

Mum told me he'd gone up to bed feeling unwell. Then he said he was going to be sick, so she went for the bucket. When she returned, he had passed away.

'What?' was all I could say.

He had seemed so well lately, yet so empty the previous night when he was telling me about the the oxygen supply. Was that it all took? Was it one dent in your recovering confidence that would finish you off or had the medics actually identified brilliantly that Dad was about to take a turn for the worse again? I would never know, of course.

Mum seemed strong. I went into organisational mode. She had her friend Scarlett to take immediate care of her while the doctors took Dad away. She said they had been very kind. I rang Sue. She said she would come and collect me. I had to call my daughters Charlotte and Kate first. Chas came out to get me because I had been gone for half an hour.

'Come inside and let's have a drink and a chat,' he tried to console me.

I don't think whatever anyone says to you at this point goes in, as well-meaning as they are. You hear them but you don't listen. You speak but you're not in a conversation. I toasted my dad. Then burst into tears. Of all the deaths, this was the only one that rocked me.

I wanted to give him a good send-off. It was 21.40 in Spain on a bank holiday weekend at home. I rang Paul Easter, who just said to go. I called the special BBC 24-hour desk and told them I had to get to Alicante in the morning – as soon as possible.

'£364,' the muppet at the end of the line stunned me. The flight would leave at 07.30.

'Put it in on the charge card for News ...' I said.

'Oh, I can't do that,' she replied. 'You have to pay for it.'

It was always the way. If I had phoned in work time, I would have sorted it because they knew me. Not on the eve of a four-day weekend, though. My mobile then rang. Monarch had declined my BBC Amex Card. Did I have a card that would cover it? How could Monarch Airline not accept the BBC credit card and what the hell were they charging that much for? You didn't need grief at a time of grief.

Sue would follow me out later.

At Mum's house, Scarlett told me the undertakers were coming that evening to sort the cremation.

'What about the insurance?' I asked Mum.

'Well, we haven't got any,' she replied.

'What about money?' I said.

'Well, we haven't got any of that either.'

I told her not to worry, and went into clinical mode. It was the only way I knew how to operate and it was the only device I had to protect myself. We drew up a list of all the things we needed to do. I told her if we didn't contact the Military Pensions, they would end up taking the money back off us.

Before I knew it, the undertaker was at the door. He was a real gentleman, speaking perfect English. He was first class, but then perhaps much of his business was elderly British people, and even in death, there was always a salesman. I was now on the receiving end of people organising death. He showed me the brochure. Unbelievably, a brochure.

I told him I was not spending thousands of pounds on a casket that was going to be burned – that was a waste of money and Dad wouldn't want that. He showed me the urns on the back page. The parents of those poor kids in Ciudad Juárez would have been through this. Drug money, though, would have paid for their send-off.

'Take me to the front page with the cheapest coffin.' I didn't want to waste any time or money.

He took me to page two. 'You know what, Mr. Summers, there's no point spending that much. You are correct. I could sit here like a salesman but that's wrong,' the undertaker said.

I told him I wanted to spend £75 and take the ashes home. It was holiday in the UK and I wanted it over as soon as possible. We settled on the Tuesday evening at 5 p.m.

'Would you like to see your dad?' he asked. I said I would.

The undertaker was supremely professional. He didn't mention money, and was efficient, thorough and had integrity. I aspired to be the same in my line of work. I respected that.

And it took me back into operational mode. I told Mum that we had to leave messages on answer phones in the morning. You heard horror stories of people getting fleeced because they had been slow to record loved ones' deaths. I said I would ring BT, the army, the Pensions, everyone. If it meant speaking into a voicemail, so be it. It was on the record that my dad had died at this time and on this day. There would be no doubt.

At 7 p.m., I drove Mum to the chapel to see Dad for the last time. The undertaker was there on schedule. Even though we had a lot in common professionally, I could never have done his job, despite having done those duties several times over. I offered him a down payment straightaway, even though he was ushering me in. In all it came in at 3,500 euros.

Then it was time to see Dad. The chapel where he lay would be the same for the service. Two young Spanish lads hustled out and said it was ready. It was all so very strange, as though the king was summoning us. Mum went in first – she hadn't seen him since he had passed away. She went in briefly but came out too upset.

Then it was my turn. I'm not religious in any way, but the stained-glass window behind the altar was stunning. It felt perfect. Then I saw the coffin and felt I had done Dad an injustice. It looked cheap. As I got closer, he looked good, absolutely brilliant – like the Dad I remembered. They had done a really good job on him.

I leant over, said very little, almost nothing, just staring at him, and walked back out. It couldn't have been ninety seconds. Despite the number of bodies that I had seen, I didn't know what to say or how to behave. In my mind, I was thinking, I'll be seeing you Dad, but I just didn't know what I was supposed to do.

Did it change my attitude to Banda Aceh, to Stuart, to Kaveh, to Kate and to all the others? I don't know. It reminded me of all those clichés about one life and all that. The difference still remained that in all those stories, I was on a job and that was what the job was. For work, there was a dead body. In real life, there was a dead body that was part of me.

The funeral was Tuesday 6 April. My daughters and Sue were over – they went straight to see Dad before they sealed the coffin. The Spaniards often leave the lid off or open but that wasn't for me. Kate went in first but came out bawling. Walking down the aisle, Charlotte said she didn't think she could do it either.

'Don't worry about it; you can,' I consoled her. 'You just have to remember Dad as he was. He doesn't look any different. Just come with me.'

I held her, walking forward to the coffin. She looked inside, saw him, and turned around in tears. 'I can't do it, Dad,' she cried.

That just left me to say goodbye for the last time. I didn't linger. I couldn't. In some ways it was easier to leave this time, because the girls needed me outside. That gave me the reason not to spend any more time than I needed to. One thing remained consistent with all the bodies that I had seen, even though this was different. There was nothing more to say. Nothing was bringing him back. I said farewell, then followed the girls out.

I didn't know how to behave – death was all about organisation, filing a report and putting recommendations for next time. I had never seen it as something close to home.

Kate wrote a poem that she wanted to read with Charlotte, I somehow composed a eulogy that I didn't realise I was capable of, and between us, we all figured out Dad would only want to go out to the sound of Johnny Mathis. Different generation!

I got talking to Mum's brother, Graham – a decent, salt of the earth guy who once had trials with Wolves. He looked up to my dad – we filled the void chatting, and he told me more than Dad ever did really, explaining how Mum and Dad got together, even recalling their first date. It took me back to how Sue and I met while I was on leave from Ireland, in the Nelson pub in Poole, Dorset.

There was time to kill before the funeral. Fifty locals of similar age to Dad were coming. I sorted the money behind the bar. I needed it over. I decided to go for a run to get it out of my system, loading up the Springsteen to clear my head. It was an odd thing to do, but I was so unused to a funeral in a personal capacity.

Dad wouldn't have wanted suits, so I insisted on smart casual and took the lead. Outside the church, dozens of friends of his, who had made up Little England along the Spanish coastline, all came to pay respects. I recognised many from the bar. They probably knew that this day would be theirs soon enough but it told me he was well liked and that made me happy. To make the move out here so late in life and then for Dad's life to have been unhappy was no way to go. I hoped he would have called these the best years of his life.

It was a strange conveyor belt process. A Spanish family were in an adjacent chapel at the same time burying their own. Sue sat with Mum on the front row. Misty was playing in the background. After a few words from the resident English vicar, it was my turn to deliver the eulogy. I didn't do this kind of thing. I delivered safety briefings and shouted a lot in tense situations. I wasn't the kind of guy to whisper gentle thoughts. Out of my comfort zone, all I cared about was not letting Dad down.

John Lawrence Bigham Summers was born in Ardrossan Scotland on the 11th of the 11th in 1930.

John was one of nine children born to Mary and Joseph and spent the early part of his life in Scotland, where after leaving school he worked on the farm looking after horses.

At the age of 18 John went into National service where he completed his two years' service with the Royal Artillery stationed in the UK. John realised that the army held a future for him and he decided to enlist full time back into the Royal Artillery.

John's potential as a sportsman shone through and he soon passed his PT exam to become the unit instructor. John loved his sport and played rugby, hockey, football and almost anything with a ball!

While serving overseas in Hong Kong he decided along with his mates to send off for pen friends and this is where Doreen came into the equation, forever the young, suave good-looking PT instructor with his film star looks, as he told everyone! The photo captured Doreen's heart and the letters quickly flowed over a period of three years, before they eventually met for their first date. It was love at first sight for both of them and they were married in 1955 after a whirlwind romance.

The next few years were spent in Malaya, Germany, which included seeing active service twice in Cyprus and Malaya.

During that time Doreen gave birth to their son, Craig, born in 1960.

John's military service came to an end in 1972 after an exemplary career of twenty-two years.

John and Doreen decided then to settle in Essex, with their son Craig, where John worked for the Post Office and then BT over the next eighteen years.

John still kept himself busy after retiring at the age of sixty. John and Doreen kept travelling the world on holidays which they both enjoyed. They returned to places that John had served in his military career to show Doreen what it was like. He also loved meeting up with his old buddies at reunions.

John was still active and enjoyed his golf and watching sports as often as Doreen would allow!

In 2001 they both moved to Spain for the sunshine and the laidback lifestyle of which they both took full advantage of until early 2005 when John was diagnosed with cancer. This was a blow to them both and affected their way of life and travel.

However, John the fighter did not show any signs of pain or let anyone know how he was feeling and the strength of the man was slowly wilting. Doreen was also fussing around him, which she is famous for with everyone, and as the years went by John slowly got worse.

In Dec 2009 he was taken to the hospital with pneumonia and a heart attack, which he pulled through and soon returned home to his loving wife.

Time was running out for this straight talking, good-looking man who told it as it was, and I believe he knew his end was near when he asked Doreen to renew their marriage vows.

And on April the first 2010 the big man could not fight any more and passed away peacefully.

John leaves his wife Doreen, son Craig and his wife Sue, and five grandchildren.

Kate and Charlotte followed, each reading half a poem. I was relieved it was over and took my place back in the front row. I was on a different sort of auto pilot to normal, wanting it finished but desperate to do it justice. I glossed over the prayers – those were for Dad and meant nothing to me. I may have changed my perspective on death, but I had seen too much for Dad's passing to show me the door to an afterlife or a religious re-birth. That was all nonsense to me.

Before I knew it, 'Time to say Goodbye' was on and it was the moment to leave. There would be another one along in a minute. That was how it was. We all filed out, leaving the coffin behind, then with great relief hit the bar. I said a few more words, thanked everyone for coming, and toasted my dad.

I was knackered, and didn't want to go through that again soon. Almost as light relief, we found Arsenal getting hammered by Barcelona in the Champions League on a TV in the next room. I asked Mum if she minded if we watched. Most of the blokes followed, and the woman stayed as one. You can justify every-thing by saying it's what Dad would have wanted, but if he had been there he would have had the game on. Of course, it took our minds off things. By half one in the morning, we called time on a long day. Tomorrow was another day.

I took Sue and the girls to the airport and spent the next twenty-four hours sorting out more paperwork, returning home on the Friday. It had been an exhausting, expensive few days.

And I knew I hadn't mourned properly. On my wall at home I hung his medals. Every picture that I would never normally glance at stared back at me. What were once passing thoughts dominated my mind. If Dad were still alive, I should have said a few things – after I split from my first wife I felt that they had taken her side. I regretted that now and wished I could put that right. I loved him more in death than in life, but then don't we all? If I had my time again, I would have found a way to love him in life, too.

SOUTH AFRICA

I tried to throw myself back in to work. It wasn't right though. Normally, I would be relishing a major football tournament overseas. The loss of Dad and Big Brother watching me at work had taken the gloss of things and by the time the departure day of 3 June came, Sue's and my prediction about both our dads had come true. Sue's dad passed away the night before.

Two in two months.

He was a typical no-nonsense working-class man, the father of nine. Life was pit, pub, dinner and sleep, taking Sue's mum out once a week. That was how it was. I got on very well with him – probably because I saw a lot of my dad in him. My relationship with them was also so much better than with my first wife's parents – they always felt she could do better than me.

Sue spent the last days with him. It was obvious the end was near, and so strange that both men went at the same time.

'I genuinely want you to go,' Sue said to me as she broke the news while I was packing for South Africa. She was upset, but it was his time. He was eighty-seven. I never really know with Sue if she means stuff like that or if she wants me to drop everything and head up to Mansfield.

'I will be back for the funeral,' I promised. So I told work that I would have to make several trips, and headed the next day to Heathrow to fly to Cape Town. At Terminal Five, things went from bad to worse – of all the days to find I was in Economy! There were so many of us flying out that day that the plane was packed. In total, the BBC flew nearly 300 people to South Africa. With my Gold Card, I had managed to pick my seat, though. The only way to do this, I thought, was more leg room at the bulk head seat and a few drinks all the way to South Africa. Grim, but beyond my control.

I had passed through immigration when my phone rang. It was the floor manager from *Match of the Day*. 'Where are you, Craig?' Chris White asked. 'We're in Wetherspoons – come and join us.' I found him there with a couple of the assistant producers. Everyone seemed to be thinking the same – down a few to knock you out for the flight.

'Why don't we use my lounge access and have a few freebies in the Business Lounge?' I warmed to the theme. We were flying out of B gate – I knew there was a lounge up there. We chewed the fat, waiting to be called, and sunk our pints. Whitey had six weeks at the World Cup, then was flying straight on to Scotland for the Open. Finally, they called us – I was dreading the eleven hours in Economy. We decided to down one final beer. I didn't do Economy.

'Help me, help me,' I suddenly heard as I was coming down the stairs out of the bar area.

Down below was a BA employee with his mouth jammed tightly. It looked straightaway like he was having an epileptic fit. I handed Whitey my bag and rushed to help. 'Have you called for paramedics?' I asked the other BA staff. 'We need to stop him swallowing his tongue or biting it off. I need something to prize his mouth open.'

The BA girl handed me a plastic fork. 'This is no good,' I looked at her unimpressed. That was the summit of her first-aid training.

'Final call for BA flight ...'

Chris picked up the tannoy among the commotion.

'Look, we're both on that,' I alerted them.

'Don't worry,' the BA staffer said. 'We'll let them know you're going to be slightly late.'

The epileptic began to respond a little once I loosened his uniform. I asked him if he was on any medication – they were in his jacket. Then he began to shake, just as the paramedic was arriving on his bike, and that was my cue to go. We were way late now.

'Thank you so much; you've saved his life,' said the BA manager who'd come over to thank me. I told them that was nonsense.

'Yeah, yeah, you saved his life,' Whitey agreed.

'I just stabilised him,' I said, calming them all down. 'We've got to board now.'

As we walked over to Boarding, I was asked if we had the tickets. 'Yeah, we're in Economy,' I replied, handing them over.

'Don't worry about that; I'll sort that,' the steward replied. I winked at Whitey.

We were the last two to board. The in-flight supervisor approached us. 'I would just like to say thank you for looking after our colleague. Come with me,' she said.

There were two Business Class seats left. We looked at each other. 'This is a great start,' he said.

'Would you like some champagne?' the stewardess offered.

'Why not?' I replied. It was the least I could do!

The rest of the BBC crew had been waiting for us back beyond the curtains. Whitey did the decent thing and popped down to tell them the story! I was shattered again, after another whirlwind twenty-four hours. In less than a week, I would have to make this trip back for the funeral. I didn't bother to ask any more questions about the BA guy back at Heathrow and temporarily parked Sue's dad in my head. I had got my seat and was heading back into the zone.

Knocking back my drinks, I ate everything they threw at me and got my head down – lights out all the way to Cape Town. I only woke as we were landing. It had been a great beginning, but it didn't feel the same. I was living every boy's dream, to be out there at a major sporting event, looking after some of my sporting heroes. Alan Hansen and Shearer, Gary Lineker, Roy Hodgson, Lee Dixon, Jürgen Klinsmann and Clarence Seedorf, among others, were all on my watch. It was a jolly for six weeks, and I knew it.

I was determined to milk it. Things had moved on so much since I filmed undercover at Euro 2000 and again at Germany 2006; my life was changing at a pace even in just the past two months, and dark forces were definitely operating within my department. This time, there was no need for undercover filming: South Africa 2010 didn't attract the scum element of the English soccer fan. Those who were there mostly had money and tickets; they went for the football – not the afters. That meant I was just a chaperone to the stars, in a country where you still needed your wits about you. Mindful of the fact that Sue was having a tough week at home, I was determined to make the most of it, in case for one reason or another it didn't happen again.

I had met many of the ex-players before in some capacity. They had all been invited to a special briefing the week before at Television Centre. I loved that. When I walked in, they had all stared at me. Those who didn't know me must have been thinking, 'Who the fuck is he?' I was that in awe that I needed a drink of water to avoid clamming up. I told them a bit about myself … how I normally went with News but this time was responsible for Sport. This was new to me – I was a bombs and bullets guy. In front of me, I had pupils Hansen, Shearer and Lawrenson in my own classroom! Gary wasn't there for some reason – golf, or a crisp advert, or something … I can't recall. They lasted about three-quarters of an hour. I'm sure this meeting was an irritation to them but they tolerated me! Millionaire ex-pros wanted to talk football on the telly, play golf, and not do much else.

My main message had been common sense. There was petty theft out here, and a little street crime. They needed to be careful in bars and be aware that credit card cloning was now rife in Cape Town – when punching in your number, make sure there was nobody at your shoulder, and don't let the waiter take the card. Use a real wallet and a fake wallet with some out of date credit cards. If you need to hand anything over at gunpoint, you hand the fake one over and you've lost nothing; if you are stopped, don't argue for a second, just give them what they want. Watch yourself in your own hotel room, too. On their salaries, the cleaners would think nothing of pinching anything. By the time they had got home and moved your stuff on, it would be long gone. I gave them each a flier with key numbers and venue info on them. We would see in time who would throw them away the minute the class was over!

Mark Bright and I chatted a lot as we had a mutual friend; Shearer asked about safes in the hotel; Hansen never said a word and Lawro chipped in with the odd camp comment, before calling time on my session and directing everyone to the bar. I would soon find out why Shearer was so bothered about the safes.

The first job in Cape Town was to pick up my accreditation and meet Ernie, whose company was to look after the main security for our roof studio. It had just been a shell when I was last out in January. Now this old morgue was to become the BBC compound. Before we had even gone on air there had already been an attempted break-in to steal a couple of air-conditioning units, of all things. I ordered sensors for the roof. The studio itself was getting a lot of stick in the press at home. We had built it on the top of Somerset Hospital, in the shadow of the new Cape Town Stadium, and had installed a lift and a walkway on the end of the building. Of course, they said we were wasting huge amounts of public money – or in fact, were we just trying to get the best backdrop to the *Match of the Day* studio? Predictably, the *Daily Mail* twisted the knife, implying that Shearer and Hansen couldn't face three flights of stairs, nor did they want to mingle with gunshot and stabbing victims, a ward where forty per cent of the children were in intensive care, or another were many of the neo-natal intake were HIV positive. Our only concerns were Gary and the lift. He had the odd vertigo issue.

It was the usual bullshit. We got it at most tournaments. The essentials were that access in and around the complex was safe, that footage of Table Mountain would be cracking, and that we didn't get in the way of the hospital. In fact, we agreed afterwards that they could take whatever they needed that the BBC didn't want and before we went live every doctor and nurse was invited in to look around.

Immediately, the atmosphere was unlike any other tournament. I would get the BBC bus in and file situation reports back to London, while still cracking on with other paperwork, waiting to see if any of my stars wandered into trouble. I wasn't singing 'No Surrender to the IRA' this time or avoiding vomit in the back of a Stuttgart police van. I was waiting for nothing to happen.

At night, I felt a little bit of a spare part. I was on a per diem allowance of £33 from the BBC. My guess was that Lee Dixon hadn't even bothered to see what expenses the BBC would offer him. It rapidly became Dicko's job to pick the wine – but only after he had consulted his iPhone to peruse the list that Heston Blumenthal had pre-selected him. There was no hovering around the £15 per bottle mark now; Lee went straight to the £200 range. Oh, and several bottles, too. When the bill came, we would all chip in. Lee or one of the other ex-pros would invariably pick up the tab for the vino, much to my relief. It was a different world. The funny thing is, I hated him as a player, being a Hammer. In the real world, he was a top bloke.

On my second day in Cape Town, I was given my toughest assignment yet. Probably worse than Friendly Fire, or hanging on for Košice, tougher than mixing it with gangs on the Czech border or protecting three legends through Surobi, more action-packed than Juárez or more discreet than Zim, this was what I was paid to do. I had to find the lads a safe bar to retreat to after the live *Match of the Day* shows.

This was important stuff. I joke, of course, but it is one of those situations where if Alan Shearer or Gary Lineker wanted to have a drink in private after the game, and they ran into a swaying mob of drunk St Georges or petty crooks, then I'd get it in the neck big time if Lineker couldn't go on air because he was too shaken or physically marked – or worse. As much as you laugh, this was my job.

289

So, in total, I visited three bars. At each, Whitey and I would sit at the counter, knocking them back, watching for trouble. Twankey's was the favourite, and often the boys wouldn't pile out of there before 01.30. There was another on the corner by a hotel, and the third was too far into town to be safe, and we didn't want to be walking there. If you like, I was a body double for Shearer's right arm that would hold his pint. But security on a petty level was key.

At the same time, I got a call from the guy I had charged with security for the Johannesburg end. Already the fun and games had begun. A BBC engineer in the suburb of Melville had been robbed of his wallet containing $200 and his iPod. Back at our studios, I felt it wasn't secure enough. Unbelievably, the security hut had been plonked at the wrong end of the compound. I had to get that moved. The next day – the Sunday – one of the engineers came up to me to say that he'd had money stolen from his hotel room on Mandela Road and that one of the girls had had an attempted break-in on her suitcase. Her loose change had been plundered. It was always the engineers.

Lots of minor time-consuming irritations were starting and we had only been here a couple of days. There was an undercurrent of opportunism – the BBC was a good target. It was time to see the head of security at the hotel, Thys Van Der Meer. He came back swiftly and refunded the money, whether or not he had the evidence. It emerged that he had a float and at the start of six weeks of the Beeb in house, he didn't want to get off on the wrong foot. I would be back and forth to see him two to three times a week. Things were bubbling.

The next day, the big guns started flying in. If my staff were being targeted in the run-up to the tournament, the whole thing was surely about to change when the millionaire household names rocked up.

On the Monday, Philip Bernie, the deputy head of Sport called me. Emmanuel Adebayor needed round the clock protection. In the January, his Tonga team bus had come under attack at the African Nations Cup in Angola – three were killed and nine injured.

'I can arrange security but what does he need it for?' I said. 'Does he really want it? Has anybody actually spoken to him or is it his agent bigging him up? And who's going to pay for it?'

Philip gave me the number of his representative.

'I'm looking after Gary and all the others here. I'll meet you at the airport and bring you to the hotel. It's safe here. If he wants to go out in the evening and wants security, we can arrange that: it will cost about $500 per day,' I broke it gently to him.

'Oh, the BBC can pay for it,' he said.

'No, I've been told they won't,' I replied. It was the usual game of bullshit with agents. I knew that they were trying it on. Did Adebayor get special protection from Manchester City? Was he armed driving through Moss Side on the way to training? No, utter bollocks. I told him to speak to Phil about the costs. I would happily arrange it, but buck-passing as to who was paying was well and truly underway. However wealthy you were, a gig on the BBC overrode any financial motive. I knew we would freeze them out and they wouldn't not show up.

On the Tuesday, Alan Shearer and Mark Lawrenson arrived. I couldn't move for golf clubs. A bus fetched them and I met them at the hotel. Shearer asked me about the standard of the hotel – his missus and his daughter Chloe were coming out. Chloe was doing work experience and he really wanted her to put a shift in and not just dine out on his name.

Then he handed me the watches. He must have had close to a hundred grand in timepieces. Hublot had rung him when he took over at Newcastle United. They wanted him to wear one on the touchline. He had been sent a catalogue to pick from and they duly obliged. All managers like to look at their wrist a lot. As it turned out, he was on borrowed time – just nine games in the job before taking Newcastle United down from the premiership. He was given a second one to wear on TV. I don't know why he brought them. They were only going in that safe he had asked about!

On the way to the restaurant that night, we got chatting for the first time proper.

'Are you our bodyguard?' he small-talked.

'No,' I refused to rise to any ego.

'Would you take a bullet for me?' he asked. He was bantering.

I told him about Friendly Fire and some of the other scrapes. I'd hated him for all the times he had scored against West Ham but I respected what he had done. I wanted the same back – so that he knew he was in safe hands rather than with some bouncer that the BBC had lifted off the streets. No, I wouldn't take a bullet for him, or any of them, I wasn't paid enough to go that far, but I would break up a scrap if it all got a bit tasty and, yeah, it was a great feeling at the bar that night getting the drinks in.

'I'll get these, Al. What do you want?'

'Craig, I'll have another one, please,' the legend replied.

Dreams – and the stuff they were made of. Just like with Dicko, I momentarily forgot that humourless celebration and all those goals that Shearer had banged in against us.

The next day I was up early to the airport – the serious players were landing. In fact, I was on almost a daily run back and forth to Cape Town International, mindful of the fact that in the next couple of days I would be coming here again alone, to abandon the World Cup temporarily for Sue's dad's funeral. But today – more golf clubs rattling their way through Arrivals – Hansen and Lineker were touching down!

There was a massive press pack there – it was also the day huge numbers of English fans were arriving. By the time the British tabloids had written this up with a picture of a beaming Lineker, I was a £1,000 per day ex-commando escorting potential kidnap victims Lineker and Hansen, five years younger than I actually was, and a fully honoured war hero.

I wouldn't argue with any of that. It was complete bullshit, of course.

With Lineker's arrival, all eyes began to focus on the first game. England were due to play the USA on the Saturday night. The boys were pretty unanimous on two issues – that Joe Hart should have been in goal and that England couldn't win the tournament. Alan Hansen, in particular, could see no way the Three Lions would triumph. With their arrival, it meant curtain up. Things were getting serious now and Cape Town was the place to be for St George. Many were based here for the better social life than Johannesburg. It was a very different clientele to Stuttgart and Charleroi. Most of the hooligans were watching back home down the pub.

Gary had a couple of hours to get settled, then it was straight out to film. Yes, there was lots of golf and wine, but we were off to Signal Hill next to Table Mountain to shoot, then to the beach before heading on to the Apartheid Museum. We had to get as much in the can as we could before a ball was kicked because then the games would come thick and fast. These were the little two- to three-minute films which would pop up from time to time, and help justify the whole BBC spend.

Alan Hansen went off to the studio to record a piece for *Football Focus*. I liked him instantly – he was just a normal, down to earth guy. He won me over straightaway when he told me about the work he had done with Help for Heroes and how important it was to him. The slightly aloof downbeat misery that you might see on the telly wasn't the real deal. He was a good man.

The atmosphere was great. Egos, as they say, were left at the door. Everyone from the talent down to the make-up girls would meet each other at night in the bar. It was one big team but with many individuals in it. Gary would have a wine and hit the sack, but then he had a much younger more gorgeous other half who required his energy; Alan Shearer and I would talk about what I was going to wager on in my Betfair account and he would shake his head jokingly; Dicko would be up most mornings cycling like a freak; and I loved having the confidence to talk football with them all. There was no 'Listen,

BODYGUARD

son, I've played the game and you ain't' about them, and they were all generous to a tee. Goodness, at one point, even Hansen put his hand in his pocket! And Lee was still loving his wine.

On the Wednesday night, I pissed myself. Heston rang! The two had owned a restaurant together and were great mates but this was big knob territory. He was on the way out as Lee's guest. It was unbelievable fantasy land. Here I was, sitting there at dinner with Lee Dixon, a man I have called a wanker from the terraces dozens of time, and Heston Bloody Blumenthal rang to discuss Lee's wine selection. You couldn't make it up.

Who would want to ever leave this or have it taken away from them because the Beeb would want them desk-bound in the future? This really was the life.

But I had to go. Sue's dad's funeral was on the Friday, and the tournament hadn't begun. I couldn't not go, nor did I want to miss it. Amid all the showbiz and good times, and the chance to follow England abroad on the BBC payroll with all my footballing heroes, I wouldn't forget that my life had turned a corner and Sue had met me round the other side. Now, she too had made that journey.

Dirk from Zim flew in for three days to stand in for me. Before I left on the Thursday, my last task was to help shoot the promo for *Match of the Day*. There I was, standing half way up a hill with Gary Lineker, waiting for the hired helicopter to fly up the hill, hover, pick up Gary, then move to the shots over Cape Beach. My job was to bring the helicopter in. I was back in the A-Team again! Loads of fans began driving up to Signal Hill. You could see Robben Island, the stadium and the whole of Cape Town from there. We had to block the road off. They all wanted a piece of Gary. He would sign a few autographs, then call a halt; do a few more then move on. It was a nightmare but Gaz was a pro.

And then I had to fly – literally.

I said goodbye to Gary, who wished me well for the funeral. Next, I briefed Dirk on Adebayor, before making it to the airport with minutes to spare. I didn't really want to leave, but it was the right thing to do. That was what partnerships were about. Lineker, Shearer, Hansen and Dixon would be there when I got back.

At the airport, maybe I was feeling sorry for myself. The Beeb had got me a hire car from Heathrow and arranged World Traveller Plus for the flight home. 'Fuck this,' I thought. 'I'm not travelling World Traveller; I'm going Business.' I marched up to the check-in desk. 'My wife's father just died,' I told them. 'And I work for the BBC ... and I'm a Gold Card holder. Is there any chance of an upgrade?'

'Look, the flight's not that full,' she replied.

'I didn't ask that question,' I said.

'I can't do it, Sir.'

This was a challenge to me – I was the King of the Upgrade. I decided to wait for the manager. 'Look mate, I'm heading up the BBC security, I'm a Gold Card holder, my wife's dad just died ...' I repeated the whole shebang.

'Look, I'm sorry, I cannot do it,' he reiterated after a quick search. 'We're not even three-quarters full in Economy; there's only one or two free in Business.'

'Well, I only need one,' I bullshitted.

He told me it was all computer-driven now and he wasn't allowed to play with it any more. 'If anything changes, I'll let you know,' he promised.

In the lounge, I resigned myself to a couple of beers and a big kip all the way home. Then there was a tap on my shoulder. 'Mr Summers,' the voice said. 'Would you come this way?' Here we go, I was thinking. 'Look, we can't upgrade you,' he began. 'But we've looked at your ticket: it should be £400 but we can sell you an upgrade at a rate of £200. That's the best we can do, Sir.'

I jumped at it, laughing all the way home, and had my fillet steak and champagne before Sue picked me up at Heathrow, driving us straight to the funeral.

We gave the old boy another great send-off. There were about 200 people there. Jack would have been proud.

The difference in the two funerals was huge – one in a foreign church with a few family and the old folk from the town, done very much the Spanish way; the other was a right big piss-up on home soil that left me with a big hangover the next morning. My dad loved a drink. He was the real life and soul of the party. It saddened me a little that because he'd moved to Spain, there weren't hundreds turning out for him. Both, despite seven years age gap, were from the no-nonsense era before PC went mad. Baa baa black sheep or the golliwog on Robinson's Jam, that was all they knew. If a police-man wanted to smack you round the lughole because you were having a crafty teenage fag then that's what happened. You got on with it and made good of the little you had. They weren't politically incorrect, bigoted, selfish or sexist. They were just plain-talking. That had rubbed off on to me. It was a miracle I had survived over a decade at the new BBC. I was the least PC person in the Corporation and I think they let it go because I did a good job. What you saw was what you got.

I saw Sue's dad's funeral as the ceremony mine would have had if he had died at home, and I took a good look at myself in the process. That gave me some comfort, and some distance. Having the two deaths so close helped me for the first time come to terms with my dad leaving us. Now it was Sue's turn to grieve and I could chan-nel my emotions through her, I was in a much better place to deal with my own dad, though, of course, two funerals in a month meant that I re-lived the whole thing again. Life had to go on, though, as much as it still cut through me when I would see a picture of Dad.

The next morning was the Saturday. England were to play the USA that night. That afternoon, the football helped me move on as I watched the Argies beat Nigeria 1–0. There would be so many games now that, actually, the funeral couldn't have happened at a better time in terms of moving on. It was very strange to have set the whole thing up and see the boys getting ready but instead be tearing back down the M1 with a sore head. I felt it was important to spend a couple of days with Sue but, of course, once the action kicked off again, I just wanted to be back out there.

I was always able to move on very quickly once a new day had started. From London, I could visualise the boys in the studio and remember their words after Robert Green's howler. They all had said Joe Hart should have been in goal, and they all turned out to be correct. I had watched Robert Green all season and knew he was a brilliant goalkeeper. Twenty-four hours after burying Sue's dad, I felt gutted for someone else – the West Ham keeper.

It had the makings of the usual England performance at a tournament. The hopes of a nation had all the potential to be crushed again. I needed to get back out there before it was all over, and by the time I was reduced to watching *Celebrity Come Dine With Me* on the Sunday, I knew it was time to go.

The plane was rammed. This time I couldn't swing it. I had to face Economy. I would rather not talk about it!

Very kindly, when I touched down hot and bothered with a sore neck, they were all there to meet me. The two Alans, Gary, Roy Hodgson, Dicko, Heston were all waiting in the hall. Were they fuck?!

I rang Dirk, my stand-in, straightaway. Emmanuel Adebayor hadn't wanted anything at all. It had all been a bit of a game – the usual bullshit and brinkmanship. His brothers were acting as security, and his middleman had backed off. It had been a quiet weekend. I had missed nothing – except the fallout from the England game. Shearer told me he felt Robert Green had looked nervous even walking out against the USA.

My first job back at the compound was to file paperwork – more bloody paperwork. The now daily Sit Rep (Situation Report) contained little, but it was done, boxed off and covered somebody's backside thousands of miles away. What I lived for was to be out and about and I couldn't have been happier when I got a message that they wanted me out with Shearer in a township.

That Tuesday we were gone for around five hours – just to make a six-minute piece. No golf for Alan that day, though he was brilliant with the crew, the locals and then, after all that hanging around, on camera, too. So many professional footballers want to be and think they can be pundits, and most can't – let alone doing unprompted pieces to camera on human stories. Alan just had that normal touch about him. Despite being able to buy the township himself, he never forgot where he'd come from; my respect for him went through the roof as he became more than just a gob on a stick and really was genuinely warm to, and interested in, the people.

The township of Khayelitsha was about half an hour away, to the left of the motorway – a shanty town that used to be a big drugs place and was well known for its violence. Literally translated, it meant New Home. It was the fastest-growing township in South Africa, one of those places that you would have seen on a Lenny Henry Comic Relief piece. The authorities would turn a blind eye. Here was a problem that they couldn't really get their teeth into – a community of helpless people born into poverty, which society was largely ignor-ing, even though it was clearly very much alive. And that was the thrust of Alan's piece.

It would be wrong to walk away from the human story while the greatest show on earth was in town. I had seen this sub-standard living so many times around the world, but it didn't half show how the other half lived. The BBC didn't want this to be the untold story of the World Cup – and rightly so. It really opened my eyes to Alan Shearer. I thought it would be beneath him. It wasn't. It was the least he felt he could do.

By that evening at a Chinese, I also really began to get a sense of how the pundits like to operate when they were out in the same restaurants and bars that the fans were in. The mob clocked their heroes straightaway. I feared the worst as they headed over to our table – each of them wanting a picture and an autograph. I asked if they could give the lads some peace, but the boys overruled me saying it was not a problem, even though Gary thanked me for putting the fans on the back foot. The rule of thumb was established. They didn't mind any of that, but when the food came they would want their privacy. I didn't want to be too heavy-handed but didn't know if I was being heavy-handed enough. Once the alcohol was flowing among the travelling support, you could never really know.

On the way out, there were more cries of 'Shearer, Shearer' and more requests for photos. I could see that the best way to deal with all of this was to take the photos myself and move everyone along. Of all my roles that I had played for the BBC, I was now acting bouncer-cum-paparazzo! The boys were grateful. They had seen all this before and fans often think they were cleverer than they actually were. It wouldn't take much for one of them to be offended or for someone's reputation to be slurred by seeming to be stand-offish.

So far, so good.

All was not well in Johannesburg, though. I got a call that two BBC 5 Live producers had been mugged the previous night.

Liam Hanley and Jacques Sweeney had been eating and drinking near to their accommodation at the 7th Street Guesthouse in Melville. For some reason, they decided not to take the usual taxi, and walk the 200 metres down the street lined with bars and restaurants up to the locked security gate and then down into their guesthouse. When they were around fifteen metres from the security gate, a black hatchback pulled up alongside them. A white Eastern European man in his thirties jumped out and pointed a handgun at Jacques. Three other men stayed in the car, shouting in a language that was neither English nor Afrikaans. The gunman rifled through Jacques's trouser pockets, removing his wallet, taking the cash before returning the wallet. He also took his passport but gave it back. Without being asked, Liam too took out his wallet and two mobiles and laid them on the street. The assailant ignored these, jumped back in the van and sped off.

He had followed my briefing to the letter. Jacques, however, got lucky. They didn't need their passports on the streets. I had made it clear that if they felt they needed their documentation, to take a colour photocopy out. We were back in the land of the schoolboy error – plus they shouldn't have changed the habit of a lifetime and should have used a taxi. It could have been a lot worse, but every time something like that happened I knew I was proving my worth, my initial briefings would be seen to be wise and, most importantly, there would be lots more paperwork for Paul Easter to drown in!

I knew word was spreading among the pros about the increasing crime threat and that I was the man to come to.

'You're the guy who's looking after everybody, aren't you?' Alan Hansen's father-in-law approached me in the Oyster Bar at the Taj Hotel. I'm not sure a specially cordoned-off VIP area at a posh South African hotel was really his scene. He was standing on his own. I think he wanted someone normal to talk to. We chatted about the army, life at the Beeb, Liverpool, Scotland, the World Cup, the England v USA game and Alan – just normal stuff. I liked him a lot.

Hansen popped over to see if he was all right.

'Yeah, I'm just chatting to Craig,' he replied.

We were there hours, knocking them back, chewing the fat, until Al called time just before midnight – his father-in-law tottering towards the stairs. What a laugh.

The next morning Hansen confirmed the damage. 'Thanks for getting my father-in-law pissed!' he laughed.

This became the routine. Joking and banter before the show, almost robotic professionalism during it, and we would always unwind together in the bar after.

Nicky Campbell was also out for 5 Live – staying in a guesthouse in Rustenburg. This is where England were based. Just like everyone else, Nicky had had all the briefing, and just like many others before him, he had gone out, leaving his iPod by the side of the bed, only to return to find it gone. I wasn't officially told about this – I think Nicky wanted to keep it quiet – but as ever, word got back to me. I joked that they would soon return it when they saw his taste in music!

It was another thing to stuff Paul Easter's inbox with. Those Sit Reps were coming thick and fast, all full of minor detail like this. Here I was doing what the BBC loved, filling in forms, while justifying my existence. Nobody seemed to realise that the more Sit Reps I filed, the more it showed that there was need for more and not less of me on the ground, and that you couldn't do the job behind in a desk in West London. Ironically, the quest for paperwork and their desire to send me in that direction proved all over again why I had been hired in the first place.

Increasingly, despite the past tricky two months and the silent pressure I was feeling from work, I knew this was a trip to savour. It wasn't that I was bogged down in paperwork; I just knew that the end was coming and that I had proven my worth time and time again from back-watcher to undercover reporter. If they were about to kill off Craig Summers by confining him to a desk back in London, then I would enjoy every last drop of this trip.

To be able to tell your mates back home that you walked Motty out of a bar pissed was the stuff I never had a shot at the day my dad marched me off to the army. This was probably the last tournament for John Motson too. John was now sixty-five and had handed over the reins as lead commentator to Guy Mowbray, but still somehow found himself on the trip. A train-spotter of useless football information, he knew everything. You had to respect him for that – statistics and turning them into poetry were his life. But just like the rest of us, he liked the odd sherbet too.

One night in Twankey's Bar, he turned to me. 'I think I've had enough, Craig. I've got to go home,' he slurred. As he turned round, he walked straight into the glass partition at the other end of the bar. He didn't hit it hard, in fact no less tamely than the shot Robert Green had let in, but because it was Motty, the whole bar cracked up. It was a classic *You've Been Framed* moment.

'Are you all right, John?' I asked him.

He told me he thought he'd had one too many. I couldn't have Motty face down in the gutter. 'Oh, Craig, that's really kind; you don't have to,' he protested. 'That's very kind, young man.' I showed him to his room and went back to the bar, laughing. That was a moment I would never forget.

On Sunday 27 June, Alan Hansen's prediction came true as Germany served notice on England's tournament. At home, a nation stopped. In South Africa not even the diehard pessimists could have foreseen such a dire England performance, torn apart by the misfortune of Frank Lampard's disallowed goal, a horror show of defending against long balls coming straight down the middle – the bread and butter of the English game served up on a plate by the Germans. We were out in the last sixteen, losing 4–1.

The atmosphere died immediately. The boys still had half a tournament to broadcast but this meant News would start withdrawing and some of the less frontline pundits began to come home. In short, the whole operation, despite months of planning and millions of pounds, came down to one thing as ever. The show was only going to be as good as long as England were in it. As a fan, I was gutted. As a professional, it meant less to do on the job and more online Scrabble to play with Colin Murray. Most England fans left the next day as many of my colleagues began to de-camp.

South Africa was still a dangerous place though – a gang of New Zealand fans, one of them a former policeman, had been raped.

And when we weren't dragging out the work, there would be the daily draw for tickets from our allocation. After England's exit there were more to go round, so long as you could handle the vuvuzela. I couldn't have had been more charged about a match when my name came out for the neutral's heaven – Argentina versus Germany in Cape Town. Every England fan would have kept any eye on this one and if I hadn't been working for the BBC and this game had been in some European hot spot, well – it's the kind of fixture when my old West Ham colours might have come out and mixed it a bit. Those days were long gone now. Instead, my ticket came with conditions. I had to chaperone Gary Lineker's and Lee Dixon's sons to the game.

And the game couldn't have had more about it. Germany won four nil – not that George Lineker would have known, texting birds on his BlackBerry throughout and wanting to leave before the end! I loved it, though. It was the game of the tournament to see the old enemy thrash ... the old enemy. Normally these matches were dogged affairs. This was a firecracker but barely consolation for the traditional English exit. That left me just killing time until the end of the World Cup. Sue asked if I would be coming home early. Paul Easter would ring me on mobile and I wouldn't take the call, later phoning him back to say I had been really busy. I hadn't been.

On 11 July, Spain beat the Netherlands 1–0 in the final. It was the pairing many wanted to see. The next day I wandered into the BBC compound for the last time. This time I took Paul's call.

'Have you done a post-deployment report?'

'Of course not,' I replied.

That was the final nail in the coffin. I told him we were flying back the next day (Tuesday).

'I need it on my desk for Wednesday,' he said, stunning me. 'I'm meeting Paul Greeves on Thursday. I can give it to him then.'

I slammed the phone down. He was taking the piss.

I rang Richard Stacey in News and Jimmy, who had been looking after Johannesburg, and told them I had twenty-four hours to turn this thing around. Two pages wouldn't do. They wanted *War and Peace*. I emailed it just before we flew.

On the Wednesday I went into Television Centre to see everyone.

'Where's Paul Easter?' I asked.

'Oh, he's not in today,' I was told. 'He's in tomorrow.'

PINSENT

I felt I had been set up – deliberately messed about. Obviously, it had been the last day of operations in Cape Town and we were packing up. Then, when I made the effort to go in just after landing, my boss wasn't even there.

It was time to go.

When I finally spoke to Paul, it was obvious he was miffed.

'You won't be going away for six-week trips like that any more,' he had pretty much said.

I began to form my exit strategy. Phil Bigwood, executive producer at *Match of the Day*, was already buzzing about the Euros in 2012, despite England's shortcomings.

'I don't think they'll allow me to do it,' I told him, knowing what was coming.

The BBC had spent half a million quid on DQF – Delivering Quality First. They had spent that much money on consultants showing them ... how to cost cut! I always used to say to John Simpson after every trip, 'What's next, John?' It was time to stop asking. They wanted me less on the road, and more at my desk, and rather than just hinting this, these were now the words coming out of people's mouths.

Despite my desire to get out of the BBC, I wasn't quite done yet.

On 29 November I flew back out to Baghdad. Matthew Pinsent had been making occasional shows for BBC World in the run-up to London 2012 – he was charting the unlikely Olympic Dream.

'There's a couple of rowers in Iraq who are going for the Olympics ... what do you think?' Kev Bishop, the producer of *World Olympic Dreams* had come to ask. We had worked together at the Euros in Portugal six years previously.

'Have you spoken to anyone else about it?' I asked suspiciously.

'No, I've come to you first,' he replied.

In some places my reputation was still right up there. I was over the moon that he had thought of me, and that I could be on the road again. Paul Easter was put in the difficult position of having to come to me to say that I had been asked for as nobody knew Baghdad better. I felt it was done through gritted teeth, which made it double the pleasure.

I rang Dylan, the head honcho in Baghdad. He knew the patch, the short-cuts, and he knew how to deal out there. I had got on really well with him over many years of visits. His response was immediate. Whatever I needed was not a problem.

What I wanted was for Matthew Pinsent, legend of four consecutive Olympic and ten World Championship Golds, to row on the famous River Tigris, the 1,850-kilometre stretch of water on whose banks Iraq's capital stands. I hoped that wasn't too much to ask.

This is where the Baghdad Rowing Club was based – one of just two clubs in the country. The Tigris itself went on into Turkey and Syria, but it still bore the marks of the brutal Saddam Hussein era. At that time, bodies would just float abandoned in the water. Even now, you couldn't row the whole stretch, a specially cordoned-off section steering you clear of the government ministries whose offices overlooked the water. This was the first problem for Iraqi rowers Haider Rashid and Hamza Hussein – the Olympic course was longer than the zone marked off for them.

Haider and Hamza had also spent much of their time on the water accompanied by a soundtrack of gunfire and explosions. In many ways, given the resources available to them and their lack of Olympic pedigree, this had the potential to be the *Cool Runnings* of 2012. It was the Jamaican bobsleigh all over again.

To put it into context, Iraq had won one medal ever, at the Rome Games in 1960. From nowhere, they produced a Bronze in weightlifting. In days gone by of course, the Olympic story was overshadowed by the fact that Saddam's son Uday was head of its committee. His way ruled, with dire consequences for failure. Seven years after his death at the hands of Special Forces, Haider and Hamza were coming out of the cold in search of their Olympic dream. These were no Redgraves, though – Haider was pushing thirty and had spent much of his life away from the troubles in Sweden. Hamza was thirty-four and the more likely of the two to get noticed on the world stage. They also had day jobs: Hamza was studying and Haider was a teacher. That was like old-school athletics – where you were officially amateur and worked an eight-hour day in a bank, bookended by four-hour training sessions either side. That was proper desire and hunger.

It was a world away from the time, resource, attitude and funding that Sir Matthew Pinsent had available to him by the end of his career.

I first met Matthew in the same way I met many other people – right after they had attended the Hostile Environments Course. He was a smart guy, taking it all in and, like Ranulph, asking the right questions – sensible stuff about the drive from the airport etc. You could tell Matthew had thought about it. If his trophy cabinet hadn't already placed me in awe, he had my respect for preparing mentally for this challenge.

The political situation in Baghdad was at its calmest in living memory, but there were still threats. There had been three democratic elections since the fall of Saddam. The situation was stable – sort of. Electricity and water were still rationed to six hours a day. The Americans were babysitting the Iraqi police and army and there would be plenty of checkpoints – there was a still real danger of kidnap. Insurgents wanted the Yanks out. They wanted their own democracy, not an American-influenced one. We had often interviewed locals who had preferred life under Saddam – they were free to roam and electricity and water weren't issues. It was an uneasy kind of peace. I briefed Matthew that magnetic (sticky) bombs were now a real issue.

Dylan told me that it would be foolish to interview Hamza at his home at Adhamiya. There were a still a lot of tensions in the north-west part of the city centre. Something going wrong would not do me, or the CV that I had been dusting off, much good for the future. In the week running up to departure alone, there had been thirteen incidents across the city. Predictably, that made me even keener to get started. Matthew, too, wanted to know the place as well as his story.

After flying ahead to double check all the arrangements, I picked him up in an armoured 4x4 on a cold and dusty day. You could see him soaking it up on that first drive – a world away from a team coach driving you to a sterile Olympic village. I laid out the map and showed him the safe areas. My brief was exactly the same as with the Three Dogs. If anything happens, you stay in the vehicle. There was no need to stop unless we had a serious accident. We had B6 ballistics all around us – that was the highest level of protection you could get at the time, and it would protect us from grenades or small pistols – but an IED (improvised explosive device) could take us out. In total, the ride from the airport to the Bureau took around forty minutes. So there was plenty of time for someone to have some fun with us.

I told him that whatever happened, I was in charge. Americans called it the most dangerous road in the world – from 2005 to 2009, there were hundreds of attacks on this stretch. I had never had a problem to date. I left him with nothing to do except stare out the window. As long as he had his wits about him, it was probably the best thing to take it all in.

Safely at the Bureau, I showed him the humble basic living quarters. He went straight to the gym. I think it exceeded his expectations, given the simplicity of the rest of the surroundings. He had nothing to train for now, but of course, it never left you.

We would begin proper work the next day. That afternoon, I took him down to the Tigris for a first look – he loved the river and its sense of history. Most people probably couldn't name it in a pub quiz but it was an iconic landmark which held a thousand secrets. We went down on foot past the checkpoint and through a park which was non-existent three years ago. Nowadays everyone would flock there on a Friday, and they greeted us warmly. Life went on – not everyone was a terrorist. They didn't really clock Matthew – they were just being polite as we were clearly guests in the country. One patrol car stopped us, concerned at which way we were filming. They didn't want us pointing the camera in the direction of the Ministry of Information.

That was no problem, we said. We were here to cover the Iraqi national sport of ... rowing? Occasionally they would come back our way and we would wave like cheesy Americans. Then we would start filming again, in the direction of the Ministry of Information.

When we weren't really shooting Matthew delivered a great line to the camera with exquisite poise. 'The acid test was what would it be like to row on that?'

A stretch of water was a stretch of water to me. Wind and currents, I understood, but at the end of the day it was just water. Matthew would have gone through this psychological preparation thousands of times, visualising his arena as great sportsmen do. This came with baggage though – the nervous energy and responsibility which any cultured individual would feel, smelling that history all around and picturing walking his equipment down to the shore, knowing that these two budding Olympians had done this time and time again in among the dead bodies of the Tigris.

That night I had a surprise for Sir Matthew. Our conditions may have been basic at the Bureau but we did share a chef with Reuters next door. He was called Ayyub-al-Obeidi. His CV was interesting. His last position of note? Well, decent staff are hard to come by these days. He was only the chief chef for Saddam Hussein, wasn't he? What a story that was. It was like one of those seven degrees of separation things, where you can trace a path to Hitler through seven connections – except this time we got there in one. He didn't speak much English, and though always friendly, his lack of communication probably was apt. I guessed there was a lot he didn't like to talk about.

Frankly, he would have been party to it all. It seems fair to suggest that the more Saddam ate, the more he bragged, and the more he drank with 'important' guests, then the more his crackpot ideas became. We all dream when we've had a few. His dreams would have become other people's nightmares. Our chef would have only been next door. He was obviously a top-drawer chef – after all, if you think that Olympic failure could mean Uday removing your hands, then clearly you didn't want to cock up the catering. In general, he was reserved. Perhaps this culture meant you had a private dignity about your past, or maybe he still lived in awe – I'm sure the effect on some Iraqis was such that they still feared that Saddam would rise from the grave at any point.

Saddam's favourite dish was Masgouf. Who could turn down that well-known irresistible fish dish? Or his other favourite – chicken stuffed with rice and peas and almonds? You've probably seen it on Jamie's TV shows many a time. I couldn't wait to try camel toe. In the end we had meatballs in batter! But it was the best – and what a story he had to tell. How wasted was he cooking up for us after all he had seen and done? I suspect he would never tell that story.

By night we retired to the back room. It was always the same wherever you found a little piece of Britain around the world – luxuries lay out the back that locals would never see. If you ever went to an embassy, the ambassador would never be short of the finest of everything. Were we the only people in Baghdad playing *Call of Duty* on the X-Box that night?

Matthew walked in to see what all the fuss was about – he had never heard of the game. Instantly, he was hooked – and he was an Olympian at that, too. Once a champ, always a champ.

The next day, we went straight to meet Hamza Hussein. Hamza had been at Beijing in 2008 along with seven other Iraqis. North

Korea had pulled out, making places available. It was Iraq's moment to not quite shine. He was due in the double sculls event. Iraq also had a sprinter, a judokaya, a discus thrower, an archer, and of course, for old times sake, the weightlifter. On 24 July 2008 the nation was banned from competing. I have no recollection of this story. The ban was because of political influence in the team – and Uday had been dead for five years! Unsurprisingly, Baghdad had been outraged. Amazingly, as far back as July 2006, several members of the Olympic Committee had been kidnapped, meaning that the IOC feared corruption in selection and that any subsequent meetings hadn't been quorate. On 29 July, they lifted the ban.

But further controversy loomed – only the track and field athletes could compete, as the Iraqi Olympic Committee had missed the entry deadlines. You could see it was nothing but a shambles.

Finally, the International Rowing Federation relented – Hamza and Haider were allowed in. They did the whole of Iraq proud. By finishing last. In the weightlifting, which had made their Olympic name (!), their only athlete, Mohammed Jassim, faced a drugs ban.

You could never be on track to Olympic glory, or indeed self-respect, if you were this much off the rails. If they ever made it to London, you just knew there would be a tube strike on the day of their event and they would never see the light of day – in fact it crossed my mind that they might just disappear and that political asylum might be the way forward. That was a throwback to another era but these two guys were certainly hindered by the details in their passport.

We went to meet Hamza at Firdos Square. I wanted to take Matthew down to see where Saddam's statue was felled by the Yanks in 2003. Just opposite the square was the Blue Mosque – the story here was that when the Americans were staging that dramatic shot, Saddam was only metres away inside it, which is staggering to think that they so nearly had him, and that he had no better plan that being underneath their noses. You would have to say it was a combination of luck and stupidity on both sides. Now, there stood some bullshit abstract green structure, supposedly intended to symbolise freedom. I didn't buy all that arty farty stuff but we couldn't have Matthew out here without attempting to do a piece to camera with that in the shadow. We had to be quick – and as he stood under where the statue had been with his own sense of history, the fate that befell many an athlete under Uday wouldn't have been lost on him.

I called it off though. It would draw too much attention to ourselves. Instead, we waited for Hamza to arrive in his Iraqi track suit. He recognised his hero Matthew instantly. What a moment that must have been for him.

Haider was at college so the plan was take a ride in the 4x4 and pick him up. En route, Matthew would be quizzing Hamza on what it took to become a rower in Iraq and how on earth he had got involved, plus what it meant to him to compete for Iraq in troubled times. Well, you can understand that it would be a welcome distraction, a chance for the world to look favourably on his nation post-Uday and for his countrymen to have something positive to unite behind.

It was a ten minute journey to the rowing club. In typical Baghdad traffic, it took forty-five. I didn't like us being sandwiched in the dust of the city, rammed in on either side, but this was daily life in Baghdad. We pulled up outside the rowing club. You would never know it was there. It opened as long ago as 1976.

Heading down through a track in between the houses in a sort of semi-industrial estate, we emerged at the river but were forced to turn right, appearing in what seemed like a huge car park built on wasteland. Then we encountered the massive gates to the club, beyond which was a different world. The lawns were smart, the gardens well-groomed and green plants were everywhere; the club itself on huge stilts. If you lost yourself for a moment, you would think you were in Kew Gardens. Even in Baghdad, the world of rowing was still for the privileged. It was incredible to think that all this existed even through wars. With Matthew in tow, the two Iraqis were in dream territory – the Olympics' worst-funded athletes coming face to face with one of the all-time greats. They were equals only in terms of passion and commitment.

Inside, they had the latest Concept 2 rowing machines and decent weights. But it was small – lino on the floor. Like every gym, the music was blaring out. I was tempted to flick the tape out and put 'Pump My Pussy' on for old times sake.

I asked Matthew what he thought of their actual boats.

'One of them is old and has been patched up a lot and that does affect it, but one is in good shape and a reasonable boat.'

You could see that their problems started here. At least this time, they had experienced the opportunity to travel to a regatta in Boston and train with the American team – a good bit of patronising PR for the Yanks, but more importantly a genuine opportunity for them to experience something close to top-flight competition. There were only so many times you could race against yourself and call yourself competitive.

But this was no Henley – there was no honours board, nor were there trophies. Ironically, there was a DIY leader board at the gym in the BBC Bureau where we would all write up our times. And if they were lucky enough to receive an overseas invitation, picking up some free kit on the way, they still came back to this. No sponsor would be paying to adorn their vests with their international brand.

Matthew thought their facilities were better than he had feared, even though it wasn't the high-tech gear he would be used to. Anyone could tell, though, that Matthew, with all his ability and strength, would have struggled to get his own Olympic dreams moving from a start like this.

All the young athletes in the gym were in awe of him, and rightly so, and even though Matty was making a documentary, there is a part of the rower that will always take over. That forty-five minutes in the car had put pressure on our schedule but it didn't matter when Matthew got lost in the rowing moment. In the heat of battle, they were all competitors. In the disproportionate world of the game of life, they were a fraternity. He wanted to talk the sport, share what he could with whoever wanted to listen, and he invited Hamza and Haider to train with him when they came to the UK for the 2012 games. He meant it sincerely. If he wanted, he could have put his hand in his pocket and funded that gym for the boys, but we all knew that wouldn't solve the problems and was nothing more than a one-off hit. It left no infrastructure. It would only create an artificial high of false dreams.

Even when it came to combining his new career of journalism and his old of rowing, his expertise was second to none. Sara, who was filming, wanted to rig up a couple of cameras to film inside the boat – Matthew took over, knowing exactly the angles to place them at. That was years of video analysis and playback which brought that superior knowledge – Haider and Hamza would never get that opportunity otherwise, and the BBC would also benefit with incredible shots. And when it came to rowing, he led the way, helping carry the boats down to the shore. He was a gent with no need to stand on ceremony. Olympic legend or not, it was the kind of singular sport that bred self-sufficiency and focus. For all those years, Matthew would have taken his own boat down to the river as he did the Iraqis'. It was that kind of sport and he was that kind of guy.

Haider and Hamza would train for four or five hours – as long as they could until the light went. You could see they were quality athletes – they carried themselves as sportsmen. They weren't Jamaican bobsleighers at all.

'They'll be lucky to qualify,' Matthew said. 'Haider might have a chance but I doubt it. Hamza is too old.'

Matthew was mindful that Hamza was still six or seven years younger than when Sir Steve Redgrave won his last gold medal but he admired them for their work ethic and their love of the sport. It wasn't their fault they would never be contenders. Every day they would walk onto a pontoon where you would be lucky not to fall over. The safety boat that followed them was nothing more than an old wreck, but it did the job.

We filmed from in there. Matthew encouraged, trained and chatted with them on camera as they went up and down the Tigris. He was impressed with what they could achieve against the odds: in this day and age, unless you are training 24/7 with enormous backing, there is always going to be somebody better than you.

'If they qualify, it's a tremendous achievement,' he confirmed but he did so out of respect, not humour.

We agreed that it was difficult to know if they knew how good they were in this context and how far they had to go to be Olympian but they were united in two things – they wanted to represent their country at the highest level and they were destined to go to the Olympics. This is why we were making the show – it was proper old school, the stuff dreams were made of. Could there be any other athlete at London 2012 whose training facilities were lined with bodies? Some days they wouldn't be able to row as they waited for the corpses to float on down the river. They couldn't touch them in case they were booby-trapped. On others, they would just push themselves off and go, making a course around them.

They lived with it. It was their day to day.

Inevitably Matthew asked both of them if any of their friends had been badly injured or killed during the troubles. They had. It brought home their Olympic dream and was a reminder to those who say sport and politics don't mix. That eternal flame burned within and gave them personal aspiration and international focus for their country – the taking part rather than the winning still did count after all. You could say, 'why bother?', but then you could argue it was more important than ever to make the effort.

Over the next couple of days, we took more general shots of Hamza and Heider in everyday life – the story was about them, after all. Who wouldn't admire them? It was one of the rare occasions in my eleven years at the BBC when I ceased to see the subjects as TV fodder and looked at them as the human beings.

Matthew, too, found the whole Baghdad experience a cultural reward. Some people come to Iraq with pre-conceptions that it is all guns blazing but he came with open eyes, listening to your every word rather than you hanging on his because of who he was. Nothing was too much for him. Without a second glance he would wash up with the crew or stick the kettle on, or fight for his life on *Call of Duty*. Yes – we asked him about Olympic glory – but the honours bestowed upon him hadn't changed him. He wouldn't talk about it unless you quizzed him but how could you sit there and not? He probably knew that, like a million times before, he would get the 'So, what was it like?' question. It was something he had done and now he was having new adventures. It had been an amazing time in his life. To win one Gold was incredible, to win four out of this world. Sir Steve Redgrave had been the best, as an athlete and as a mentor. He'd had a fantastic opportunity in life and worked his butt off to maximise his talent, and probably we wouldn't see that era of rowing again, even though the bar was so high that we now took success for granted. He was aware that their combined legacy created a massive pressure for the next generation.

To be in his presence as an athlete and as a human being, to sit down at the end of the day and hear him say all this, was awe-inspiring. I showed him the ultimate respect of not asking him about his own coxless pairs. I am sure he had heard that joke a million times. He had no self-doubt but not a whiff of arrogance, despite the fact that he was an old Etonian and a descendant of – get this – William the Conqueror.

For different reasons, we have both lived the dream. And it had taken this trip with Sir Matthew Pinsent to bring it all home. It was almost like the Beeb had laid on a final jolly for me, knowing that I would quit the next year. None of my previous thirty visits to Iraq had been like this.

What a contrast to when I first touched down on Iraqi soil back in 2003. I had seen it all, from Stuart's foot to the Yanks nearly killing the World Affairs editor. We were bombed again a couple of years later in the Sheraton – a bus opposite the hotel fired shells into our floor as we woke one morning. John Simpson emerged in his boxers on to our floor as we came under attack – these were the daily perils that we brushed off as minor details.

Then there was all the filming with John at the Al-Yarmouk Hospital in Baghdad on the day hundreds of bodies were brought in and all we could see were the feet bobbing up and down off the end of the truck. Much of what we did was about the dead. I had seen more corpses than I knew people alive. I will never forget going to Halabja where Saddam gassed the Kurds or visiting Fallujah with John filming all the babies born with birth defects because of chemical weapons. There was Ali Abbas, who in 2003 suffered 35 per cent burns and the loss of his arms – not to mention his family being wiped out and his house destroyed. He was just twelve years old at the time and had become the face of the war. In July 2009, we took him home for the first time.

To have been there at the first democratic elections meant nothing to me personally but I knew it was a Berlin Wall moment for the Gulf, and I loved walking in the footsteps of history. Not to have been there when Saddam was hung close to New Year 2006 remains a regret, but nobody saw it coming and we already had four security guys out there by the time John arrived. I say nobody saw it coming. Obviously some of the American guards who filmed it on their phones knew what was happening.

John and I were there for Saddam's trial, but it was a closed shop. Correspondents were carefully selected to report and for us it was John, of course. I never saw Saddam himself – John would be dropped in the Green Zone within a mile or so of the court and taken on a coach to the building where the done deal was being done. I loved even being that close. We were at the equivalent of Hitler's trial, even though I would sit and drink coffee all day waiting for him. I was both on the doorsteps of history and the doorsteps of Starbucks.

To see John in there made me proud. As the only BBC man inside, he was in with some of the world's finest, and each night, he would meet us with tales of Saddam's blasphemy and his disregard for the legitimacy of the trial itself. There was little unrest on the street but inside it was a circus. There had been a $25 million bounty on Saddam's head. The word was that a family member had ultimately sold him down the same River Tigris that Sir Matthew Pinsent had showcased the Olympic dreams of two his countrymen on.

Baghdad and I were done. It had been one hell of a journey and this was the last ride on the Craig Summers rollercoaster. It was time to go home, and it was time to go home for good.

REACH FOR THE SKY

I knew it was over.

Sue was fully supportive. 'If you want to do something else, that's fine. I'm right behind you,' she had said. That was the way it had always been and I loved her for it. She never questioned me and she didn't ask when I was away. She trusted me unconditionally and knew that I had been given two second chances in life.

In her, there was somebody who accepted who and what I was and took it at face value, while professionally, the Beeb had fulfilled all my dreams way beyond my expectations from those early days of back-watching for Nicholas Witchell.

I was as married to the job as I was to Sue.

'I'm going to take redundancy,' I told her in the spring of 2011. It was on offer. I'd had enough.

'Well, look, we'll just work something out. Let's see what comes up,' she said, brilliantly on side. She hadn't ever tired of all the trips, even though after Friendly Fire I promised I would try to keep them down to two or three weeks. She would always say be careful but she knew I wouldn't tell her the real story – Friendly Fire and the Tsunami excepted – and even then I was clinical on the detail.

It was after the Pinsent trip that I finally made up my mind, and the BBC accepted my forms the following June. On 19 August, I left the BBC for the final time.

My very last trip was straight after to Ukraine to recce the Euro 2012s – something I had already had a whiff of a story on for whoever would hire me next. If nobody did, then I had plenty of stuff to go freelance on. I'd had a great run. But I wasn't going to ride a desk for the next decade.

In my mind, I knew I had a great reputation and everything said go. John was coming towards the end of his time; Paul Easter was changing my department; finance and expenses were under scrutiny; Health and Safety was king; and crucially both Sue's and my own dad had passed away.

When a mutual friend insinuated that there was something going at Sky and I could work with the brilliant Stuart Ramsay and Alex Crawford, both of whom had done the ultimate in the modern era in penetrating the Taliban, my journalistic taste buds were whetted again. Years of John not wanting to be embedded turned in seconds to respect when I saw the work that those two were doing for Sky. It was a no-brainer. I had to play the game one more time. Get my money from the Beeb. Then wait for Sky to call.

I would miss some of the characters – people who had made the BBC what it was, not those who had recently been seen to make it what it would become.

I'd had only had two proper jobs, and I had no regrets.

John wrote me a reference and I knew our paths would cross again. Being nominated for an Emmy for Ciudad Juárez and being short-listed for the Rory Peck Award for Friendly Fire said it all.

Job done.

It was time for the Bodyguard to reach for the Sky. I had been honoured and absolutely loved my life on the front line. Now, new challenges lay ahead with another major international broadcaster.

I couldn't wait to go to the next level.

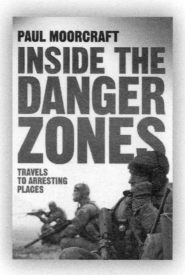

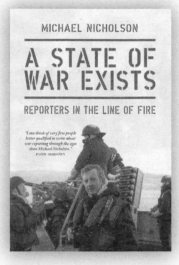